CHILDREN'S LITERATURE IN PRIMARY SCHOOLS

CHILDREN'S LITERATURE IN PRIMARY SCHOOLS

2ND EDITION

DAVID WAUGH,
SALLY NEAUM and
ROSEMARY WAUGH

Learning Matters
An imprint of SAGE Publications Ltd
1 Oliver's Yard
55 City Road
London EC1Y 1SP

SAGE Publications Inc.
2455 Teller Road
Thousand Oaks, California 91320

SAGE Publications India Pvt Ltd
B 1/I 1 Mohan Cooperative Industrial Area
Mathura Road
New Delhi 110 044

SAGE Publications Asia-Pacific Pte Ltd
3 Church Street
#10-04 Samsung Hub
Singapore 049483

Editor: Amy Thornton
Development Editor: Jennifer Clark
Production Controller: Chris Marke
Project Management: Deer Park Productions
Marketing Manager: Lorna Patkai
Cover design: Wendy Scott
Typeset by: C&M Digitals (P) Ltd, Chennai, India
Printed and bound by CPI Group (UK) Ltd, Croydon, CR0 4YY

Library of Congress Control Number: 2016940059

British Library Cataloguing in Publication Data

A catalogue record for this book is available from the British Library

ISBN 978-1-4739-6901-8 paperback
ISBN 978-1-4739-6900-1 hardback

At SAGE we take sustainability seriously. Most of our products are printed in the UK using FSC papers and boards. When we print overseas we ensure sustainable papers are used as measured by the PREPS grading system. We undertake an annual audit to monitor our sustainability.

Contents

The authors

David Waugh is subject leader for Primary English at Durham University. A former deputy headteacher, David worked in ITT from 1990 at the University of Hull, where he led the PGCE course and became Head of Department. In 2008 he was appointed as National Strategies Regional Adviser for ITT. As well as his educational writing, David also writes children's stories, including *Jessica's Other World* published in 2016.

Sally Neaum is a Lecturer in Education. Sally has worked as a nursery and primary school teacher, an early years and inclusion advisory teacher and in initial teacher training. Her areas of research include the pedagogy of early literacy and the professional development of early years practitioners.

Rosemary Waugh is a linguist and classics teacher at Queen Margaret's School, York. She collects children's literature and lectured on the subject for the University of Hull. She also contributes to conferences and publications on children's literature.

Acknowledgements

We would like to thank all the trainee teachers who shared their classroom experiences to help us to write this book. Particular thanks go to Molly Hill and Surindar Kaur, both of whom wrote their case studies for us. We are also grateful to Cliff and Dot Robson, Debbie Ling and Kirsty Anderson for their suggested books for Appendix 1. We are especially grateful to Amanda Swift, Headteacher of Easington CE Primary, and Angela Gill of Durham University, who contributed reviews of books for Appendix 1.

Introduction

Story is the most powerful means for teaching anything. No wonder then that most commercials construct stories to promote their products. Think of the fairy tale world built around the launch of the latest car, which takes the new owner to undreamed of fulfilments. Banal these narratives may be, but they work!

(Carter, 2000, p.24)

Reading widely and often increases pupils' vocabulary because they encounter words they would rarely hear or use in everyday speech. Reading also feeds pupils' imagination and opens up a treasure-house of wonder and joy for curious young minds.

(DfE, 2013, p.14)

For many children, reading is part of their way of life. At home, they are surrounded by books and they have parents, carers and elder siblings who are eager to share stories with them. For many adults, reading is a natural part of every day, whether it involves reading a novel as they commute to and from work or reading in bed at the end of the day. However, for too many other people, reading, especially fiction and poetry, does not feature strongly in their lives. Our aim with this book is to ensure that teachers and trainee teachers, the very people who are entrusted with the literacy and literary development of our children, are people who enjoy books, and who are enthusiastic and knowledgeable about children's literature.

We are all experienced educators who have, for many years, shared our love of children's literature through our work in schools and universities. Usually, we find trainee teachers enthusiastic and eager to find out more about children's literature. We know that teachers are a powerful influence on children's attitudes to reading and on their literacy skills. So, if we are to do the very best for children, it is vital that teachers and trainee teachers communicate enthusiasm and engagement with books and reading to hook children into books.

In writing this book, we have drawn heavily upon our knowledge of children's literature and the way in which it can entertain, engage and enthral young readers. We have made extensive use of case studies of trainee teachers' work with literature in schools to show the potential for literature to be both entertaining and informative. We have supported our claims with references to an established body of research which explores children's literature and teachers' knowledge and understanding of it. We hope that readers, including even the most reluctant, will find here ideas for working in the classroom, as well as an introduction to texts they may never have read.

In this second edition we have, by popular request, added an Appendix in which we have suggested books, no more than one per author, which might be of particular interest to readers. Any such list is bound to cause controversy: *Why this author and not that one? Why that book by that author and not one of her others?* We hope that you will join the debate and will send us your own suggestions, but that in the meantime the list might inspire you to read something you hadn't previously tried or even to revisit some old favourites.

In Chapter 1, we look in more depth at how we can develop a love of reading in children and why it is so important that teachers, too, enjoy and are knowledgeable about stories and poems. Chapter 2 explores ways in which we might share literature with children, through both reading aloud and developing follow-up activities, including drama and writing.

Chapter 3 explores ways in which literature can enhance children's learning across the curriculum and provides several examples of stories which might be used for different subjects. In Chapter 4, we look at the importance of books for younger children and provide examples of activities and texts. Chapter 5 examines the place of picture books: texts we normally associate with inexperienced readers, but which we show have value for all readers as they seek meaning from texts.

Chapter 6 focuses on stories and poems from different cultures. We live in a multicultural society and literature can provide an important meeting point between different ethnic groups, who can better understand each other's heritage through sharing their literature. Stories and poems from other countries also help us to understand how others live and enable us to see our own lives in a wider context.

In Chapter 7, we look at the place of traditional tales, including fairy stories. We find out how they have been passed through generations and across cultures, while considering their place in today's curriculum. Chapter 8 examines the role of fiction which addresses issues children may face, as well as those at a wider level. This is a genre which has developed recently and which attracts young people as they develop their understanding of themselves and the world around them. Some of the selections in Appendix 1 have been made to reflect the way in which society is changing, and literature is playing a role in developing our understanding and tolerance of different ways of living.

Magic and fantasy feature strongly in modern children's literature, with the *Harry Potter* series (Rowling, 1998–2009) having broken sales records and developed an unprecedented level of interest in books for children. This is the subject for Chapter 9. Chapter 10 focuses on so-called classic children's literature. There has been much discussion recently about whether there are books all children should have read. This chapter examines some of those which are frequently mentioned, while looking at the place of classics in the classroom.

In Chapter 11, we look at what we have termed everyday fiction: stories in which there is no magic or fantasy but which often involve a group of characters who embark on a range of adventures in a series of books. Last, and by no means least, we look at poetry in Chapter 12.

Our research for this book has led us to feel that poetry is often neglected in books about children's literature. We hope, through this chapter, to encourage you to look at the huge potential of poetry as both being pleasurable to read and having potential to develop children's language skills.

Each chapter helps you to address the Teachers' Standard:

3. Demonstrate good subject and curriculum knowledge

    - have a secure knowledge of the relevant subject(s) and curriculum areas, foster and maintain pupils' interest in the subject;

    - demonstrate an understanding of and take responsibility for promoting high standards of literacy and articulacy.

Throughout each chapter you will find research focus sections that provide details of research on children's literature, case studies that describe classroom activities, references to the *National Curriculum* (DfE, 2013) and activities, all of which will help you to link the advice and guidance in this book with your teaching. Curriculum links features also suggest ways in which the literature described might be used across the curriculum. You will find a list of references and recommended reading at the end of each chapter.

We hope that you will enjoy reading the book as much as we have enjoyed writing it. For us, it has been an opportunity to revisit and to discover a wealth of interesting stories and poems, while exploring the range and scope of classroom activities which even relatively inexperienced teachers and trainees have devised to bring literature to life for children. We are confident that you will find similar pleasure in children's literature if you adopt the same enthusiastic approaches.

David Waugh
Sally Neaum
Rosemary Waugh
June 2016

References

Carter, D. (2000) *Teaching Fiction in the Primary School.* Abingdon: David Fulton.

DfE (2013) *The National Curriculum in England: Key Stages 1 and 2 Framework Document.* DFE-00178-2013. London: DfE.

1 Developing a love of reading

Learning Outcomes

By reading this chapter you will have considered:

- how you can make reading an appealing activity;
- why it is important for teachers to be active readers with a wide knowledge of texts;
- strategies for developing children's enthusiasm for and engagement with reading;
- gender issues in reading.

Introduction

The best teachers of literature are those for whom reading is important in their own lives, and who read more than the texts they teach …. Being a reader of literature gives a teacher the confidence to teach powerfully.

(Martin, 2003, p.6)

Why is it important to develop a love of reading?

For many people, like the 'best teachers of literature' Martin describes, reading is as much a part of life as eating and watching television. They always have at least one novel on the go and they buy books regularly, either in hard copy or electronically. Look around a bus or train and you will see that many people are reading novels, newspapers and magazines, or are reading from an electronic device. Some may be texting or sending e-mails, while others may be solving word puzzles. In fact, anyone new to a place like Britain would probably assume that it is a nation of readers, and enthusiastic readers at that.

However, many people are not so enthusiastic about reading and while most may engage in reading activities at a functional level by texting, e-mailing, etc., they may not read novels and poems. They may struggle with reading and find it challenging, but more likely they lost whatever enthusiasm they may once have had for literature while still at school. Does this matter? After all, if people have reading skills which are adequate for their daily lives and their reading preferences do not include fiction and poetry, shouldn't we simply respect their choices? Are they actually missing anything if they choose not to read novels and poems? Is there anything which these genres can offer which cannot be found in other media, including theatre, films and television?

Research Focus

Fiction and non-fiction

Researchers at the University of California, Berkeley, conducted a study of 94 people and measured the extent to which they read fiction and non-fiction. Through conducting tests which included showing participants video clips of people interacting and then asking them questions, they discovered that people who read predominantly fiction had greater social abilities, for example in guessing the mental states of people in photographs and in matching children in videos to their parents. The researchers argued that while non-fiction increases expertise in topics such as cookery, genetics or whatever the subject matter of the books was, fiction develops expertise in empathising and socialising.

(Oatley, 2009)

So perhaps there are sound reasons why teachers should foster a love of reading in children. Apart from providing entertainment, information, pleasure and relaxation, stories and poems can help us to look at the world around us in a more reflective way, and be better able to consider people's motives for actions. Indeed, DiYanni (1997) argued that besides entertaining and enlightening us and engaging our imaginations, stories *enlarge our understanding of ourselves and deepen our appreciation of life* (p.27).

As you will see in Chapter 8 on issue fiction, sometimes authors set out to address a current issue or scenario with the specific aim of getting readers to explore their views. Often authors set up moral dilemmas which force readers to consider how they would react to situations and to compare their own solutions to problems with those of fictional characters. Indeed, it has been argued that most fiction can be viewed in terms of 'facts' about characters. Peha (2003) maintains there are five facts of fiction:

Fact 1: Fiction is all about a character. Who is your main character? What does he or she look like? Can you describe your character's personality? How did this character get to be this way?

Fact 2: Fiction is all about what your character wants. What does your character want more than anything else? Why does your character want it? Some characters want a lot; some want a little. It doesn't really matter as long as what your character wants is extremely important. The more important it is, the more your character will do to get it, and that's what makes the plot so interesting.

Fact 3: Fiction is all about how your character gets or does not get what he or she wants. Is your character successful? Or does your character's quest end in failure? Either way, it can still be a great story. The trick is to understand how your character succeeds or fails. What obstacles does your character encounter? What solutions does your character craft to meet the challenges of his or her world?

Fact 4: Fiction is all about how your character changes. How does your character change as a result of what happens? What was your character like at the beginning? What is your character like at the end? What has your character learned? What did you learn from reading the story?

Fact 5: Fiction is all about a world an author creates. How did the author create the world of the book? What kinds of people, places, things and ideas did the author include? What successes, disasters and conflicts does this world have? What are the good things in this world? What are the bad things? Complete the following sentence: 'This is a world where ...' Remember: the story is made up, but it is also true to its world.

Activity

Look at Peha's *Five Facts of Fiction* and apply them to a character in a story you know well. How well do they work? Is this a model you could use in the classroom? How might you adapt it for different age groups?

What Peha's model achieves is to make us think about the potential of literature for helping us to think more deeply about character and to give us ideas for how we might explore this with children. Through reading and discussing what we read, we can develop an understanding of ways in which problems can be tackled and learn how other people live or used to live. And literature can help us in all sorts of other ways. Through reading, we broaden our knowledge and understanding of language, our vocabularies and our appreciation of different ways of expressing ideas. This helps us when we write as well as when we hold conversations.

As teachers, we can enhance work across the curriculum by introducing children to relevant stories and poems. For example, for history we might look at some of the following to add interest to studies of different periods.

Aiken, Joan	*Black Hearts in Battersea*	nineteenth century (historical fantasy)
Avery, Gillian	*The Elephant War*	nineteenth century
Bawden, Nina	*Carrie's War*	Second World War
Boston, Lucy M	*Children of Green Knowe*	seventeenth century
Dickens, Monica	*The Great Fire*	seventeenth century
Jones, Terry	*The Saga of Erik the Viking*	Vikings
Kerr, Judith	*When Hitler Stole Pink Rabbit*	1930s refugees
King, Clive	*Stig of the Dump*	present and Stone Age
Lively, Penelope	*The Ghost of Thomas Kempe*	today and seventeenth century

Morpurgo, Michael	*Friend or Foe*	Second World War
Sutcliffe, Rosemary	*The Eagle of the Ninth*	Romans
Treece, Henry	*Children's Crusade*	thirteenth century

(See Chapter 3 for further ideas and suggestions.)

Given the huge potential of literature, it is worrying that some teachers do not appear to value children's literature or have a wide knowledge of it.

Research Focus

Teachers and reading

Concerned by evidence from such sources as PIRLS (2006; see Twist, et al., 2007) that children in the UK increasingly found less pleasure in reading than those in other countries, Cremin, et al. (2008) undertook a survey of teachers' reading habits, preferences and knowledge of children's literature. While they found that most of the 1200 teachers who responded to their questionnaire were regular readers who made use of stories and poems which they had enjoyed as children, the researchers had significant concerns about their findings.

Teachers were asked to name six children's authors, poets and picture book makers. The researchers concluded that:

> … it is questionable whether they know a sufficiently diverse range of writers to enable them to foster reader development and make informed recommendations to emerging readers with different needs and interests. The lack of professional knowledge and assurance with children's literature which this research reveals and the minimal knowledge of global literature indicated has potentially serious consequences for all learners, particularly those from linguistic and cultural minority groups who may well be marginalised unless teachers' own reading repertoires can be expanded. Furthermore, the infrequent mention of poetry in teachers' personal reading and their lack of knowledge of poets, as well as the relative absence of women poets and poets from other cultures writing in English, is also a concern, as is the dearth of knowledge of picture book creators, and the almost non-existent mention of picture book writers for older readers.
>
> It is debatable therefore whether teachers are familiar with a wide enough range of children's authors in order to plan richly integrated and holistic literacy work. The evidence suggests that if units of work or author studies are undertaken they are likely to be based around the work of writers from the canon, whose writing may already be very well known to children. The wide popularity and teacher reliance on the prolific work of Dahl may restrict children's reading repertoires, since child-based surveys suggest he is also a core author of choice for children. This convergence of choice by adults and children is likely to narrow the range still further.
>
> (p.458)

Cremin, et al. (2008) provide a disquieting view of the consequences of some teachers' lack of engagement with literature. It is therefore important that as teachers train they develop a knowledge and understanding of children's literature, as well as an enthusiasm for sharing it with children, which will enable them to broaden children's reading horizons. In the case study below, you will see that tutorial discussions about children's literature revealed that some student teachers claim that they never read children's literature and that it doesn't appeal to them.

Case Study

Trainees who don't read children's novels

Some students also said that they had few recollections of reading stories as children and only did so later in order to pass English Literature GCSE. Other students asserted that those who didn't read and didn't know about children's literature were not only missing a treat but were also going to be ill-prepared to be primary teachers. The tutor, seeking to avoid a potentially unpleasant argument, suggested a challenge: she asked if two people who did not read children's literature would agree to sample a selection made by others in the group. Josh and Lauren agreed and were asked to say what their hobbies were and what kind of stories appealed to them in films and on TV so that the others could discuss in small groups some stories which might appeal to them. The tutor suggested there should be six recommendations each for Josh and Lauren and that these should include at least one which would appeal to Key Stage 1 children and should not include two books by the same author.

Josh enjoyed adventure movies and sport. He said that he liked stories which had clear endings in which everything was sorted out and he thought he would be unlikely to persist with a book which didn't have plenty of action. Lauren liked to travel and enjoyed movies set in other countries and those which addressed social issues and made her think. She asked for stories in which girls were central characters and were 'feisty and had opinions'.

The other students held lengthy discussions about a wide range of stories and agreed to narrow their selections down for the following week and to bring in copies of the chosen stories. The top six recommendations for Josh and for Lauren were as follows.

Josh	Lauren
Billy the Kid by Michael Morpurgo	*The Gruffalo* by Julia Donaldson
Goodnight Mr Tom by Michelle Magorian	*Matilda* by Roald Dahl
Diary of a Wimpy Kid by Jeff Kinney	*Bill's New Frock* by Anne Fine
Cliff-hanger and *Buried Alive!* (sequel) by Jacqueline Wilson	*The Boy in the Dress* by David Walliams
A Series of Unfortunate Events by Lemony Snicket	*Sylvia and Bird* by Catherine Rayner
The Owl Who Was Afraid of the Dark by Jill Tomlinson	*Precious and the Monkeys* by Alexander McCall Smith

Activity

How many of the stories above do you know?

Which other stories would you recommend for Josh and Lauren?

What would you recommend for each of the following:

- a Year 3 girl who is a proficient reader but doesn't read for pleasure – she likes horses and enjoys soaps on TV;
- a Year 5 boy who likes football, action films and computer games.

Guiding children to reading

Research focus

What do we know about children's love of reading?

The National Literacy Trust (NLT) has conducted a national annual literacy survey since 2010. Their annual report outlines findings about the reading habits, and levels of enjoyment, of children and young people aged eight to 18. Their 2015 report contains findings from their survey conducted in November and December 2014.

Overall, it is good news. In 2014 children and young people's level of daily reading increased across all formats, and 60 per cent of children reported having a favourite book. Many thought positively about reading, many reported reading for fun, and children and young people's enjoyment of reading improved (Clark, 2015). However, despite these positive shifts in attitudes, there are still only just over 50 per cent of children who report that they enjoy reading, and there are some significant differences between groups of children: overall girls enjoy reading more than boys, and socio-economic status remains a factor in reading frequency and enjoyment. Additionally, technology-based reading (websites, social networking and messaging) remain the most commonly read material outside the classroom.

Clearly, if we are to be able to help our pupils to broaden their knowledge and experience of literature, we need to develop our own knowledge and experience. If you look at an online bookseller site you will see that whenever you locate a book you are interested in buying you will be shown examples of other books which people who bought your choice also bought. It is part of our role as teachers of reading to guide children to the range of children's literature which is available. This means that we need to have a broad knowledge of different texts and we also need to develop strategies for enabling children to share their recommendations. To help develop your own knowledge of texts, build a literature portfolio.

Activity

Creating a literature portfolio

Look at charts of best-selling children's books both current and over time (you will find lists on several websites) and identify those which you haven't read. Make brief notes on the books as you read them, commenting on the following:

- age groups which might enjoy the book;
- how the book might be linked to work across the curriculum;
- whether the book would have wide appeal and be suitable for reading to a whole class or whether it might be one which only some readers would enjoy;
- other books that someone who enjoyed the book might like to read.

Build your portfolio throughout your teaching career and include poems as well as stories and you will find not only that your own knowledge of children's literature broadens, but also that you have a useful resource for finding stories and poems for the children you teach and the student teachers you will help to train. As you can see from the case study below, a literature portfolio can be an invaluable resource.

Case Study

Changing children's attitudes

At a school in the northeast of England the literacy co-ordinator was concerned that so many children rarely read except when directed to do so. Children's reading performance was below the national average and the teacher felt that it would improve if children's attitudes to reading for pleasure improved. She asked the English tutor from a local university for suggestions as to how to go about changing children's attitudes. It was agreed that the tutor would seek volunteers from the Postgraduate Certificate in Education (PGCE) course to attend the school on Wednesday afternoons, when they had no workshops or school visits, to act as reading role models.

As part of their course, the students produced children's literature portfolios which were placed in the course VLE to share with others. At an exploratory meeting between the tutor and the volunteer students, it was suggested that a starting point for work with the children could be to share with them some of the stories and poems the students had included in their portfolios, even where these might be more appropriate for younger children. It was hoped that sharing some of the books which the students loved, and which, perhaps, the children had enjoyed when younger, might be a good way to get them to talk about stories and poems and what they enjoyed.

$\longrightarrow$

In all, 17 student teachers volunteered to work in the school over a four-week period, taking with them some of the books they had reviewed and being prepared to share and discuss them with Year 5 and Year 6 children. Most children responded very well to working in pairs with a student and enjoyed the attention they received and found revisiting old favourites enjoyable. The students discussed with the children what they enjoyed reading and made notes which they could compare with other students. In a plenary session after the children had gone home, students and the tutor and literacy co-ordinator discussed and suggested stories which might engage different children, given their expressed preferences. Students went away to find copies of stories in readiness for the following week's visit.

Curriculum Links

Literature portfolios can be an excellent resource for noting stories and poems which might enhance learning across the curriculum. Try creating a spreadsheet which you can use to pick out selections of texts relevant to different topics. This can be added to as you discover new stories and poems and could become a shared resource for a school staff or a group of trainee teachers.

Activity

In the next chapter, you will find strategies for sharing literature with children. Before reading the chapter, consider how you would share stories with Year 5 and Year 6 children in a school with a similar situation to that described in the case study above.

Further strategies for developing a love of reading

Reading groups

Another way of increasing knowledge of books is to arrange children into reading groups which meet to discuss what they have read. Encourage them to prepare for these meetings and to share excerpts from books they enjoy, as well as to try out some of the recommendations of other group members. For some meetings, ask everyone in the group to read the same book in advance and be prepared to discuss it. The BBC Radio 4 programme, *A Good Read*, is an excellent model for this. The programme is especially interesting when each of the three panel members shares a favourite book, which the others also have to read in advance, and some love the book and others hate it!

If you look in many bookshops you will find a section of shelves on which members of staff have placed cards with their own comments about the books. Try this with your class, asking each child to choose and display a book and write on a postcard-sized sheet their opinions on it and to whom they would recommend it.

Shared and guided reading

Another simple way to introduce children to different books is to use excerpts in shared and guided reading. While it is good practice to choose extracts from books which children will read from beginning to end, it can also be a very good strategy to show them passages which may encourage them to find the book and read it in full. It is important, therefore, to have available copies of any books which you select excerpts from for shared reading.

Guided reading, too, can provide opportunities to whet appetites, especially when the parts children read can be discussed and children are asked to make predictions about what might happen next. They can subsequently read the rest of the books independently to see how their predictions matched the authors' decisions.

However, you need to exercise caution when conducting guided reading sessions. Guided reading enables us to:

- help children to apply newly learned skills in context;
- meet the needs of individuals, or groups of individuals working at the same level;
- guide children through a text;
- prompt children to apply the knowledge and skills they have learned elsewhere;
- encourage and extend independent reading skills on new and increasingly challenging texts.

But it can also put some children off reading stories if they feel that the only reason to do this is to engage in analysis of the text. It is important to balance direct learning with giving children opportunities to enjoy stories for their own sake.

Dialogic book talk

A possible alternative to guided reading, which enables children to have greater ownership of discussions, is dialogic book talk. This has been described as a collaborative act of enquiry, in which participants:

- use language for thinking;
- make connections to things they already know;
- ask questions of the book;

- explore the book at different levels;
- give reasons for what they say.

(DCSF, 2008, p.1)

Sessions might begin with you reading to the children or the children may read independently or in pairs. Books may be full of pictures or could be prose, depending upon the age and abilities of the children.

Books can be fiction or non-fiction but should make the reader ask questions. To plan for sessions you need to think about possible questions and opportunities for children to have differing views about aspects of the text. They might discuss:

- the setting for a story and how this affects characters and events;
- the characters and their relationships with each other and importance to the story;
- events: do they like the way things turned out? Can they suggest alternatives?

Rather than having a prepared script for the discussion, it may be better to anticipate what children may wish to discuss and to prepare some prompts to move things on as they exhaust topics. You should avoid simple questions such as 'Who is that?' or 'What is he doing?', which result in simple answers, and instead prompt children to think and discuss. Important things to consider when using dialogic book talk include the following.

- Allow pauses and thinking time – don't rush in to fill gaps in the talk.
- Try to use prompts such as 'I wonder why … ' rather than direct questions such as 'Why does …?' This suggests that you really want to know, rather than that you already have the answer and are checking whether or not the children know it.
- You need to be ready to move things on if children have nothing to say or are going round in circles.
- Expect children to listen to each other first time round rather than making them repeat what they've said, or repeating it for them, though you may wish to recast it in order to encourage other children to contribute.
- Listen carefully to everything the children say – be ready for the flash of insight from the child who doesn't seem to have been listening at all.
- Be prepared to let the conversation go in directions which you hadn't expected.
- Encourage children to go back to the book to look again at pictures, and re-read for them bits they refer to. The activity is not a test of memory, and going back often gives an opportunity to go deeper or change your mind.
- Stop when the children start to show that they have had enough.

Using excerpts to whet appetites – the DVD approach

In the days when renting videos and DVDs was a regular activity for many people, the first thing we saw after inserting the film into our machine was a series of highlights from other films. These excerpts were short and designed to tempt us to go out and buy or rent the films or watch them in the cinema. While there are many occasions when we may wish to avoid sharing only small passages from books with children, there is also a place for the DVD approach, which can show children a range of potentially interesting and exciting stories. Do be careful not to give too much of the story away since children, just like most adults, may not wish to read a story if they know how it ends.

In the case study below, you will see how Asif, a newly qualified teacher working in a small rural school and teaching a Years 3–4 class, sets about raising the profile of books for his class.

Case Study

A book week

After discussing his ideas with the other staff members, it was decided that a whole-school book week would be planned. Asif was given responsibility for co-ordinating it.

Asif had experienced a book week in one of his placement schools during training and contacted the literacy co-ordinator there to ask for a meeting so he could find out about some of the practicalities of arranging one for his school. He was advised that if the book week was to be really successful he would need at least three months' preparation time in which to do the following.

- Invite a local children's bookshop to set up a stall offering discounts to parents and children.

- Invite a local children's author and establish that she has a DBS certificate.

- Hire costumes for teachers who would take on roles from well-known stories.

- Involve parents and carers.

- Plan activities and competitions including designing book covers; best book-related costumes; book quizzes, etc.

- Invite an English tutor from the local university to speak to parents at an evening meeting about ways of sharing literature with children.

- Put up displays of extracts from books, poems and plays.

Asif took his former colleague's advice and added further ideas of his own, including a school performance for parents in which each class divided children into groups to enact scenes from stories, read poems chorally, sing songs from *Charlie and the Chocolate Factory* and hold a *Who Wants to Be a Millionaire*-style quiz on children's literature for volunteer children and parents.

The week was a great success and there was a noticeable increase in many children's engagement with fiction in the weeks which followed.

Research Focus

Reading and ebooks

The impact of ebooks on reading motivation and reading skill of children and young people (Picton and Clarke, 2015)

> *I like reading now, it's more simple, it's easier to use – I read a lot more at home even. I'm more comfortable reading online, I'm not sure why. I read at home on my phone, my ipad, my brother's game console … a lot more people should give it a try.*

> (Picton and Clarke, 2015, p.6)

This study investigated the impact of ebooks on reading motivation and skill over the period of an academic year. Schools from across the UK provided attitudinal and attainment data before and after running an ebooks project with a group of pupils. Practitioners and pupils were also interviewed and took part in focus groups to explore the initial findings in more depth.

The key findings from the study relating to children's enjoyment of reading were as follows.

- Enjoyment of reading increased significantly over the course of the project activities.

- More pupils thought reading was cool after the project.

- Fewer children said that they found reading difficult or that they couldn't find things to read that interested them.

- Positive attitudinal changes were more pronounced for boys than girls.

- Reading enjoyment increased, in particular for boys who started the project with the lowest levels of reading enjoyment.

- Most pupils preferred reading using technology but a higher proportion didn't have a preference for the format they read on.

- 84.6 per cent of practitioners felt that the ebooks project had increased pupils reading enjoyment and motivation.

Curriculum Links

Book weeks can be themed to link them to topics and subject areas being studied by different classes. As you will see in Chapter 3, there is great potential for enhancing work across the curriculum through the use of stories and poems. For example, in Asif's book week teachers and children dressed in costumes related to stories. These costumes could have been related to historical periods, with a Second World War topic being enhanced through the creation of a school museum with artefacts borrowed from library services and children's families, and children discovering novels about the period, such as Michele Magorian's *Goodnight Mr Tom* and Nina Bawden's *Carrie's War*.

Reading into writing – teaching sequence for writing

The success of Asif's book week demonstrates that enjoying literature can to lead to other activities, one of which is writing. However, not all teachers make the link effectively, perhaps because of a limited knowledge of children's literature or because they fail to see the opportunities available, as the conversation below illustrates.

These children have no imaginations. They can't write stories!

These were the words of an experienced teacher who despaired of her class's inability to write the kind of imaginative, exciting tales which she claimed children would have been capable of producing when she began teaching 30 years earlier.

How often do you read to them? I asked.

Well, I read to them in shared reading, but there's no time for reading stories in lesson time these days. We've got SATs to practise for and there aren't enough hours in the day to spend time reading stories to them.

> ### Activity
>
> How could the teacher above help develop children's imaginations so that they could write more exciting stories?

In fact, the *Talk for Writing* (DCSF, 2008b) shows us that reading is the essential starting point for writing. Just as the BBC's *Blue Peter* always showed 'one I made earlier' before demonstrating how to make a model, so teachers need to show children examples of the genres they wish them to use in their writing. By reading stories and poems we provide ideas for content and structure for children's writing.

A further challenge

You have seen in this chapter the importance of teachers developing a wide knowledge of children's literature. Through doing this they can help inspire and engage their pupils. However, international studies (Twist, et al., 2007; OECD, 2010) consistently show that there is a particular challenge in engaging boys with reading.

Research Focus

Boys' and girls' reading

A study in Finland, which also looked at research from elsewhere, is worth considering as we look for strategies to address many boys' lack of enthusiasm for reading. In Finland boys achieve higher than boys in other countries yet achieve significantly lower than Finnish girls, according to PISA (the Programme for International Student Assessment, of the Organisation for Economic Co-operation and Development) (OECD, 2010). Finnish children perform significantly better than their peers in almost all other countries and have a high level of interest and engagement in reading outside school. The PISA assessment showed that they borrowed books from the library more frequently than in any other OECD country and 41 per cent of boys reported that reading was one of their favourite pastimes, but for girls the figure was 60 per cent.

Merisuo-Storm (2006) studied 145 ten- and eleven-year-olds (67 boys and 78 girls) from a Finnish comprehensive school in order to:

- explore fourth-grade pupils' attitudes towards reading and writing;
- find out what texts pupils would choose to read and write and which materials they did not find attractive;
- find whether girls and boys enjoyed reading different texts. (p.115)

Merisuo-Storm's (2006) conclusions accord strongly with those of Cremin, et al. (2008) described earlier in this chapter:

> The teacher's love for literature, and ability to find reading and writing material that interests pupils, are crucial.

> (p.114)

> It is crucial that the teacher gathers information about his or her pupils' interests. With interesting reading material it is possible to encourage even the most reluctant reader to read.

> (p.124)

Activity

Have you found in your experience in schools that boys tend to be less enthusiastic about reading than girls?

Do you think teachers need to take into account gender differences when planning reading activities?

Discuss your views with a colleague.

Conclusion

As you will see in Chapter 10 on classic texts, literature permeates our culture. We know things about stories which we have never read, and not only because literature so often becomes films, television programmes, musicals and plays. We use phrases and names in everyday life which refer to novels and poems. Sometimes these come from Shakespeare or Dickens and many people can complete lines even if they have never read a play or novel. If we say *To be or not to be*, people will very probably know that the next words are *that is the question*, even if they have never read or seen *Hamlet*. If we say *Romeo, Romeo* people will continue with *wherefore art thou Romeo?* We refer to mean people as *Scrooge* even though we may never have read *A Christmas Carol*, and if anyone says *Please sir, I want some more*, many people will know the line comes from *Oliver Twist*.

Literature is, then, part of our heritage. We live in a highly literate society with texts all around us. Many texts are used functionally and enable us to go about our daily lives getting from place to place; filling in forms; responding to messages; and keeping up to date with events. We can function in our society without necessarily having a love of reading, but many would argue that life is richer if we read for pleasure as well as purpose.

For children acquiring reading skills, having teachers whose enthusiasm for reading is infectious can be just the incentive they need to make progress. If they know what a good story can sound like because a skilled reader has shared it with them, they are more likely to want to read stories independently. Just as people who want to be top athletes will spend hours practising the skills of their sports so that they can perform at the highest level, so children are more likely to work hard to develop the reading skills which will enable them to enjoy exciting stories if they can see a purpose for their endeavours. As Rose (2006) maintained: *it is important to make sure that, over the course of acquiring phonic skills, children are also given every opportunity to enjoy and benefit from excellent literature* (para 116, p.36).

Learning Outcomes Review

You should now have ideas for making reading an appealing activity and recognise the importance of being an active reader with a wide knowledge of texts. You should also be aware of strategies for developing children's enthusiasm for and engagement with reading, and for developing both girls' and boys' love of reading.

Self-assessment questions

1   What are the key features of dialogic book talk?
2   Why is it important for teachers to have a wide knowledge of texts?

Further Reading

Rose, J. (2006) *Independent Review of the Teaching of Early Reading, Final Report, March 2006* (The Rose Review – Ref: 0201–2006DOC-EN). Nottingham: DfES Publications.

Most initial teacher education courses make the Rose Review essential reading. It is important to understand that while there is a strong emphasis in the review on phonics, this is set within the context of an emphasis on the importance of providing children *with every opportunity to enjoy and benefit from excellent literature* (para 116, p.36).

References

Clark, C. (2015) Children and Young People's Reading 2014. Findings from the National Literacy Trust's annual survey. Available at: www.literacytrust.org.uk/research/nlt_research/6646_childrens_and_young_peoples_reading_in_2014 (accessed 12.04.16).

Cremin, T., Mottram, M., Bearne, E. and Goodwin, P. (2008) Exploring teachers' knowledge of children's literature. *Cambridge Journal of Education*, 38(4): 449–64.

DCSF (2008a) *The National Strategies – Early Years: Communication, Language and Literacy Essential Knowledge.* Reference: 00159-2008EPD-01.

DCSF (2008b) *Talk for Writing*. London: DCSF.

DiYanni, R. (1997) *Literature: Reading Fiction, Poetry, Drama and the Essay.* Boston, MA: McGraw-Hill.

Martin, T. (2003) Minimum and maximum entitlements: Literature at Key Stage 2. *Reading Literacy and Language*, 37(1): 14–17.

Merisuo-Storm, T. (2006) Girls and boys like to read and write different texts. *Journal of Educational Research*, 50(2): 111–25.

Oatley, K. (2009) The mind's flight simulator. *The Psychologist*, 21: 1030–32.

OECD (2010) *PISA 2009 Results: Executive Summary.* Available at: www.oecd.org/pisa/pisaproducts/46619703.pdf (accessed 12.04.16).

Peha, S. (2003) What Can You Say About a Book? Available at: www.ttms.org/say_about_a_book/facts_of_fiction.htm (accessed 12.04.16).

Picton, I. Clark, C. (2015) The impact of ebooks on the reading motivation and reading skills of children and young people. Available at: www.literacytrust.org.uk/research/nlt_research/6975_the_impact_of_ebooks_on_the_reading_motivation_and_reading_skills_of_children_and_young_people (accessed 12.04.16).

Rose, J. (2006) *Independent Review of the Teaching of Early Reading, Final Report, March 2006* (The Rose Review – Ref: 0201–2006DOC-EN). Nottingham: DfES Publications.

Twist, L., Schagen, I. and Hodgson, C. (2007) *Readers and Reading: The National Report for England 2006* (PIRLS). Slough: NFER/DfES.

2 Sharing literature with children

Learning Outcomes

By reading this chapter you will have:

- considered strategies for sharing literature with children;
- looked at ways of responding to reading;
- considered ways of reading to children.

Introduction

Teacher training should always include modules dedicated to developing the teachers' own appreciation of literature, so that when they come to read to the children or to recommend a book, it is meant, and the children know it. To use books simply as a teacher's tool is unlikely to convince many children that books are for them, particularly those that are failing already, many of whom will be boys.

(Morpurgo, 2012)

In the previous chapter, you looked at the importance of developing a love of reading in children. In this chapter, you will explore ways in which you might share literature with them.

It may seem that there is a perfectly straightforward way of doing this: you either read lots of stories and poems to your class or you provide lots of stories and poems for them to read, or you do a combination of both. Many teachers have done just that with success. However, there are further activities which will also engage children's interest and develop both their love of reading and their awareness of different genres. Some of these will be discussed later in this chapter, but first let's look at three strategies.

Shared reading enables teachers to model the reading process for children and involves children following text as the teacher reads it and then reading with the teacher. By showing how they approach unfamiliar words and phrases and by modelling expressive reading, teachers can show children how a text can be brought to life as they follow it and then join in.

Guided reading enables us to focus on texts which groups of children read and to look at them closely and discuss textual features (see Chapter 1). Both shared and guided reading help children to develop strategies which they can use when reading independently, but they are not simply stages on the route to independence. Even the most able readers can benefit from discussing texts and examining the ways in which they are constructed. Shared reading is not simply for younger children. As children's reading develops and they meet new and more challenging texts, you will need to model ways of approaching them. As you will see in Chapter 12 on poetry, there are skills and techniques which need to be deployed which many adult readers, including some teachers, have not acquired.

However, shared and guided reading are strongly associated with literacy lessons in which they may feature as part of a sequence of activities. Michael Morpurgo, quoted at the beginning of this chapter, warns against using books simply as teachers' tools and it is important that we use strategies which engage children rather than put them off reading. Another approach, which has been part of classroom practice for many years, involves simply reading to children, although this may well be accompanied by associated activities.

Reading to children

The advent of a rather overwhelmingly demanding National Curriculum in 1988, followed by National Strategies for literacy and numeracy and numerous revisions of the National Curriculum have been blamed for the reduction in time devoted to reading to children. For many years trainee teachers, urged by their tutors to read to children, have sometimes been thwarted by teachers who protested that there simply wasn't time in the day for such 'frills'. With SATs to prepare for and an emphasis on structured literacy hours in which extracts from books were used to study language, from 1998 teachers' priorities often relegated story time to a rather lowly status. However, there are some very important reasons why reading stories and poems to children should be an integral part of children's literacy development and a key feature of the school day.

- If teachers, who should be able to provide a model of good reading, do not read stories to children, how will children know what a well-read story or poem can sound like? For those children who read haltingly and focus heavily on decoding words, there can be immense pleasure in hearing a skilled reader bringing a text to life.

- Once children hear stories and poems read well, they will be more likely to want to read them themselves, even if this is with the help of a more able reader. Next time you read a story to your class, notice how often children ask if they can read the book too.

- By reading to children we can introduce them to texts which they could not read easily independently. They can then enjoy being 'lost' in a story and experience the delight of desperately wanting to know what happens next.

- Reading stories and poems to children provides them with ideas for their own writing: not only plots and themes, but also ways of describing events, interesting vocabulary and different ways of phrasing.

- Whole-class story time provides an opportunity for the class to come together for a common and pleasurable purpose. It also provides lots of opportunities to involve children at different levels.

The case study below demonstrates some of the ways in which a trainee teacher turned story time into a participative and interactive activity.

Case Study

Daily stories

Helen, a School Direct PGCE trainee with a love of children's literature from her own childhood, wanted to share her favourite children's novel, Roald Dahl's *Danny the Champion of the World*, with her Year 4 class. The class teacher was reluctant to allow Helen to spend more than 30 minutes a week reading to the children, but Helen persuaded him to let her show how spending 15 minutes a day reading to children could be both highly productive and enjoyable for children. The teacher agreed, but insisted that this would only be tried for two weeks and that if story time was 'no more than a pleasant diversion from the curriculum' the time spent would be reduced.

Helen re-read the book carefully, making notes on how different parts of the story might involve children in a range of ways and where there were opportunities to link the reading to other aspects of the curriculum and to literacy lessons in particular.

She decided that reading the story to the children could, besides being a pleasurable and entertaining activity, involve focusing on the following:

- investigating hunting and discussing the pros and cons of breeding pheasants and other creatures for game;

- drama including children working individually on Danny's drive to rescue his father; Danny and his father finding pheasants falling from trees; an argument between Mr Victor Hazel and Danny's father;

- investigating dialects after looking at Sergeant Samways' dialogue;

- creating interesting fact boards like the one suggested by Danny.

The children were captivated by the story and Helen discovered that it not only provided opportunities for a series of purposeful activities, but also had the unexpected by-product of helping with class management. The children were so keen to hear the next episode of the story that Helen was able to use it as an incentive for good working habits: 'If you work really hard in maths, we'll stop five minutes before playtime and hear what happened to Danny!'

Curriculum Links

The National Curriculum for England (2014) emphasises the importance of reading aloud to children at both ends of the primary school:

Year 1 programme of study: Non-statutory notes and guidance

By listening frequently to stories, poems and other books that they cannot yet read for themselves, pupils start to learn how language sounds and increase their vocabulary and awareness of grammatical structures. In due course, they will be able to draw on such grammar in their own writing.

(DfE, 2013, p.22)

By listening frequently to stories, poems and non-fiction that they cannot yet read for themselves, pupils begin to understand how written language can be structured in order, for example, to build surprise in narratives or to present facts in non-fiction.

Years 5 and 6 programme of study: Non-statutory notes and guidance

Even though pupils can now read independently, reading aloud to them should include whole books so that they meet books and authors that they might not choose to read themselves.

(DfE, 2013, p.45)

Research (see below) suggests that many children do not have stories read to them at home. This, therefore, makes it all the more important that they have this experience at school.

Research Focus

A picture of literacy in the UK

Deeqa Jama and George Dugdale (2010) produced a report for the National Literacy Trust, *Literacy: State of the Nation – A picture of literacy in the UK today*, in which they looked at children's reading habits. Their findings on literacy in the home and reading and writing frequency are particularly interesting.

- 73 per cent of parents and carers say their child often reads (p.25).

- Age is closely linked to attitudes towards reading and reading behaviour. 30 per cent of five- to eight-year-olds read a book every day compared with only 17 per cent of 15- to 17-year-olds (p.26)

→

- However, teenagers are more likely to read other materials such as blogs, websites and newspapers (p.27).

- 14 per cent of children and young people in lower-income homes rarely or never read their books for pleasure (p.28).

- Parents are the most important reading role models for their children and young people. 71 per cent of young people say that their mothers are their most important role model for reading and 62 per cent say their fathers (p.29).

- One in five parents easily finds the opportunity to read to their children, with the rest struggling to read to their children due to fatigue and busy lifestyles.

- Of the parents that read to the children, 67 per cent are mothers compared to just 17 per cent of fathers [sic] (p.30).

The importance of sharing literature with children is recognised internationally. In Canada, the Ontario report of the expert panel on early reading, *Early Reading Strategy* (Ontario, 2003), stated:

> *Reading aloud to children helps them to develop a love of good literature, motivation to pursue reading on their own, and familiarity with a variety of genres, including non-fiction. It provides them with new vocabulary, exposes them to a variety of literature, and contributes to their oral and written language development. Reading aloud should occur every day in the early stage of reading instruction to stimulate the children's interest in books and reading.*

(p.24)

Interestingly, given the prominence accorded to systematic synthetic phonics in England, the United States National Reading Panel, which reviewed a wide range of research on the teaching of reading, concluded in its Executive Summary:

> *Phonics instruction is never a total reading program. In 1st grade, teachers can provide controlled vocabulary texts that allow students to practice decoding, and they can also read quality literature to students to build a sense of story and to develop vocabulary and comprehension. Phonics should not become the dominant component in a reading program, neither in the amount of time devoted to it nor in the significance attached.*

(NICHHD, 2000, pp. 2–97)

And while the Panel was strongly in favour of phonics being a key strategy in teaching reading, it also emphasised the importance of story:

> *Knowing the structure of the story and its time, place, characters, problems, goals, solutions, and resolution facilitates comprehension and memory for stories. Stories constitute the bulk of the texts used in elementary school reading.*

(NICHHD, 2000, pp. 4–91)

However, as you will see later in this chapter, sharing literature with children still figures prominently in the English National Curriculum and in the key review of early reading (Rose, 2006), which led to a strong focus on phonics. But while systematic synthetic phonics is central to developing children's reading, there is also an abundance of research which advocates sharing stories with children as a key element of developing their reading and understanding of texts. It is important, therefore, that teachers are confident in their ability to do this.

Strategies for reading aloud

For some people who wish to become teachers, reading is one of the first activities in which they participate. Visits to schools to gain experience before applying for a training course may involve listening to individuals or small groups reading and, perhaps, as the class teacher recognises the aspiring teacher is ready to take more responsibility, reading to a group or even a whole class. For some, this is a wonderful experience in which they first realise that they have the ability to hold children's attention, make them laugh or make them concerned about the fate of characters. For others, this can be a testing occasion and children may exploit any weakness or nervousness to disrupt proceedings. If the latter was your first experience of working with a large group you might be forgiven for becoming anxious about the prospect of repeating it. For some teachers, reading aloud to children lacks appeal, perhaps because they fear children may be restless or disruptive. But there are simple techniques which skilled readers use to gain and hold listeners' attention, and some of these are discussed in the case study below.

Case Study

The art of reading aloud

At a primary school in the north of England a supply teacher, Jeff, who was also a part-time actor, worked for three weeks during a Year 4 class teacher's absence. It quickly became apparent from what children told other teachers that Jeff's story and poetry reading was captivating the children. The headteacher observed one of Jeff's story sessions and asked Jeff if he would read a story in a school assembly so that the whole of Key Stage 2 could enjoy the experience. Jeff read a short story, The Fib, by George Layton and kept 200 children and eight teachers enraptured throughout. He involved children, regularly paused to ask questions, varied voice tone and level and accent, and built up tension through facial expression and pace.

At the end of Jeff's stint at the school the headteacher asked him if he would return to do a workshop for staff on the art of reading to children and story telling. Jeff agreed to do this but asked if the staff would prepare by reflecting on their own story telling and that of their

→

colleagues, taking turns to observe each other to identify the features of successful story telling. He asked that they:

- observe each other for short periods and then discuss what they had seen and talk about strategies which were successful and those which might be developed;

- note children's responses to being read to and hearing stories and poems.

The staff agreed to do this and it was emphasised by the senior management team that the observations were not to be assessments but simply opportunities for colleagues to work together to develop their practice.

When Jeff returned to lead an in-service event, the staff had prepared a short presentation to begin the day in which they described some of the most successful techniques they had seen and the effect these had had upon the children's response. They distilled these into five bullet points.

- Voice variation engaged children.

- Involving children through questioning and actual participation was very effective in holding their attention.

- Including artefacts such as those found in story sacks helped children to follow stories and held their interest.

- Manageable time slots for both teachers and pupils were important – too long and children lost attention; too short and they didn't have time to become engaged.

- Some successful strategies were age- and class-dependent while others seemed to apply universally.

Jeff discussed some of the strategies he had learned as an actor and teachers were encouraged to try these. Throughout the day, teachers took turns to read their favourite poems and stories aloud and to discuss these with colleagues.

As a result of the story telling day, the school built story time into every class's timetable and teachers and teaching assistants (TAs) grew in their confidence about sharing literature with children.

Curriculum Links

In the light of what teachers learned about reading aloud in the case study above, you might consider implications for developing children's ability to read aloud too. Children are often asked to read aloud in a range of subjects and could be helped to develop their confidence if good techniques were shared and discussed.

Research Focus

Prosodic and paralinguistic cues

Gamble and Yates (2002) argue that reading aloud could be a dramatic event in which the reader could use *paralinguistic* and *prosodic* cues to help the listener to understand the narrative.

Prosodic features How the words are spoken	Paralinguistic features The behaviour of the speaker beyond the words
Intonation, pitch, melody	Timbre – tone of voice, whisper, etc.
Loudness	Gesture
Stress, accent	Facial expression
Tempo	Body language
Rhythm	Pauses

It is the features above which, according to Gamble and Yates, *provide a 'soundtrack' which could be likened to the background music in a film* (p.122). Not only do the reader's methods of reading engage and interest the reader, but they also help bring text to life and enable children to understand text which might otherwise prove difficult to interpret. Consider your own response to Shakespeare. Simply reading a play may prove difficult because of the antiquity of some words and phrases and the need to interpret motives of characters and unfamiliar settings. However, when you watch a play performed live or as a film, the actors' tone, stress, gesture and body language make understanding the plot much simpler. As a teacher who is skilled in reading aloud, you can bring stories to life in similar ways.

Following shared reading experiences

The school described in the case study above went on to explore ways of following up reading to children to exploit the enthusiasm which it generated among children. In this section, some possible ways of doing this are explored.

Drama from stories and poems

When considering ways in which drama might emerge from reading it is important to recognise that this does not have to involve everyone leaving the classroom and going to the school hall. Many drama activities can take place while children are sitting in the classroom. For example, after an exciting passage in *Charlie and the Chocolate Factory* in which the hero discovers the golden ticket which will admit him to Mr Wonka's factory, children could be asked to show in facial expressions how Charlie might have looked. They could take turns with a partner to be Charlie and to share their good news.

Drama can involve hot-seating, with children taking on the role of characters and answering questions from classmates. This encourages children to think carefully about the text and the motivations of characters.

Another simple way of introducing drama into story time is to ask some children to 'be' characters in the story and for you to pause when the characters have dialogue so that they can say their lines. If you tell the children in advance they can read ahead and practise their lines, looking out for punctuation such as question and exclamation marks, and adverbs and verbs which will tell them how the lines might be spoken.

Poetry can lead to drama as children mime actions or say lines, especially where these are dialogue. Try involving your class in reading *Please Mrs Butler* by Allan Ahlberg (Ahlberg, 1984) with different children taking on the roles of three different complainants about the naughty Derek Drew, you or another child being the weary teacher responding to the children's grumbles, and someone else being the silent but mischievous Derek.

Continuing stories – teaching sequence for writing

An essential prerequisite for writing is reading. As you saw in Chapter 1, children need to know and understand different genres of texts if they are to be able to write their own. After reading an absorbing opening to a story to children, you might ask them to create their own story openings after investigating a selection from well-known books. Alternatively, children might write the next part of the story. Before writing, ask them to tell the next part of the story to a partner or a small group. Encourage them to make a plan or brief notes to help them to focus their thoughts and ideas. The activity below provides an example.

Activity

A story opening

Look at the opening chapter of a story below then consider the questions which follow:

CHAPTER ONE: **IN THE WOODS**

Darkness enveloped her like a blanket. The smells of night time woods filled her nostrils: damp grass, sweet and musty leaf mould. Above her, the branches of hundreds of trees creaked and swayed in the light breeze. There were other noises too. Small scurrying sounds as woodland creatures sought food or shelter. Lottie thought many of them were keeping an eye out for the owls she had heard hooting a few moments earlier. Daytime woods were friendly, inviting places to play and hide in. She had never realised that they changed character at night.

But it wasn't the woodland creatures or the darkness which Lottie feared the most as she snuggled into the moist bracken which she hoped would hide her. It was the three people who were out there somewhere looking for her. She knew they couldn't be far away, and she listened for footsteps, breaking twigs and alarm calls from birds. When a nightjar screeched as it flew through a nearby clearing, she caught her breath and felt the pain of fear deep in her stomach. Then there was a rustling in the undergrowth behind her and she turned as quietly as she could, terrified that it might be the kidnappers, to find herself staring through the darkness at three roe deer.

They stood, alert and still, checking for their own safety, unaware that she was watching them. Despite her predicament, despite her pounding heart and dry mouth, she was entranced by their beauty. Like her, they were constantly afraid of being captured or killed, but, unlike her, they knew the woods and the places to hide from hunters and other predators. If they had to run, they would know where to run to: if Lottie had to run, she would have to blunder her way through brambles, overhanging branches and thick undergrowth.

Suddenly, the deer pricked up their ears and, as one, galloped away from the clearing. Lottie looked around to see what had startled them and saw, perhaps fifty metres away, the silhouettes of two men. She had to make a decision: run like the deer or stay in her hiding place and hope they didn't find her.

(Waugh, 2015)

After reading the story opening to your class, consider the following questions.

- What would you discuss with them?
- Which words and phrases might you focus upon?
- How would you follow up your reading using drama, discussion and writing?

The story opening could lead to some of the following activities:

- a continuation of the story, either orally or in writing, and perhaps involving children in drama and movement;

- discussion about similes such as *enveloped her like a blanket* and *run like the deer* and asking children to think of other possible similes as they describe the next episode;

- discussion about fear – an exploration of a range of words and phrases used in the text to indicate Lottie's fear and a look at the origins of other words often used to denote fear, such as terrified, petrified and horrified;

- looking at some of the words and phrases which may be unfamiliar to some children and talking about ways in which they are used in the text and could be used in different situations, for example: *enveloped, musty, changed character, screeched, alert, predicament, entranced, predators, silhouettes;*

- first-person writing – asking children to write about the scene or a subsequent episode as if they are Lottie;

- comparison with other stories and poems in which someone is afraid and/or being pursued.

Alternative endings

There is a well-documented history of writers responding to popular demand for alternative endings to stories. Arthur Conan Doyle had decided to kill off his hero Sherlock Holmes so that he could focus on other writing, and although Holmes appeared to die at the Reichenbach Falls in *The Final Problem* as he fought with his arch enemy Moriarty in 1891, Conan Doyle brought the character back to life eight years later in the face of public pressure. The TV drama, *Dallas*, also saw a reincarnation of Bobby Ewing, who emerged from the shower more than a year after his 'death', and the explanation that the storylines of the 1985–86 series, including the accident, were a lengthy dream sequence.

With such famous reincarnations available as examples, together with alternatives to well-known fairy tales such as those found in Dahl's *Revolting Rhymes*, there is great scope for discussion of alternative endings for stories. This might take the form of discussion or could involve drama or writing.

Sequels and prequels

Just as alternative endings might be discussed, so you might also talk with children about sequels and prequels. The sequel is a well-known literary device which has been used by many authors. Dahl's Charlie Bucket, from *Charlie and the Chocolate Factory*, goes on to feature in *Charlie and the Great Glass Elevator*, C.S. Lewis wrote seven books in his Narnia series, and Philip Pullman wrote *His Dark Materials* trilogy between 1995 and 2000, but then produced *Once Upon a Time in the North* as a prequel in 2008.

Sequels are sometimes produced by other authors long after the original has died, and prequels, although less common, are still a significant genre sometimes written by different authors. Charlie Higson's Young James Bond series, for example, tells tales of Bond's schoolboy adventures.

With such well-known examples available and the possibility of sharing film footage of some episodes, sequels and prequels can provide a rich vein of ideas for discussions and writing.

Tell rather than read a story

Oral story telling has a strong tradition in most societies and, as you will see in the chapter on fairy stories, has been the source for many of the tales which we know well and which appear in many countries in varying forms. There is an art to telling a story without a text and you may wish to invite a story teller to school so that children and staff can experience this. However, you may wish to use oral story telling to enable you to share some more challenging literature with your class. As Grainger asserted:

> *The oral tradition of storytelling underpins and complements the growth of language and literacy. Its spellbinding power can liberate children's imaginations, release their creativity and enable them to weave dreams together, as they journey along the road of never-ending stories.*

(Grainger, 1997, p.10)

Many schools now use Shakespearean plays as starting points for drama and writing. However, parts of the plays can prove almost incomprehensible to Key Stage 2 children and they may need to be told those parts of the tales, while other passages can be read to them. This can apply, too, to works by Robert Louis Stevenson and Mark Twain, all of whom wrote stories which are engaging for modern children but which are written in a style which is no longer easily accessible.

Use narrative poems as starting points for stories

As you will see in Chapter 12 on poetry, there are many narrative poems which might be introduced in the primary school. Rather like some of the stories mentioned above, some of these are written in a style which can be difficult to decipher, but when read aloud the poems offer a rich source of imagery and adventure which can lead to discussion, writing and drama. Gibson's *Flannan Isle*, written in 1912 and based on a real event in 1900, tells the story of the mysterious disappearance of three lighthouse keepers from an island in the Outer Hebrides. It offers wonderful opportunities for children to discuss, dramatise or write mystery stories. This can be supported by viewing film about the disappearance from YouTube (www.youtube.com/watch?v=DxXCTFQ-BiM – accessed 12.04.16) and investigations into what is known about the events. There are other sources in popular culture too. A section of the poem even appears in an episode of *Dr Who* (*Horror of Fang Rock*). In 1967, the rock band, Genesis, recorded a song: *The Mystery of Flannan Isle Lighthouse*. There is also an opera based on the incident called *The Lighthouse* by composer Sir Peter Maxwell Davies.

Draw and paint pictures of key events/characters in stories and poems

Poems such as *Flannan Isle* lend themselves to other creative activities, including art. Try reading the poem as children sketch images, perhaps using dark blue paper, chalk and charcoal to capture the mood of the deserted island.

Children might also draw pictures of characters from stories and poems where these are not illustrated in publications. This can encourage them to read and listen carefully to descriptions so that they can produce plausible pictures.

Characterisation

Providing children with opportunities to discuss characters' features, both personal attributes and physical, offers an opportunity for them to reflect upon their behaviour and motivations. A simple starting point could be to create adjective charts in which characteristics are written around a character's picture or name. For example, for Lottie in the story opening above, we might use words and phrases like: afraid, terrified, nervous, tense, shaking with fear, worried.

Role play and hot-seating might follow, with children assuming the role of characters and answering questions or, if appropriate, 'entering conscience alley', whereby the class lines up in two rows, one of which tells the character to take one course of action while the other gives an opposing view. As the character walks slowly between the rows, children make suggestions to them. Afterwards, the character can be interviewed as a hot-seating activity to talk about what he or she has decided to do and why.

Work on characters can be developed in a range of ways, depending upon the age and ability of the children, but it offers a powerful opportunity to engage more closely with a text as well as a potential stimulus for drama and writing.

Research Focus

Planning for reading

The Ontario Report of the Expert Panel on Early Reading, *Early Reading Strategy* (Ontario, 2003) stated:

The teacher should provide children with planned activities for before, during, and after reading. For example:

- *Before beginning to read, the teacher and students establish the purpose for reading. Together they consider what they already know about the topic or genre and use the title, headings, table of contents or index, and new, unfamiliar vocabulary to enhance their predictions.*

- *During reading, the students respond to the text by searching for meaning, identifying the main ideas, predicting and verifying predictions, and building a coherent interpretation of the text. Students bring their experiences of the world and literature into the reading activity. The teacher directs the attention of students to subtleties in the text, points out challenging words and ideas, and identifies problems and encourages the students to predict solutions.*

$\longrightarrow$

- *After reading, the students reflect on their learning as they apply the knowledge acquired during reading, or transfer that knowledge to other contexts (e.g., by retelling, summarizing, creating graphic organizers, or putting pictures in sequential order).*

- *No single skill in this complex interaction is sufficient on its own, and the teacher must be careful not to overemphasize one skill at the expense of others.*

- *With all of this instruction, the teacher provides continuous role modelling, coaching, guiding, and feedback, and is always building on the children's prior knowledge and experiences. The teacher also ensures that children are focused and engaged in the reading process, and monitors their time on task.*

(p.22)

Bearing in mind some of the suggestions made in the Ontario report, consider how you could develop focused activities based upon the text in the activity below.

Activity

Granddad

Read the extract from a story below and consider how you would:

- activate children's prior knowledge;
- discuss any new or unfamiliar words and spellings;
- discuss the use of dialect (*learn us tables, when I were a lad, gi' you a thick ear*, etc.) and the way in which accent is indicated through words such as *wi'*, *gi'* and *t'teachers*;
- look for meaning;
- explore the subtleties of the text. Consider, in particular, Chris's use of anachronisms;
- follow up reading with other activities including drama and writing, and research.

(Please see further ideas below the extract.)

I loved my granddad, but that didn't stop me from amusing my mum and dad by impersonating him.

'Teachers,' I'd say, putting on Granddad's Yorkshire accent, 'they're not like t'teachers we had when I were a lad. If you mucked about in class in my day, they'd gi' you a thick ear. Now they daren't even look at the kids with a cross expression in case some daft parent sues them!'

(Continued)

(Continued)

My parents usually laughed out loud when I did this, even if my mum, who was Granddad's daughter, did say things like, 'Ooh Christopher, you shouldn't make fun of your granddad like that!' But their laughter would encourage me to go on, despite my mum's protests.

'And another thing,' I'd continue, the Yorkshire voice getting deeper, 'they don't teach them properly nowadays. We had to learn us tables and write wi' an ink pen. We didn't have any of these fancy calculators and computers in my day. And we had to help us parents by going out hunting for dinosaurs!'

'Oh Chris, you are daft!' my mum would say.

'And we thought brontosaurus burger was a treat in those days. And my mother used to make a smashing pterodactyl stew. We didn't have any of the fancy pizzas and curries you lot go in for!'

Of course, my granddad didn't really say things like that about dinosaurs, and he knew very well that dinosaurs had become extinct thousands of years ago, but he did go on about how everything was better when he was a child.

The extract could lead to some of the following activities.

- Activate children's prior knowledge: show a YouTube clip of Clive Dunn singing Granddad and look at the lyrics. What do grandparents often talk about? Do they complain that things are not as good as when they were children or do they think that life is easier now? How was life different when they were children?

- Discuss any new or unfamiliar words and spellings.

- Discuss the use of dialect (*learn us tables, when I were a lad, gi' you a thick ear, mucked about*, etc.) and the way in which accent is indicated through words such as *wi'*, *gi'* and *t'teachers*. How would these words and phrases be written or spoken in Standard English? Which dialect phrases and words do children know or use? Are there words which their grandparents use which are no longer commonly used, for example 'wireless' for 'radio'?

- Look for meaning. Why does Chris exaggerate what his granddad says? Does Chris like his granddad?

- Explore the subtleties of the text. Consider, in particular, Chris's use of anachronisms. What is an anachronism? Relate this to a historical period they have studied – what would they not expect to see in, say, a Victorian street scene?

Conclusion

This chapter has emphasised the importance of sharing literature with children. This has become, in some schools, a rather limited activity with a strong focus on shared reading and textual analysis in literacy lessons. However, you have seen that sharing literature can be much more than that and has the potential to develop children's language and literacy skills as well as their affection for literature. It is worth quoting at length from Rose's *Independent Review of Early Reading* (DfES, 2006), which has been widely misinterpreted as being all about phonics. Rose repeatedly refers to a broad and rich language and literature curriculum and states:

> *In the best circumstances, parents and carers, along with settings and schools, do much to foster these attitudes. For example, they stimulate children's early interest in literacy by exploiting play, story, songs and rhymes and provide lots of opportunities, and time, to talk with children about their experiences and feelings. For the youngest children, well before the age of five, sharing and enjoying favourite books regularly with trusted adults, be they parents, carers, practitioners or teachers, is at the heart of this activity. Parents and carers should be strongly encouraged in these pursuits and reassured that, in so doing, they are contributing massively to children's literacy and to their education in general. However, there are significant numbers of children who, for one reason or another, do not start with these advantages.*

(DfES, 2006, p.4)

Rose's *Independent Review of Early Reading* is required reading for most teacher training programmes and it is pleasing to note its strong emphasis upon sharing literature with children as a way of developing their literacy skills and positive attitude to literature.

Learning Outcomes Review

In this chapter you have seen that reading aloud to children is not only a good way to alert them to a range of literature, but also a way of enabling them to enjoy stories and poems which might normally be beyond their reading abilities. You will be aware that reading aloud demands high levels of skills from teachers and that when these are used well there is great potential for follow-up activities with engaged listeners. Stories and poems not only bring pleasure to listeners and readers, but also enable us to develop our knowledge and understanding of the world around us.

Self-assessment question

1   How would you justify spending time reading stories and poems to children if a parent or colleague questioned your approach?

Further Reading

Jolliffe, W., Head, C. and Waugh, D. (2004) *50 Shared Texts for Year 1*. Leamington Spa: Scholastic.

This book and others in the series give ideas for looking closely at texts and provide photocopiable sample texts.

Newton, L. (ed.) (2012) *Creativity for a New Curriculum.* London: David Fulton.

See Chapter 2, 'Creativity in English', for ideas for sharing texts.

References

Ahlberg, A. (1984) *Please Mrs Butler*. London: Puffin.

Dahl, R. (2001) *Revolting Rhymes.* London: Puffin.

DfE (2013) *The National Curriculum in England: Key Stages 1 and 2 Framework Document.* London: DfE. Available at: www.gov.uk/government/uploads/system/uploads/attachment_data/file/335133/PRIMARY_national_curriculum_220714.pdf

DfES (2006) *Independent Review of the Teaching of Early Reading (Final Report by Jim Rose).* Ref: 0201/2006DOC-EN. Nottingham: DfES.

Gamble, N. and Yates, S. (2002) *Exploring Children's Literature.* London: Paul Chapman.

Grainger, T. (1997) *Traditional Storytelling in the Primary Classroom.* Leamington Spa: Scholastic.

Jama, D. and Dugdale, G. (2010) *Literacy: State of the Nation – A picture of literacy in the UK today.* National Literacy Trust, 30 March 2010.

Morpurgo, M. (2012) We are failing too many boys in the enjoyment of reading. *Guardian.* Available at: www.guardian.co.uk/teacher-network/teacher-blog/2012/jul/02/michael-morpurgo-boysreading (accessed 12.04.16). (See his seven tips for engaging boys with reading.)

National Institute of Child Health and Human Development (NICHHD) (2000) *Teaching Children to Read: An evidence-based assessment of the scientific research literature on reading and its implications for reading instruction. Report of the National Reading Panel.* (NIH Publication No. 00–4769).Washington, DC: US Government Printing Office.

Ontario (2003) *Early Reading Strategy – The Report of the Expert Panel on Early Reading in Ontario.* Available at: www.edu.gov.on.ca (Ontario Ministry of Education) (accessed 12.04.16).

Rose, J. (2006) *Independent Review of the Teaching of Early Reading, Final Report, March 2006* (The Rose Review – Ref: 0201–2006DOC-EN). Nottingham: DfES Publications.

Waugh, D. (2015) *Lottie's Run.* Bishop's Castle: Constance Books.

3 Literature across the curriculum

Learning Outcomes

By reading this chapter you will:

- understand why we use children's literature across the curriculum;
- have considered what to look for when choosing books to use in different curriculum areas;
- be able to reflect on how children's literature can be used to support the teaching of science and maths;
- have identified some appropriate books for use in the different curriculum areas;
- have reflected on how individual books encourage learning across different curriculum areas.

Introduction

Using children's literature in your teaching does not have to be limited to the English curriculum. Children's literature has the potential to be used across all curriculum areas. You may be aware of examples of this in practice, for example reading or listening to Jacqueline Wilson's (1998) *Lottie Project* to explore the life of a house maid in Victorian times, or reading *Handa's Surprise* (Browne, 2006) to open up discussion about different foods in different parts of the world. This same approach can be used across all curriculum areas; stories and poetry can be used as a wonderful stimulation for learning whatever the subject. Additionally, children's books and poems can be used as stimuli for cross-curricular thinking, as they bring together themes that straddle curriculum subject divides.

So, what are the benefits of using literature as a stimulus to learning across the curriculum? And how do we integrate literature in our teaching?

Why use children's literature across the curriculum?

Using literature across all areas of learning has the following benefits.

- Engages children: Hayes observes that *joyful teaching does not happen by chance. It blossoms where pupils and adults enthusiastically engage with learning* (2007, p.8). Books and stories have the potential to do this in all areas of learning. They can arouse and excite children's (and adults') imagination and stimulate a sense of enquiry, and, in doing so, provide an immediate and powerful hook into the subject.

- Promotes enquiry: Books and stories engage with our imagination and set our minds running. This is a wonderful way to start or enhance a lesson.

- Contextualises learning: Books and stories provide an authentic context for learning. Stories frame the themes and ideas in a concrete way that enables children to discuss and apply their learning in a realistic context.

Research Focus

Discussing The Creation

Evans' (2016) research investigated children's responses to the text *Die Schöpfung* (The Creation) by Waechter, published in 2002. Evans describes the book thus:

This is a picture book of great quality, dealing with one of life's big unknowns in a thought provoking, humorous, and at times, irreverent manner. At first glance this large size picture book appears simple and child-like with dreamy naïve illustrations executed in soft earthy colours – pinks, browns, blues and sepia, juxtaposed with the characters depicted in a cartoon-like style. All the ingredients needed to create the world are in place – chaotically – and need to be brought together to make a cohesive whole. However, the appearance of simplicity is deceptive. The German title Die Schöpfung *has a double meaning – it is a play on words – meaning to create but also to ladle or scoop. This is reflected in the images and storyline ... especially at the beginning of the book where the first huge double page spread depicts a young girl in pigtails ladling some kind of liquid.*

(p.61)

Before reading the book the children looked at the front cover and predicted what they thought it might be about. Much discussion followed the reading, many comments were made and rhetorical questions asked. The children then reconsidered their initial predictions and summarised the story. Evans characterises the discussion as *rich discussion that released previously untapped thoughts and emotions allowing the reader to reflect on life and its vagaries* (2016, p.64). She concludes that, among other things, the children's engagement with this text gave them the opportunity to:

- empathise with characters;

- philosophise about 'big' questions in life, in particular where they came from, and how the world came to be;

- work collaboratively, offering and sharing points of view;

- really enjoy reading and responding to a thought-provoking book.

- Enhances children's learning: Kelly (2007) describes the natural, everyday ways in which we learn as *ubiquitous learning and intuitive learning*. These he describes as learning that happens as we engage in everyday life and activities: learning is intuitive, as we don't consider it as it is happening, and ubiquitous, as it happens all the time. He contrasts this with school-based learning, which tends to be explicit and formal and regarded as happening at certain times and in certain places. Kelly (2007) illustrates these concepts with research by Nunes (1993 cited in Hayes, 2007, pp11–12), who examined the mathematical competencies of Brazilian street children who traded in goods that they bought from wholesalers. The children, many of whom had almost no formal education, had high levels of mathematical ability, which then translated into a school environment and mathematical tasks. They had acquired this high level of skill by living the experience. In a similar way, a book or story provides for learning that is holistic, ubiquitous and intuitive. We can use this aspect of books and stories in our teaching to enhance children's learning.

- Integrates and enhances literacy: Using literature across the curriculum enables children to integrate and adapt their literacy skills across their learning.

Research Focus

How did the bird die?

Hayes (2007) details this account of a dialogue between a teacher and her class stimulated by a picture book.

The teacher read the book Frog and the Birdsong *(Velthuijs, 1991). It tells the story of a group of animals who come across a blackbird lying on the ground. They are not sure what is wrong but eventually decide that the bird is dead. They bury it and put flowers on the grave. On the way home they play happily together and the final illustration shows a tree with a bird in it accompanied by the text.* There in the tree was a blackbird singing a lovely song – as always. *The class of six-year-old children were asked to think about what interested them in the story. One child commented,* I think the bird in the tree was the one in the hole *and the children quickly became interested in how the other animals could tell that the bird was dead. They were then asked to draw pictures or write about their ideas.*

When they came together as a class, the teacher wrote their ideas on the board, creating a web of ideas about how the animals knew the bird was dead. This included:

- *the eyes were open;*

- *you can check the heartbeat;*

- *doctors can make your heart start again.*

As they talked the children consistently referred to the text to confirm or refute their ideas. The discussion was ultimately inconclusive and the children went out to play.

(p.21)

→

- Compare this study with the list of reasons for using children's books on pages 37–8.

  The teacher's use of Frog and Birdsong *is clearly an enjoyable and engaging activity for the children. It promoted enquiry in a contextualised way. These young children had an actual situation to discuss and ponder. It concretised aspects of their learning in line with learning theory and in doing so enabled them to identify and discuss issues that opened up their thinking and learning.*

- Explain how the other criteria are fulfilled in the teacher's use of *Frog and the Birdsong*.

- If you were to categorise the children's learning into curriculum areas, which ones could this dialogue include?

Choosing books for use across the curriculum

There are many important principles to consider when choosing books to use in a chosen subject area (Schiro, 1997; Price and Lennon, n.d.; Mayer, 1995).

1. The book must have accurate subject content. All writers who discuss this issue cite texts in their subject area where the content is incorrect: the maths concepts are misunderstood, or the history is inaccurate, or the geographical facts are wrong. The content must be accurate in both the text and, where appropriate, the illustrations. Where the content is discovered to be inaccurate this can serve as a way to identify errors and misconceptions but the teacher must use it in this way (Mayer, 1995; Sackes, et al., 2009).

2. The subject content must be visible in the story. Ideally the content to be taught should be presented without significant distractions from surrounding detail.

3. The book needs to be developmentally appropriate to enable children to access the content.

4. The illustrations should complement the text and reflect and/or present information correctly and with clarity.

Where books don't meet these criteria it is probably advisable not to use them to teach a particular concept. However, this is not to say that books only have value if they are wholly, factually accurate. Some books and stories that cannot be used in this way remain good books and stories for children to read and enjoy, and should continue to be used as such.

Using children's literature in the curriculum areas

Children's literature has the potential to be used across all curriculum areas. It is perhaps reasonably straightforward to see how fiction can be incorporated into the teaching of certain aspects of the curriculum such as history, geography and the creative arts. Fiction lends itself to both the content and the affective aspects of these curriculum areas. Maths and science, however, are two curriculum areas that perhaps do not immediately, or obviously, lend themselves to the use of fiction. This chapter therefore will look in more detail at using literature to support learning in maths and science.

Mathematics

Since the 1990s there has been growing interest in using picture books as a stimulus for mathematical learning. It is recognised that children's literature has many positive benefits (see research focus below) (van den Heuvel-Panhuizen and van den Boogaard, 2008). However, Schiro (1997) cautions that the books must be carefully selected to be mathematically accurate; he cites, for example, a book in which the text refers to a child having two arms around the teddy bear but the illustrations only show one. In another text cardinal numbers (1, 2, 3) are used to depict the order in which animals enter a room. Ordinal numbers should have been used (1st, 2nd, 3rd). Another text he cites refers to the ingredients in a recipe in which *Mrs Bear never counts anything properly, because Mrs Bear cannot count.* As Schiro (1997, p.78) notes, Mrs Bear shouldn't be counting the ingredients; she should be measuring them.

Research Focus

The benefits of using literature to teach mathematics

Picture books as an impetus for kindergarteners' mathematical thinking.
Van den Heuvel-Panhuizen and van den Boogaard (2008)

The purpose of this study was to learn about the kind of cognitive activity that is evoked by children's books and the way in which the maths comes into play. The focus was on the responses that the books can elicit directly from readers rather than responses prompted by adults. The researchers wanted to understand what mathematics-related thinking a book evokes on its own during the process of reading the book to young children.

The researchers investigated children's invisible mental process by observing the overt reactions that showed engagement with the book's mathematical phenomena, for example counting down on seeing a rocket, indignation when things are not shared fairly, or recognising that something is upside down. The assumption made was that the more the children were cognitively engaged in mathematical phenomena while being read the book, the more the book could contribute to children's mathematical development.

The researchers found that the children did engage in child-initiated mathematical thinking. Spatial-orientated utterances exceeded number-orientated utterances, which were predominantly cardinal rather than ordinal references. They conclude that:

→

the mathematics-related thinking that could be identified in children's utterances gave support to the idea that children can be mathematically engaged by being read a picture book. This is true even when the reading session does not have an instructional purpose and the book has not been written with the intention of teaching mathematics and does not explicitly display mathematics, for example, by means of number and number symbols and shapes.

(Van den Heuvel-Panhuizen and van den Boogaard, 2008, p.367)

In terms of teaching, in their discussion of the findings, they conclude that a parental-type interaction that seamlessly integrates maths into the talk seems to be effective, and that teachers should exercise restraint, not overload children with questions and explanations, but think about making use of the power of the book.

For the youngest children there are many books that introduce numbers and can be used to develop mathematical knowledge and understanding. *My Granny Went to Market* (Blackstone and Corr, 2006) is a wonderful example of a counting book to ten. Granny spins round the world buying kites from Japan, masks in Mexico and drums in Kenya. The book is written in rhyme and is vibrantly illustrated. *One Moose Twenty Mice* (Blackstone and Beaton, 2000) has a similar vibrant presentation, with numbers up to 20. *Counting Cockatoos* (Blackstone and Bauer, 2007) engages children with bright illustrations of tumbling tigers, happy hippos and rumbling lions, and on each page, two cockatoos. This provides an excellent opportunity to talk about numbers, including addition and subtraction. *Hidden Hippo* (Gannij and Beaton, 2011) also provides opportunities for discussion of early mathematical concepts. The book journeys through the plains and rivers of Africa in search of a hidden hippo. Each page has bold, distinct drawings of small groups of different animals. These illustrations could be used in many ways: to count, to discuss concepts of more and less, and to calculate.

For older children, books such as *One Hundred Hungry Ants* (Pinczes, 2000), *How Big is a Million* (Milbourne and Rigliotti, 2007) and *Centipede's 100 Shoes* (Ross, 2003) can be used to explore larger numbers.

Books can also be found that deal with concepts of time, shape and space, money, and engage children in using mathematical language. These include: *The Doorbell Rang* (Hutchins, 1996), a tale about baking batches of biscuits that will be shared among children, but more and more children arrive which means that there are fewer and fewer biscuits for each child; *The Great Pet Sale* (Inkpen, 2006), in which a boy has £1 to spend in the pet sale and has to consider which pets to buy; and *A Cloak for the Dreamer* (Friedman and Howard, 1995), in which three brothers, whose father is a tailor, are tasked with making a cloak. The older two make beautiful cloaks using triangles and squares. Misha, the youngest son, who dreams of travelling far and wide and making his own way in the world, makes a disastrous cloak, from circles. The book is a wonderful stimulus for exploring the properties of shapes. *The Lion's Share* (McElligott, 2012), a book described as *a tale of halving cake and eating it too,* can be used to teach fractions.

The case study below shows how a book can be used as a starting point for teaching mathematics. Notice how the teaching is given a context: the children use number operations to make calculations about the guests and the catering.

Case Study

Using a story book to consolidate number operations

To start a lesson in which her aim was to consolidate calculating with different number operations, Ruby, a third-year student, read *Night Noises* (Fox and Denton, 2001). In it the old lady, Lily Laceby, whose hair was as *wispy as cobwebs in ceilings and whose bones were as creaky as floorboards at midnight,* is treated to a surprise 90th birthday party. A huge number of people turn up: her sons and daughters, grandchildren, great-grandchildren, great-great-grandchildren and friends.

At the end of the story, Ruby wrote the numbers on the board. The children were given a whiteboard and put in small groups and asked to work out how many people came to the party. Once they had had a chance to work it out, each group was asked to say how many people came to the party, and show everyone else how they had worked it out. This gave Ruby and the TA the chance to see what the children knew and understood and what else needed to be a focus in the lesson.

She then modelled a way to calculate the number at the party and the children checked their working and the answer. Ruby extended the task by adding onto the story the scenario of calculating how many buns and cups of tea would be needed at the party, as the visitors had travelled a long way to the party and were hungry and thirsty.

The next part of the lesson was for the children, in groups, to write a similar scenario for another group to calculate. They could use any setting but large numbers of people were to be involved.

Ruby differentiated the task according to ability, with some of the groups being asked to include more complex calculations, such as people leaving as well as arriving, and problems to solve about resources in the scenario (modelled in the group by working out how many buns and cups of tea would be needed).

Ruby was able to target her teaching according to what she knew and what she had observed in the first part of the lesson. She grouped the children carefully and worked with two identified groups. The TA focused on individual children who had been identified as needing support or extension.

The children's scenarios were then swapped between groups and they worked out each other's calculations. The groups had to show each other how they had worked out the answer.

The scenarios were then collected in, word-processed and made into a book that was put in the classroom for the children to have a go at each other's calculations.

(Ruby's lesson was adapted from an idea by Burns, 2005)

The use of children's literature in this maths lesson offered children a meaningful context in which to situate their learning. The teacher used the initial ideas in the book and then extended them to ensure that the lesson was matched to the range of abilities in her class.

Science

Science in school aims to encourage children to be curious about things that they observe and experience: to explore, ask questions, consider ideas and to communicate this using scientific language. Hincks (2007) argues that *science is about real life, that learning needs to be 'situated in contexts which offer worthwhile experience, in accessible forms'(Gura 1994)* (p.106). Using children's literature is one of the ways in which teachers can stimulate this curiosity and engage in the exploration of ideas. It is important to acknowledge that there are a significant number of excellent non-fiction science books for children, most notably those shortlisted for the Royal Society science book prizes. However, this chapter considers how fiction and poetry can be used in the science curriculum. Fiction books can be used in several ways in the science curriculum: they can be read aloud to introduce a science topic, read to answer or stimulate further questions about a topic, or to explore a topic in combination with hands-on experiential science activities. The nature of the book and how the scientific concepts are conveyed will determine how it can be used.

Fiction books for the youngest children can stimulate their curiosity and encourage them to begin to ask questions about the world in which they live. The skill for practitioners and teachers is to identify the potential within a book to elicit, and answer, why and how questions. *Grandpa's Garden* (Fry and Moxley, 2012) tells the story of Billy and his grandpa planting and tending his vegetable patch from early spring to late summer, when they pick the fruit and vegetables that they have grown. The story offers opportunities for discussion about the features of living things, about similarities and differences, patterns and change. Chamberlain's (2006) *Mama Panya's Pancakes* opens up possibilities for exploring why things happen. The story is set in East Africa and Mama Panya goes to market for ingredients and cooks pancakes over an open fire for her family. The story, in combination with making pancakes, would enable exploration of why things happen and how things change. Morpurgo, et al.'s (2012) *Where My Wellies Take Me* is part fiction, part poetry anthology and follows Pippa on her walks in her wellies in the countryside. Alongside her we see the natural world in her environment. This would be a wonderful introduction to children's own 'welly-walks' when they could explore, observe, ask questions and record plants and animals in their local environment.

For older children, *Watership Down* (Adams, 2012), *The Animals of Farthing Wood* (Dann, 2006), *Tarka the Otter* (Williamson, 1995) and *Winter Shadow* (Knight and Johnson, 2011) can introduce and stimulate interest in the environment, habitats and life cycles and open up discussion about interdependence and adaptation. *The Snowstorm* (Riel and Cann, 2012), in which four children travel through the Arctic region with a dogsled team, can be used to stimulate discussion about characteristics of materials and keeping warm, and even as a provocation to explore forces and movement.

Poetry can also act as a stimulus to thinking and asking questions about science topics. *My Shadow* (Stevenson, 2008) explores the idea of a shadow, how it is *very very like me from the heels up to the head*, how it *sometimes shoots up taller like an Indian rubber ball and sometimes gets so little that there's none of him at all*, and finally:

> *One morning, very early, before the sun was up,*
>
> *I rose and found the shining dew on every buttercup;*
>
> *But my lazy little shadow, like an arrant sleepyhead,*
>
> *Had stayed at home behind me and was fast asleep in bed.*

This poem has the potential to be used at all levels, with very young children to describe shadows and how they work, and with older children to explain and investigate light and shadow. In Carol Anne Duffy's collection *The Hat* (2007), the poems *The Song Collector, The Sock, Touched* and *Your Dresses* are powerfully evocative of our senses and provide an excellent stimulus for exploring ourselves. Similarly, *The Rings* opens up possibilities for discussion about materials: *Silver* evokes rivers, moonlight and midnight hours, and *Ruby*, passion, poems and magic spells.

On a more humorous note, Pam Ayres' (n.d.) poem *Oh I Wish I'd Looked After My Teeth* looks at the impact of what we eat on our teeth. Michael Rosen's nonsense poem *Do You Know What* (Rosen and Mackie, 1997) introduces the notion of a skeleton, while Tony Mitton's (n.d.) *Grown Out Of* considers what would happen if we grew out of our skin like we grow out of our clothes – a wonderfully thought-provoking poem for considering growth and change.

A more philosophical approach to scientific issues is provided in Dawkins (2011) *The Magic of Reality. How do we know what's really true?* Dawkins combines philosophy, culture and science to consider how human beings have explored the natural world over time. He illustrates these ideas partly in factual discussion but also through the use of stories.

Research Focus

**Using children's literature to teach science concepts in early years
(Mayer, 1995; Sackes, et al., 2009)**

The aim of the study was to identify appropriate literature through which to teach science. The researchers identified and examined 73 children's books and aligned them with common themes from different states' science standards (the study was conducted in America).

→

Examples of their findings include the following.

Author	Title	Science concept	Application	Limitation
Asch, Frank	*Moonbear's Shadow*	Shadows	Looks at position of light source and direction of shadow Can compare actual observations at noon to the illustration	Concept misconception: very few places have no shadow at noon when the sun is directly overhead
Carle, Eric	*Little Cloud*	Weather, clouds, the relationship between clouds and rain	Exploring the relationship between clouds and rain	Content: anthropomorphised clouds Concept misconception: clouds don't get darker while they rain Illustration: fantastical cloud shapes

The researchers found that they had difficulty in identifying books in particular areas of science, namely physical science concepts. Additionally, they found that many books contained misconceptions, anthropomorphism and inaccurate illustrations. Although they regard accurate books as preferable, they conclude that books that have misconceptions and inaccuracies can be used to create opportunities for discussion and analysis of the misconception.

Activity

- Select a range of children's books that initially appear to be suitable to teach science concepts.
- Examine the books carefully and identify the science concept, the application and the limitations.
- Decide whether they are suitable books to use to teach science.
- Outline how you would use them in your teaching.

The case study below demonstrates how children's literature can be used to support teaching in science. Notice how Adeeba uses the story to stimulate interest in the topic, extends an aspect of the story to engage the children in finding something out through experimentation, and then returns to apply the knowledge within the context of the story.

Case Study

Teaching melting and freezing using children's literature

Adeeba, a Schools Direct trainee, had been asked to teach a series of science lessons about melting and freezing. The teacher had decided that this was a good topic to explore as winter had begun and ice and snow were forecast. Adeeba decided that using snow and snowmen would engage the children and provide a concrete example of melting and freezing. She listed a number of ideas that she wanted to use so that she could discuss them and shape them into lessons with the teacher.

- To watch *The Snowman* DVD based on Raymond Briggs' book *The Snowman* (1978).

- To focus the discussion at the end of the DVD on what happened to the snowman, and why, to elicit the children's understanding of the process of freezing and melting.

- To set up some experiments with the children in which toys are frozen inside ice cubes and the children are tasked with different things to do, ranging from extracting the toy quickly to keeping the toy frozen inside for as long as possible.

- To write and read children a short story in which two children wonder what to do next to keep their snowman from melting. The class would then be asked to advise the children about what to do next and what not to do next, based on what they had found out in the experiments.

- To record this advice in a display entitled 'What would happen if…?'

Curriculum Links

As mentioned earlier, using fiction and poetry isn't confined to science and maths. All curriculum areas can be enhanced by the use of fiction. There are books and stories available that stimulate thinking about history, geography and religious education. Similarly, fiction and poetry are excellent stimuli for the creative arts, art, drama, dance, music and design. As a teacher, you need to have a good knowledge of children's literature to enable you to make the best use of it in your teaching (see Chapters 1 and 2). This includes an ability to identify themes, ideas and subject knowledge in literature to enable you to use it across all aspects of the curriculum. The case study below is an example of using children's literature in another curriculum area: geography.

Geography

Case Study

Using children's literature to teach geography

While visiting a school a third-year trainee, Harry, noticed a display that tracked a cycle journey the length of Africa. Intrigued, he asked the teacher about it.

It had been created in response to a book. The class had listened to the teacher read *The Boy Who Biked the World* (Humphreys and Morgan Jones, 2011), a story about a boy, Tom, who wants to be an explorer, declares that he is going to cycle around the world and begins by riding the length of Africa.

In response to the book the children had traced his journey on a map and annotated it with the various adventures and insights in the book. Once this was complete, the class teacher had set up a series of groups to investigate further aspects of Tom's journey. They returned to the book and read identified extracts carefully and used this information as a starting point for looking in more detail at the landscape, people, climate, flora and fauna that Tom encountered on his journey through Africa.

The teacher had then returned to the book and read the extracts of Tom's adventure to the class and each group talked about what else they now knew about that part of Africa. This information was then recorded by the children and used to enhance the information on the display about Tom's journey.

This children's book provided an excellent opportunity for the children to explore a different locality, one that contrasted with their own. They were able to use different ways of finding out the necessary information and apply what they had learned in an enjoyable and meaningful context.

Curriculum Links

Identifying cross-curricular themes in fiction

As well as supplying books to support learning in particular subject areas, fiction also has the potential to integrate learning in different curriculum areas. Fiction takes no account of school curriculum boundaries, in the same way that curriculum areas don't determine children's lives beyond school; fiction integrates knowledge in an authentic way. Michael Morpurgo's books are a good example of this. Morpurgo is one of the most prolific current children's writers, having written more than a hundred books, many of which have great potential for cross-curricular study and follow-up. In each of his books Morpurgo addresses a particular issue, but within this he incorporates a range of themes and ideas that offer opportunities for discussion, investigation and study. However, Morpurgo's work should be seen as much more than a stimulus for wider study. His novels are as busy and active as those of Enid Blyton, but he never writes down to or patronises the reader. The language is accessible, but Morpurgo does not avoid more challenging vocabulary and concepts. He also often provides an explanation at the end of his books of the inspiration for the story, and even some background information about some of the issues raised.

Running Wild (2010) is one of several of Morpurgo's stories which centre on animals. Its hero is Will, a nine-year-old, who goes to Asia for a holiday with his mother as they try to come to terms with the death of Will's father in the Iraq War. Unfortunately, the holiday coincides with the 2004 Boxing Day tsunami which killed thousands, destroyed property and dramatically changed landscapes. The tsunami struck as Will was riding on the beach on an elephant while his mother sunbathed. The elephant, Oona, senses the imminence of the tsunami and carries Will into the jungle to safety. There Will spends many months living wild and eating fruit, fish, and drinking coconut milk, cared for by Oona, while all the time grieving for his mother whom he is sure was killed when the tsunami struck. He encounters a tiger and struggles to fight off the leeches which feed on him.

Most dramatically, he is captured by a band of men, led by an Australian who boasts about destroying the rainforest to plant palm trees and catching wild animals, including orang-utans, to sell. Will escapes his cruel captors along with three young orang-utans, whom he cares for after the killing of their parents by the men, and eventually, seriously ill, is brought by Oona to a sanctuary for orang-utans run by Dr Geraldine.

The story is gripping, often intense, and yet imbued with tenderness and reflection on animal life, relationships and moral issues, as well as loss and environmental issues. At the end, Morpurgo explains that his inspirations for the story were the true story of a boy who was saved from the tsunami by an elephant, and William Blake's poem *Tyger Tyger*. He provides short postscripts on the Iraq War, the Boxing Day tsunami, deforestation and orang-utans, as well as a map of the area affected by the tsunami.

Running Wild has, then, great potential for promoting drama, discussion, investigation and further study. Indeed, Morpurgo has already begun the process for readers. There are opportunities here to explore many themes including:

- climate and climate change;
- animal life, life cycles and food chains;
- care of the environment;
- bereavement;

(Continued)

(Continued)

- conflict and war;
- geography – maps and environments;
- diet – what we need to stay alive;
- dilemmas – growing food and fuel versus protecting rainforests;
- poetry – Will finds solace in memorising *Tyger Tyger*.

Many of Morpurgo's other stories are equally rich in potential for promoting and enhancing cross-curricular study.

- *Kensuke's Kingdom* (2000) focuses on a boy cast away on a desert island who, like Robinson Crusoe, finds he is not alone.
- *Friend or Foe* (2007a) tells of two boys who rescue a German airman during the Second World War.
- *Private Peaceful* (2004) tells of two brothers fighting in the First World War, one of whom is charged with disobeying an order.
- *Cool* (2007b) tells the story of a boy in a coma as he recovers from a traffic accident.
- *Billy the Kid* (2009) features an old man who lives on the streets in London, who turns out to be a former professional footballer for Chelsea.
- *Twist of Gold* (2007c) begins with the Irish Potato Famine and goes on to mass migration to America.

Conclusion

Children's literature can thus be seen to be an effective way to engage children in learning in all curriculum areas. Used in this way it has the potential to capture children's interest, to contextualise their learning, to promote enquiry, and to integrate and enhance their literacy skills. It is also a way of integrating children's learning across the curriculum, as fiction, like life, takes no account of curriculum areas.

Learning Outcomes Review

You should now have an understanding of why, and how, we can use children's literature across the curriculum. You should be aware of the importance of checking the subject content before using a book, usually to ensure that it is correct but perhaps, at times, to identify and discuss misconceptions and errors. You should be able to identify some books and poems for different age ranges in maths and science and have considered appropriate books for other curriculum areas. Finally, you should have learned about how children's literature integrates themes in an authentic way and therefore its potential for cross-curricular study.

> **Self-assessment questions**
>
> Consider your last teaching placement.
>
> 1 Identify a successful lesson that you taught. How could you have enhanced it by including the use of children's literature?
> 2 Identify a lesson that could have been better. How could you have used children's literature to improve the lesson?

References

Adams, R. (2012) *Watership Down*, reissue. London: Penguin Books.

Ayres, P. (n.d.) *I Wish I'd Looked After My Teeth.* Available in the Children's Poetry Archive at: http://childrenspoetryarchive.org/solr-search/Oh%2C%20I%20Wish%20I%27d%20 Looked%20After%20Me%20Teeth (accessed 12.04.16).

Blackstone, S. and Bauer, S. (2007) *Counting Cockatoos.* Oxford: Barefoot Books Ltd.

Blackstone, S. and Beaton, C. (2000) *One Moose Twenty Mice.* Oxford: Barefoot Books Ltd.

Blackstone, S. and Corr, C. (2006) *My Granny Went to Market.* Oxford: Barefoot Books Ltd.

Briggs, R. (1978) *The Snowman.* London: Picture Puffin.

Browne, E. (2006) *Handa's Surprise.* London: Walker Books.

Burns, M. (2005) Lessons by Marilyn Burns. Using Storybooks to teach Math. *Scholastic Instructor*, p.27. Available at: www.mathsolutions.com/documents/2005_Teach_Math_ Article. pdf (accessed 12.04.16).

Chamberlain, M. (2006) *Mama Panya's Pancakes.* Oxford: Barefoot Books Ltd.

Dann, C. (2006) *The Animals of Farthing Wood.* London: Egmont.

Dawkins, R. (2011) *The Magic of Reality. How do we know what is really true?* London: Bantam Books.

Duffy, C. (2007) *The Hat.* London: Faber and Faber.

Evans, J. (2016) Who am I? Why am I here? And Where do I come from? Responding to philosophical picture books. *Education, 3–13*, 44(1): 53–67.

Fox, M. and Denton, T. (2001) *Night Noises.* Harcourt Australia.

Friedman, A. and Howard, K. (1995) *A Cloak for the Dreamer.* Leamington Spa: Scholastic Press.

Fry, S. and Moxley, S. (2012) *Grandpa's Garden.* Oxford: Barefoot Books Ltd.

Gannij, J. and Beaton, C. (2011) *Hidden Hippo.* Oxford: Barefoot Books Ltd.

Hayes, D. (ed.) (2007) *Joyful Teaching and Learning in the Primary School.* Exeter: Learning Matters.

Hincks, R. (2007) Joyful teaching and learning in science. In Hayes, D. (ed.) (2007) *Joyful Teaching and Learning in the Primary School.* Exeter: Learning Matters.

Humphreys, A. and Morgan-Jones, T. (2011) *The Boy who Biked the World.* Much Wenlock, Shropshire: Eye Books.

Hutchins, P. (1999) *The Doorbell Rang.* New York: Greenwillow Books.

Inkpen, M. (2006) *The Great Pet Sale.* London: Hodder Children's Books.

Kelly, P. (2007) The Joy of Enhancing Children's Learning. In Hayes, D. (ed.) *Joyful Teaching and Learning in the Primary School.* Exeter: Learning Matters.

Knight, R. and Johnson, R. (2011) *Winter Shadow.* Oxford: Barefoot Books Ltd.

Mayer, D. (1995) How can we best use children's literature in teaching science concepts? *Science and Children,* 32(6): 16–18.

McElligott, M. (2012) *The Lion's Share.* London: Walker Books.

Milbourne, A. and Rigliotti, S. (2007) *How Big is a Million?* London: Usborne Books.

Mitton, T. (n. d.) *Grown Out Of.* Available in the Children's Poetry Archive at: http://childrenspoetryarchive.org/solr-search/Grown%20Out%20Of (accessed 12.04.16).

Morpurgo, M. (2000) *Kensuke's Kingdom.* Glasgow: Egmont Books.

Morpurgo, M. (2004) *Private Peaceful.* London: Harper Collins.

Morpurgo, M. (2007a) *Friend or Foe.* Glasgow: Egmont Books.

Morpurgo, M. (2007b) *Cool.* London: Harper Collins.

Morpurgo, M. (2007c) *Twist of Gold.* London, Glasgow: Egmont Books.

Morpurgo, M. (2009) *Billy the Kid.* London: Harper Collins.

Morpurgo, M. (2010) *Running Wild.* London: Harper Collins.

Morpurgo, M., Morpurgo, C. and Lomenach Gill, O. (2012) *Where My Wellies Take Me.* Dorking: Templar Publishing.

Pinczes, E. (2000) *One Hundred Hungry Ants.* New York: Houghton Mifflin.

Price, R. and Lennon, C. (n.d.) Using children's literature to teach mathematics. Durham NC: MetaMetrics. Available at: www.quantiles.com/resources/literaturemathematics.pdf (accessed 12.04.16).

Riel, J. and Cann, H. (2012*) The Snowstorm.* Oxford: Barefoot Books Ltd.

Rosen, M. and Mackie, C. (1997) *Book of Nonsense.* London: Hodder.

Ross, T. (2003) *Centipede's 100 Shoes.* New York: Henry Holt and Company.

Sackes, M., Trundle, K. and Flevares, L. (2009) Using children's literature to teach science concepts in early years. *Early Childhood Education Journal*, 36(5), 415–22.

Schiro, M. (1997) *Integrating Children's Literature and Mathematics in the Classroom.* NY: Teachers College Press.

Stevenson, R.L. (2008) *A Child's Garden of Verses.* London: Puffin.

Van den Heuvel-Panhuizen, M. and Van den Boogaard, S. (2008) Picture books as an impetus for kindergarteners' mathematical thinking. *Mathematical Thinking and Learning,* 10(4): 341–73.

Williamson, H. (1995) *Tarka the Otter.* London: Puffin Modern Classics.

Wilson J. (1998) *The Lottie Project.* London: Yearling.

4 Books for younger children

Learning Outcomes

By reading this chapter you will:

- understand why books and stories are important for young children;
- recognise that books have an intrinsic value as a pleasurable activity;
- recognise the importance of books for young children's language and literacy learning and development;
- understand aspects of story time and story telling for young children;
- know why books for babies are important.

Introduction

Even the briefest glance into the children's books section in a bookshop or library will reveal a bright colourful world of many books: books that are written and designed to provoke children's interest and delight in words, stories and pictures. For the very youngest children there will be board and cloth books and interactive pop-up and flap books, for toddlers books of pictures and photographs, and for children of all ages a wealth of picture books. There will be book characters that children become familiar with, such as Spot and Alfie; books with archetypes such as witches, fairies and dragons; traditional tales and fairy stories; books based on children's TV programmes; and books that are considered to be part of a canon of children's literature, such as Beatrix Potter books and *Winnie the Pooh*. There will be abundant anthropomorphism and a wide range of illustrative techniques and innovative presentation of stories, and new books will be added all the time. So why is there such rich provision for very young children? Why are books important at this early stage of life? And how do we engage children with books and reading in ways that excite their imagination and begin their journey into literature?

The importance of books and stories for young children

Books engage children at both a cognitive (intellectual) and affective (emotional) level. They are enjoyable, emotionally resonant, and support emerging linguistic and cognitive understanding and skill. Engagement with books brings significant rewards.

- Books are a rich source of engagement and enjoyment.

- Listening to (and eventually reading) and creating stories is, for many children, a flow activity (see research focus below).

- They are a source for the expression of a wide range of emotions.

- They provide an opening for sensitising children to the needs and feelings of others.

- They open up experiences beyond the child's own experience.

- They provide a safe way into understanding experiences beyond a child's own experience.

- They enable children to see social patterns and relationships beyond their own experience.

- They are a connection to children's own cultural heritage.

- They can connect children to a range of different cultural heritages, both in the content of the story and different cultural patterns of stories and story telling.

- They offer an authentic way of extending and enhancing children's language capability.

- They encourage focused listening.

- Children who engage in 'storying' in their play and responses to books and story telling absorb and explore notions of story structure, language and plot.

- They are an authentic introduction to literacy.

Books as a rich source of engagement and enjoyment

First and foremost stories and books are important for very young children simply because they are fun, engaging and enriching. Books and stories have the potential to create joy and meaning. They provide pleasure and satisfy our human need for connection and creativity. Books for very young children have the potential to open up their lives to a wide range of feelings and experiences. Children may laugh at the antics of the chaotic *Large Family* and the spirited *Princess Smarty Pants* (Cole, 1986), or delight at the anticipatory rhyming language and creative twists in Julia Donaldson's books. They may feel an engaging sense of tension that is heightened and then resolved in a narrative. This is evident in Burningham's (1996) book *Cloudland*. In this book a little boy, Albert, falls off a mountain when out walking with his parents and is rescued by the Cloud Children. He joins them to play among the rainbows and clouds but eventually longs to go home. But how will he get home? The book explores Albert's adventure away from and back to his parents.

The narrative in books may enable children to enter the experiences of others and begin to connect with how others feel. In *Albert Le Blanc* by Nick Butterworth (2002), Albert is described as having the *saddest eyes you ever saw, his head hangs low, his shoulders are hunched and his arms flop loosely by his sides.* The book encourages children to see what this may mean, and what the other toys think this means, and whether they are right. Children are gently led through these questions in the storyline to an unexpected joyful ending.

Books can also allow children entry to imaginative worlds and experiences beyond their own lives. Sheldon and Blythe's book the *Whale Song* (1990) tells the story of a little girl who listens to her grandmother's stories about gifts she gave the whales in the ocean near their home and the songs they occasionally offered in return. Lily dreams of the whales and longs to hear them sing. The storyline and illustrations are wonderfully evocative of Lily's hope and longing.

These opportunities to experience pleasure from reading are the first steps of becoming someone who identifies themselves as 'a reader': a lover of books and reading. If we can provide opportunities early on in their life and young children can learn to love books and stories, this will open up their world to an on-going rich source of pleasure. In Antonia Fraser's book *The Pleasure of Reading* (2015), authors discuss how they began their journey into literature, how they came to books and reading, and which books inspired them to become readers and writers. Without fail, all the authors tell stories of their early encounters with books and how these books excited their imagination and set the mind dreaming. How they loved the feel and smell of them. How they puzzled over myths and fables, quests and hunts, magic and truth. How individual books are evocative of times, places and people. How books and stories assuaged loneliness and isolation. How words and language were talismanic and transfiguring. The effect of this deep connection with books and reading often results in the reader 'losing themselves' in the activity: becoming engrossed in what they are reading and in doing so becoming less aware of the passage of time. This deep engagement with an activity is called *flow* (Czikszentmihalyi, 2008). Flow can be experienced across many activities which we engage in as children and adults. Flow activities have been shown to deepen and enhance our quality of life.

Research Focus

Flow

The Psychology of Optimal Experience, *Mihaly Czikszentmihalyi (2008)*

Czikszentmihalyi (2008) describes the state of flow as being completely involved in an activity for its own sake. This results in a state where the ego falls away, time flies and every action, movement and thought follows inevitably from the previous one, like playing jazz music. When in flow your whole being is involved, and you are using your skills to the utmost.

Flow has its origins in the desire to understand the phenomena of how the people involved in something creative could persist single mindedly, disregarding hunger, fatigue and discomfort, yet rapidly lost interest in the product once it had been completed. Flow research had its genesis in the desire to understand this phenomenon of intrinsic motivation, in activity that is rewarding in and of itself quite apart from its end product or any good that may come from completing the activity.

→

Being in 'flow' has characteristics such as:

- intense and focused concentration;

- merging of action and awareness;

- loss of awareness of self as a social actor;

- feeling that one can control one's actions in the sense that one can, in principle, deal with the situation because one knows how to respond whatever happens;

- distortion of temporal experience (typically a sense that time has passed faster than normal);

- experience of the action as intrinsically rewarding, for example often the end goal is just an excuse for the process.

The major contribution of flow activities and being 'in-flow' is to quality of life: periods of time of deeply resonant experience.

Books and language development

Language enables us to communicate and to think; it enables us to enter the experiences of other people and other worlds, both real and imagined. Children learn language. They are born unable to communicate through language and in the first years of their life acquire the language (or languages) that are spoken in their social world. This acquisition of language occurs through the interplay of an innate capacity for language and social interaction in a social context. Children need to hear and use language to acquire and develop their language skill. Language in books is enriching, as it goes beyond our everyday use of language. It is considered and used carefully to convey meanings and create experiences. Book reading provides an enjoyable and authentic way for enriched language experiences. It introduces children to new and different ways of using language including an enhanced vocabulary.

Written language in texts is not just spoken language written down; it is a different way of using language and has a different function from the everyday. It includes different vocabulary, different patterns and rhythm of language use, rhyme, repetition and word play. Julia Donaldson's books are an excellent example of this. There is *The Gruffalo* (Donaldson and Scheffler, 1999), whose *eyes are orange, his tongue is black, he has purple prickles all over his back.* There's *Room on the Broom* (Donaldson and Scheffler, 2001) in which a beast rises from a ditch *and its terrible voice when it started to speak, was a yowl and growl, and a croak and a shriek.* And then there's the ongoing confusion between the Night

Monkey and the Day Monkey (Donaldson and Richards, 2002). *'Hey!' said Day Monkey. 'There's a banana! How can it manage to fly?' Night Monkey laughed and said, 'Don't be daft, that banana's the moon in the sky.'* Donaldson's twists and turns in the rhyme and the rhythm of the language are delightful and open up a new and different way for young children to experience and respond to language.

Research Focus

Talking about picture books

Torr (2005) and Morgan (2005) both undertook studies to look at qualitative aspects of reading books to young children. Both studies aimed to understand the nature of reading interactions that supported language and literacy development. They each began their study with stating how important books and stories are for the development of young children's language and early literacy development.

Morgan's study looked at the shared reading interactions between mothers and pre-school children from disadvantaged communities. Torr (2005) looked at qualitative aspects of picture book reading with reference to the influence of maternal education on children's talk with mothers and pre-school teachers.

Both studies conclude that there were qualitative differences in the interactions when reading books to children and recognise that this has important implications for children's developing language and early literacy. Torr (2005) observes that children of tertiary-educated mothers were encouraged to use a range of strategies to respond to and interpret the meanings in picture books. Therefore they were able to make comparisons, inferences and generalisations, ask questions and offer explanations during shared reading. They made *frequent intertextual connections and drew on their understanding of the alphabetic principle and sound/symbols correspondence to explore characteristics of the printed text* (Torr, 2005, p.204). In contrast, Torr found that children of early-school-leaving mothers were encouraged to listen quietly to stories and interact occasionally often by naming (labelling) what they could see in illustrations.

Morgan (2005) concluded differently. Her study focused more on the dynamic relationship between mothers and children from disadvantaged communities when reading books. She concludes that, while she observed less sophisticated interactions such as questions about illustrations on the page to elicit labelling responses, she also observed sophisticated interactions between mother and child, and concludes that we must move away from the over-simplistic assumptions about who does what with their children.

However, both studies, while differing in their conclusions and recognising the limitations of the study, acknowledge that reading books with young children is a particularly effective way to encourage the development of language and literacy skills.

Activity

Find the two studies (referenced at the end of this chapter). Although they draw different conclusions about the nature of interaction between mothers and children from different socio-economic groups, they both recognise the significance of book reading for children's language and literacy development.

- Read the studies carefully and identify the significant aspects of reading books with young children that scaffold children's learning and so have an impact on children's language and literacy development.
- How could you incorporate these aspects of story book reading into your teaching?

Books as an introduction to literacy

As well as acquiring and developing spoken language, young children are in the process of learning to read and write. In order to become a reader and a writer children need to acquire a whole range of knowledge and skills. Books and stories have an important role to play in this process. As well as introducing children to new and different ways of using language, outlined above, children who engage in 'storying' through books and story telling absorb and explore notions of story structure, language and plot. These are important underpinning understandings in learning to read and write. Books provide an easy and authentic way to acquire this knowledge as children will absorb the language and structure of stories just by hearing them. Additionally, this exposure to books will alert children to other important early knowledge about books and reading, including:

- an awareness of the narrative arc in stories;
- an awareness of archetypal characters in stories;
- an awareness of typical plot structures;
- an awareness of the forms of reading: book structure, page turning, top-to-bottom and left-to-right orientation, identification of print;
- the development of a language for reading: letter, word, sentence, story, character and event;
- knowledge of letters (graphemes) and letter sounds (phonemes).

This 'book knowledge' is vital prior to a child beginning the more formally taught aspects of learning to read and write. The case study below demonstrates how this can be taught. In the case study the teacher articulates how she weaves knowledge about books and reading into her story telling. As you read through, notice how the teacher offers a model of this knowledge within the authentic context of reading a story.

Case Study

What young children can learn from hearing stories

Andrew, a second-year trainee, was in a Reception class for the first time. In the serial days before his block placement began he listed the range of activities that he wanted to closely observe the teacher doing as a model for his practice. One of these was story time. Andrew was aware that the teacher had a particular way of reading to the children and he wanted to understand exactly what this was and why she did things in this way.

Andrew observed a number of story times and noted the following things.

- The teacher spent some time settling the children first and made her expectations clear about what the children should do. This included, for the initial reading, listening to the story all the way through without interruption.

- She held the book up so that the children could see the print and the illustrations.

- On some pages she tracked her finger along the print as she read it.

- She told the story expressively, using different voice and facial expressions to create tension and anticipation and to reflect the emotional landscape of the story.

- After the first time through, she repeated the story but this time encouraged the children to fill in the narrative at the points when she stopped. Andrew noticed that many of the children mimicked her expressive way of telling the story.

After the observation Andrew asked the teacher why she read the book in this way. The teacher explained that she initially wanted the children to hear the story all the way through so that they got a sense of the narrative arc: that stories typically have the pattern of exposition, complication, climax and resolution. Hearing many stories with this narrative arc meant that when the children came to tell stories, or enact them in their play, this arc was evident; the children had come to know it through exposure to stories and storying. The second reading of the story enabled the children to demonstrate their knowledge of this pattern in the story. Holding the book up and tracking were processes to demonstrate to the children the physical aspects of books and reading: pictures, print, tracking, pages, etc. The repetition of this meant that most children developed this knowledge through their exposure to books and she could use and build on this in her literacy teaching. The teacher also explained that she told the story expressively to engage and entice the children into delighting in books and stories. All the pleasure and benefits from reading could only be available to the children if they enjoyed and engaged with books and stories. Therefore her aim was to encourage this strongly through making story time an enjoyable and significant activity for the children.

The teacher in this case study demonstrates how children learn about aspects of books and stories that support their early literacy learning and will inform their own writing as they progress through school. The pedagogical approach is developmentally appropriate, and the children's learning is situated in a clear, authentic context.

Curriculum Links

This approach to telling stories enables children to develop knowledge about books and stories identified in the Early Years Foundation Stage (EYFS) (DfE, 2012).

EYFS (2012) Reading

Children:

- listen to stories with increasing attention and recall;
- describe main story settings, events and principal characters;
- show interest in illustrations and print in books;
- use vocabulary and forms of speech that are increasingly influenced by their experience of books;
- know that print carries meaning and, in English, is read from left to right and top to bottom;
- enjoy an increasing range of books.

Similarly, reading aloud to children enables them to develop pleasure and motivation to read. As the National Curriculum for English Key Stages 1 and 2 (DfE, 2013) states: *By listening frequently to stories, poems and non-fiction that they cannot yet read for themselves, pupils begin to understand how written language can be structured* (p.22). These are all essential aspects of language which children will be able to draw on in their own writing (see also Chapter 2).

Children's engagement with books and reading enables them to engage with the potential of reading. For very young children and beginning readers it acts as an apprenticeship to reading. Chambers (1991 cited in Goouch and Lambirth, 2011) compares reading to children as a *loaning of consciousness* (Vygotsky, 1978) in that the parent or teacher engages children in an activity that they are unable, at that moment, to undertake on their own. In doing so they entice children into the rich potential of being able to read stories in books (Goouch and Lambirth, 2011).

Research Focus

Roots of literacy

'Roots of literacy' is a metaphor used by Yetta Goodman (1986). Goodman suggests that as we observe children we can see them inventing, discovering and developing understandings about literacy as they grow up in a literate environment. Her work on early literacy also concludes that children are alive to literacy and developing skills and concepts long before they become conventionally literate.

→

Goodman argues that the beginnings of literacy occur as children become aware and begin to realise written language makes sense and simultaneously begin to wonder how it makes sense. It is through this exploration of the literate environment that children develop their 'roots of literacy'. These roots include:

- print awareness in situational contexts: children become aware that print carries meaning as they see it used in day-to-day situations such as on packaging, signs and logos;

- print awareness in connected discourse: children become aware of the print in written material such as books, magazines, newspapers, letters;

- functions and forms of writing: children become aware of the many ways in which we use print in our day-to-day lives; they begin to notice how we write and read, and that reading and writing are different;

- oral language about written language: children begin to talk about reading and writing, which reflects their growing awareness of the uses of reading and writing in a literate society; they begin to learn words that refer to language such as letter or word;

- metalinguistic and metacognitive awareness about written language: children develop the conceptual ability and the language to enable them to talk about language – this means that they are able to conceive of language as something that can be talked about, both in terms of its constituent parts (a word, a letter) and about how and why it is used.

Goodman continues her metaphor of 'roots' in her observation that children need the fertile soil of a literate environment in which to grow and learn. In this way early literacy will emerge as children seek out and explore literacy practices. The knowledge and skill that arises from this engagement is often referred to as emergent reading and writing.

This process of children's gradual engagement with print and its meaning is called emergent reading. It begins with a child noticing print in their everyday lives and, through increasing sophistication in their awareness and ability to understand and make meaning of print, results in a child becoming a reader. Children's earliest engagement with print is likely to be with environmental print. Environmental print is the print that children are surrounded by in their daily lives. It is often a combination of words, colours and images and can be found on packaging; as advertising; on household appliances and controls; as print on clothing; on labels, branding or captions; through digital technology on phones, computers and other hand-held devices; and as shop signs and logos. This print becomes meaningful to children as they see and use it in their everyday lives. However, this does not necessarily mean that children can read the print; they can recognise it and know that it carries a particular meaning, but they are heavily dependent on the context of the print. Goodall (1994) found that children can often recognise words when they are in their usual context, for example a slogan on a particular item of clothing or the name of a product on a package, but are not able to read the word without these contextual clues. This is to be expected at an early stage. The important conceptual development is that print carries meaning and by reading the print we can understand that meaning. This conceptual development underpins learning to read. Additionally, environmental print can stimulate questions and discussion about reading: about why we read; about how we read; about letters and sounds; and about meanings, of words, print and books.

Alongside children's exposure to environmental print, one of the most important ways in which children engage with, and learn about, reading is through story books. Learning to read needs to be more than just learning the skill of decoding text – reading, in the fullest sense, is engagement with the purposes and pleasure of reading as well as developing the skills necessary to read. Engagement with story books enables children to develop an understanding of the full range of knowledge, skills and affective aspects of reading.

Sulzby and Rockafellow (2001) provide a framework that traces the development of emergent reading from the earliest engagement with story books through to independent reading. They observe that children's reading of books emerges initially through simple labelling and commenting based on the pictures, through a series of stages in which a child learns and refines story telling language, to reading that uses emerging understanding of phonics and other word recognition skills to support story telling from a book.

STAGES OF EMERGENT READING
Picture-governed attempts
Labels or responds to the pictures on each page with little or no understanding of the whole story.
Telling the story based on the picture in front of them. The story told is based on the actual story but the language of story telling and the book are not used.
Children will tell the story using both the pictures and the language of the story that they have learned from hearing the story over and over again. Their emergent reading begins to sound like conventional reading. This indicates that the child is becoming aware of, and making a transition between, oral language and written language.
Print-governed attempts
Children will attempt to read the book using the print. This indicates that they have learned that it is the print that carries the story when adults read rather than the pictures. Some children will have remembered the story exactly and appear to read the print; others will insist on reading the print but still struggle to decode it.
Children will bring together what they know about print and what they remember of the text and pictures to read the text conventionally.

Home, pre-school settings and schools play a key role in emergent literacy. What can be observed is that the more literacy knowledge children have in their earliest years, the more likely it is that they will do well in becoming literate. The most striking implication of this is the importance of ensuring that literacy, including lots of experiences with books and stories, is embedded in very young children's lives. So what does this look like in practice? What provision and interaction best supports young children's emerging literacy? And how do books for very young children contribute to this?

Most children will grow up with literacy practices in their homes as part of their everyday lives prior to attending a pre-school or school: talking and listening; environmental print; reading and writing. However, just being exposed to literacy practices has limited benefits for literacy development; parents, practitioners and teachers need to mediate these experiences to engage young children in literacy practices. With regard to books and stories for young children this requires that children have books read to them. They need to experience the delight in books and stories and to talk about them. They need time to go back through and over stories to label, discuss, comment and recall the story. They need to be offered opportunities to understand inferences and make generalisations from the text, to ask and answer questions, and to make intertextual links between books and stories. They need to be introduced to book structure through use of appropriate terminology and to story language and structure through hearing stories. They need to be encouraged to get involved in story telling, initially through looking at the pictures and then by recalling and retelling the story.

In addition to reading in the home, books and stories need to a have a high priority in settings and schools. They need to be used and available across activities and curriculum areas as an integral part of teaching. They need to be made accessible and enticing to children to encourage them to enjoy books and stories. Story time is an important part of how we introduce children to books and stories and inspire them with enthusiasm and, done successfully, can be an important part of a child coming to love books.

Story time for young children in settings and schools

Story time is a time to listen to a story, with the aim of engaging children in an enjoyable and enriching experience. Goouch and Lambirth (2011) argue passionately for the importance of seeing books, stories and storying as valid in themselves and not just a means to an end to meet learning outcomes; seeing story telling as an experience of what words can do in the form of rich narratives; exciting children about the potential of being a reader; and opening doors and enticing children into the exciting and emotional world of books and stories.

In addition, as outlined above, engagement with books will also have a range of other effects on children's developing literacy. It is interesting to consider the direction of this effect. If children enjoy books and story time they are more likely to become involved and interested in books and stories, which then supports other knowledge and skills. This is an important distinction.

Too easily books can be used in functional ways to teach other skills, losing all connection with reading with and for pleasure. But reading without pleasure is eventually likely to result in not reading, so it seems that reading with and for pleasure should be the priority.

Story time for very young children, whether in a group or with an individual, needs to be considered as carefully as any other activity. The table below will help you in your planning and teaching.

The choice of book or story	Is it matched to the children in the group?
	Does it have an engaging storyline?
	Look at the language potential. Does it enrich and enhance the children's experience of language, either through the language used, the text and/or the illustrations that support the text?
Preparation	Consider whether the book is better read or told to the children – or a combination of both.
	Read the book through, or learn the story well if you are telling it, so that you know it well enough to tell it fluently and dramatically, and use any props effectively.
	Think about props that you could use to read, tell or retell the story engagingly, for example puppets, a story chest, storyboard or music.
	Consider whether the session would be enhanced by using a 'big book' version of the story if it is available?
	Before you begin reading, be explicit about what you want the group to do. Do you want them to listen all the way through first? When can they ask questions or make comments? Do you want them to notice anything? Or anyone?
Reading the story	Tell or read the story enthusiastically. Children will pick up on your enthusiasm.
	When reading, let the children see the book's pages as you read it.
	If you are reading a story, at points in the story trace your finger along the text. This alerts children to the difference between illustration and writing, it communicates one of the functions of writing (recording stories to be read) and it demonstrates left-to-right tracking in reading and writing.
	Read or tell the story all the way through at some point in the session. This enables children to hear and absorb the narrative arc in stories and allows them to immerse themselves in the story.
Following up the story telling	Talk about the story when you have read or told it all the way through. You could:
	• look more closely at certain events or aspects of the story;
	• talk about similar things that have happened to the children;
	• continue parts of the story with 'What could happen next?' or 'What if?' questions;
	• make up different endings;
	• introduce rhymes or songs that link with the story;
	• retell the story using props.

The case study below shows how staff in a Foundation Stage unit considered and planned how to follow up story telling to encourage children to become engaged with the story of *Goldilocks and the Three Bears.* Notice how the staff use different play-based activities to enable the children to become familiar with the story and the characters in anticipation of a theatre group visit.

Case Study

Using props to tell a story

A theatre group was going to visit the Foundation Stage unit to do a performance of *Goldilocks and the Three Bears.* The theatre group wanted the children to be involved in the performance and so the practitioners thought that it was important that the children were familiar with the story before the theatre group's visit.

Initially one of the practitioners read the story to the children. The following day she used a story chest to retell the story for the children. In it she had a wig, hats, bowls, spoons and a pillow. She used the props as she retold the story much to the children's delight. She then retold the story again, encouraging the children to use the props when appropriate in the story.

The props were then put into the role-play area, which was set up as the three bears' house. Other opportunities were available in the setting for the children to engage with the story and characters, for example in the dolls' house, in a small world play set-up as a forest with a woodcutter's hut, making porridge, drawing the story on a long reel of paper mounted on the wall, and in role-play to act out and record on digital cameras.

When the theatre group came in to do their performance the children were able to become fully involved in the experience as they were familiar with the story. This made the experience enjoyable and engaging, and it formed positive associations with books, stories and theatre and contributed to the children's language and communication skills.

- Why was it important that the children were familiar with the story before the theatre group came to the school?

- Why do you think props were an effective way of retelling the story?

- Why did the staff use the props and provide other activities around the story?

- What would you do next to continue this enthusiasm that the children had for traditional tales?

The staff in this case study employed a range of pedagogical approaches to support the children's learning of the story of *Goldilocks and the Three Bears* so that the children could make the most of the theatre group's visit. The provision of play-based activities enabled the children to rehearse a storyline, to understand characters in the story and to begin to use the language of stories in their play.

Curriculum Links

This series of readings, activities and theatre visits addresses key elements of the EYFS (DfE, 2012) and National Curriculum for English (DfE, 2013). The EYFS (DfE, 2012) identifies a number of important aspects of children's development that support reading, including becoming aware of the way stories are structured, describing story settings, events and principal characters, and using vocabulary and forms of speech that are increasingly influenced by books and stories. The play and performance aspects of the activities also contribute to the expressive art and design area of learning which aims for children to be able to *represent their ideas, thoughts, feelings through design and technology, art, music, dance, role play and stories* (DfE, 2012, p.46).

The National Curriculum (DfE, 2013) requires children in Year 1 to listen to and discuss a range of stories at a level beyond which they can read independently and become very familiar with key stories, fairy stories and traditional tales.

Babies need books

The close physical contact and individual attention that is involved in reading to babies builds positive associations for them towards books and stories. They offer opportunities for children to interact – verbally and non-verbally – in a calm and focused way. This positive orientation towards books as something enjoyable and worthwhile is immeasurably important as children grow and learn. Books intended for babies provide a range of ways for them to engage with the book. There are wordless picture books often with bold, single focus illustrations. These are often associated with everyday items to identify and name, and with counting and the alphabet. Interactive books are also offered for the very young to enable them to interact with the book. Goodwin (2008) identifies the array of possibilities for the child to lift flaps, pull tabs, spin discs, remove items from integrated pockets or envelopes, unfold hinged pages, look through holes and turn over half-pages. In addition children can put fingers through holes in pages, run their fingers over textured sections of pages, push buttons to listen to sound effects, and move characters, attached with ribbons, around scenes in the book. Many books like these are read rather differently from other books as there is often no narrative: they are intended for interaction and discussion, often as children's first words appear. For example, *Cleo's Alphabet Book* (Mockford, 2007) has boldly outlined, brightly coloured line drawn illustrations of things beginning with a particular letter. This is accompanied by a verbal clue such as *C moos when he says hello, D barks as he plays.*

Where these interactive books do have a narrative it is important to consider how this is used, as the stop–start effect produced by the interactive elements means that the sense of a story can be lost in the engagement with the features. For example, *Dear Zoo* (Campbell, 1982) tells the story of suitable and unsuitable pets. It follows the narrative arc of: exposition (wanting a pet and writing to the zoo to request one is sent); complication (a series of unsuitable pets); climax (exasperation at the trail of unsuitable pets, and so the zookeepers think very hard); and resolution (receiving a perfect pet). At each stage the child has a flap to raise to look inside the package and see what has been sent. Consideration perhaps needs to be given to ways in which the child can follow the storyline as well as lift the flaps, rather as if it is a toy or game.

However, despite these minor reservations, these early books clearly appeal to babies and very young children and therefore provide an excellent introduction to the enjoyment to be had from books and stories.

In addition to the affective aspects of children's engagement with books and stories, books support babies and young children's language acquisition and development. Evidence suggests (Saxton, 2010) that children are born with the potential to acquire language and this potential develops through interaction with others. So babies have the capacity to learn language but they need to hear and use language to acquire and develop language. Reading books to babies provides one of the rich language experiences necessary for this. This includes an enjoyable and authentic engagement with the prosody of language. Prosody refers to the 'music' of spoken language: the appropriate pitch, loudness, speed and tone of voice. These are all learned from social interaction with others and vary within different social and cultural contexts. Hearing this will introduce children to these aspects of language. Through their involvement with books, babies and very young children not only have the opportunity to hear and tune into everyday language, but also begin to hear and tune into the language of books, and of stories in books.

Activity

Choose an interactive book for babies or young children that has a narrative.

- Identify the narrative in terms of the narrative arc (exposition, complication, climax, resolution).
- List different ways in which you could use this book with very young children.
- Highlight the ways that would enable the children to engage with the story as a whole.
- Why is this important at this stage of engagement with books and stories?

The importance of books in supporting babies' and very young children's development is recognised in the Bookstart project. The evaluation of their initial work (Moore and Wade, 2003), in which they gave books to families with babies, outlined the importance of books for babies, demonstrating the impact that they had on children's and families' engagement and interest in books and reading.

Research Focus

Bookstart

In recognition of the importance of books to babies and young children the Bookstart project began in the early 1990s in Birmingham. Children received free books and parents received advice on reading to babies and young children from health visitors (HVs). Evaluation of the project compared children of two to three years old who received Bookstart packs with a sample of children who didn't receive Bookstart packs. It showed that:

- 68 per cent of Bookstart children looked at books as one of their favourite activities (21 per cent for non-Bookstart children);

- 75 per cent of Bookstart parents said they bought books as presents for their children (10 per cent for non-Bookstart parents).

Researchers observed parents sharing a book with their children, again comparing Bookstart families with a non-Bookstart sample. Their results showed that:

- 83 per cent of Bookstart parents read the whole text compared with 34 per cent of non-Bookstart parents;

- 64 per cent talked about the story, compared with only 24 per cent;

- 43 per cent encouraged the child to join in, compared with only 27 per cent;

- 68 per cent encouraged the child to make predictions, compared to 38 per cent.

Bookstart families share more books but these findings also illustrate that the quality of the interaction between the parent and child is enhanced.

Additionally:

- All the professionals involved in the project were overwhelmingly positive about the value of giving books to babies.

- Interviews with library staff demonstrated their firm commitment to the role that book sharing has to play in children's early development.

- The role of HVs was crucial in introducing and explaining the pack – HVs saw an increase in parental interest in books and skill in sharing books with their children.

- Some parents that were harder to reach may need more support in using the gifts of books effectively.

- Greater awareness of the needs of parents who have English as an additional language was needed.

→

Overall:

- Bookstart was successful in generating positive attitudes to, and an interest in, books and book sharing in a wide range of families.

(Moore and Wade, 2003)

The initiative was extended to become a national programme in which packs of books are given to young children. The packs contained:

- Bookstart baby pack;

- Bookstart+ for toddlers;

- Bookstart Treasure Chest for three- to four-year-olds.

Book packs are also available for children with additional needs: *Bookshine* for children who are deaf and *Booktouch* for children who are visually impaired. Dual language packs are also available. Bookstart also endorses the value of reading and rhyme through locally provided groups and sessions to promote books and reading.

This commitment to providing books for babies and very young children is indicative of the importance that is placed on introducing and engaging children in books as early as possible to, in the words of Bookstart's slogan, *inspire a love of books in every child.*

Conclusion

Books for younger children can be seen to be important, not only for the development of literacy but also as an enriching and enjoyable activity. Early interaction with books, as a baby, begins this process of hooking children into books, stories, words and language, and opens up all the possibilities that children's literature holds.

Learning Outcomes Review

You should now understand why books and stories are important for young children. You should be able to recognise that engaging with books has an intrinsic value as a pleasurable activity and is significant in young children's language and literacy learning and development. You should know why books for babies are important, including how they can engender a love of books and stories. You should be aware of the important features of story time for young children including some qualitative aspects of discussion around texts to support children's learning. You should have some awareness of research that supports these understandings.

The case studies, activities and examples of texts throughout the chapter should support this understanding and make links between what we know and our practice as teachers.

Self-assessment questions

1   Choose a book for babies or young children. Identify the benefits of that book for children's enjoyment and engagement with books and stories and suggest how it might support language and literacy development.
2   Refer to Wade and Moore's (2003) evaluation of Bookstart. What are the implications of their findings for Early Years policy?
3   Recall a story time that you have led for young children. Undertake an analysis of your planning, preparation and delivery of the session. What worked well? What could have been better?

Further Reading

Gamble, N. and Yates, S. (2008) *Exploring Children's Literature. Teaching the Language and Reading of Fiction.* London: SAGE.

Styles, M., Bearne, E. and Watson, V. (eds) (1992) *After Alice. Exploring Children's Literature.* London: Cassell.

References

Burningham, J. (1996) *Cloudland.* London: Red Fox Books.

Butterworth, N. (2002) *Albert Le Blanc.* London: Collins.

Campbell, R. (1982) *Dear Zoo.* London: Puffin.

Cole, B. (1986) *Princess Smarty Pants.* London: Harper Collins.

Goouch, K. and Lambirth, A. (2011) *Teaching Early Reading and Phonics. Creative Approaches to Early Literacy.* London: SAGE.

Czikszentmihalyi, M. (2008) *The Psychology of Optimal Experience.* London: Harper.

DfE (2012) Development Matters in the EYFS. Available at: www.foundationyears.org.uk/files/2012/03/Development-Matters-FINAL-PRINT-AMENDED.pdf (accessed 12.04.16).

DfE (2013) *The National Curriculum in England: Key Stages 1 and 2 Framework Document.* London: DfE. Available at: www.gov.uk/government/uploads/system/uploads/attachment_data/file/335133/PRIMARY_national_curriculum_220714.pdf (accessed 12.04.16).

Donaldson, J. and Richards, L. (2002) *Night Monkey, Day Monkey.* London: Egmont.

Donaldson, J. and Scheffler, A. (1999) *The Gruffalo.* London: Macmillan Children's Books.

Donaldson, J. and Scheffler, A. (2001) *Room on the Broom.* London: Macmillan Children's Books.

Fraser, A. (2015) *The Pleasure of Reading.* London: Bloomsbury.

Goodall, M. (1984) Can four year olds 'read' words in the environment? *Reading Teacher,* 37(6): 478–89.

Goodman, Y. (1986) Children coming to know literacy, in Teale, W. and Sulzby, E. (eds) *Emergent Literacy Reading and Writing.* Norwood, NJ: Ablex Publishing Corporation.

Goodwin, P. (2008) *Understanding Children's Books.* London: SAGE.

Goouch, K. and Lambirth, A. (2011) *Teaching Early Reading and Phonics. Creative Approaches to Early Literacy.* London: SAGE.

Mockford, C. (2007) *Cleo's Alphabet Book.* Oxford: Barefoot Books.

Moore, M. and Wade, B. (2003) Bookstart: A Qualitative Evaluation. *Educational Review,* 55(1): 3–13.

Morgan, A. (2005) Shared reading interactions between mothers and pre-school children: Case studies of three dyads from a disadvantaged community. *Journal of Early Childhood Literacy.* 5: 279. Available at: http://ecl.sagepub.com/content/5/3/279 (accessed 12.04.16).

Saxton, M. (2010) *Child Language: Acquisition and Development.* London: SAGE.

Sheldon, D. and Blythe, G. (1990) *The Whale Song.* London: Red Fox.

Sulzby, E. and Rockafellow, B. (2001) Sulzby classification scheme instructional profiles. Available at: www.binghamtonschools.org/Downloads/Sulzby'sEmergentStoryBookReading. pdf (accessed 8.2.12).

Torr J. (2005) Talking about picture books: The influence of maternal education on four-year-old children's talk with mothers and pre-school teachers. *Journal of Early Childhood Literacy,* 4: 181. Available at: http://ecl.sagepub.com/content/4/2/181 (accessed 12.04.16).

5 Picture books

Learning Outcomes

By reading this chapter you will:

- understand what is meant by the term 'picture books';
- know why we use picture books with children;
- recognise that picture books are for children of all ages;
- understand the importance of visual imagery to children's meaning-making;
- recognise some of the complexities of looking at pictures;
- know about different ways of looking at pictures in books;
- be aware of aspects of the illustrator's craft that contribute to illustrative styles.

Introduction

When you think of a picture book what do you imagine? What are the features of it? Who do you assume it is for? Many of us will imagine some of the fabulous books now produced for young children, texts such as Helen Cooper's (1998) *Pumpkin Soup*, and Lauren Child's (2012) *Who's Afraid of the Big Bad Book?*, both richly illustrated and beautifully presented texts. Naturally much of what we see, and our own experiences, will have been that picture books are for the very young. Booksellers and libraries offer a huge range of these texts that are designed to appeal to young children (and their parents), and so encourage them to become engaged with books and stories at a young age. Illustrations in picture books provide an immediate connection with the narrative for very young children: one that doesn't require them to be able to read. Then, as children become readers, the pictures support and enhance their involvement with the book in different ways. Additionally, and despite our immediate assumptions, picture books also have the potential to engage and enrich older children's interactions with books and narrative: books such as those by David Weisner. Weisner writes and illustrates fantastical picture books which depict extraordinary events. For example, *June 29th 1999* (Weisner, 1992) depicts the day that we learn the results of Holly's science project: results unprecedented in scale and fantastical in scope. In *Flotsam* (Weisner, 2006), a boy discovers incredible happenings under the sea when he finds a barnacle-encrusted underwater camera among the flotsam on a beach.

What do we mean by picture books?

The term 'picture book' can be understood in a number of ways. This is because pictures in books interact with the narrative in different ways. In all cases they are, at least, equally as important as the text, and, in some cases, the pictures take precedence in the interaction between narrative and illustration.

Lane (1980) outlines three different ways in which the pictures can interact with the narrative.

1. Graphic decoration – the illustrations add little to the meaning; they beautify the text.

    My Dad's a Birdman by David Almond (2007) and illustrated by Polly Dunbar exemplifies this. The text is brought to life by occasional, beautifully stylised illustrations of Elizabeth, her dad, Aunt Doreen, Mr Poop and the great human bird competition.

2. Narrative illustration – the illustration mirrors the words.

    In *Mrs Armitage and the Big Wave* (Blake, 1997), Blake's colourful pictures, completed in his recognisable style, track the narrative of Mrs Armitage and her adventures on a hot sunny day, out on the sea on her surf board.

3. Interpretative illustration – the illustrations expand the text and add another layer of meaning or a richness of meaning.

    Hey, I Love You! (Whybrow and Reeve, 2005) is an excellent example of how illustrations expand the text. It tells two stories in parallel. One story, in the text, tells a tale of a mouse following his mum from the safety of his den into the world because he forgot to tell her that he loves her. The other story is told through the illustrations; it is the tale of a cat following the mouse who is following his mummy, close on his tail ready to pounce at any moment. *Monkey Puzzle* (Donaldson and Sheffler, 2000) tells the story of a monkey looking for his mummy. In his text the illustrations add another meaning to the text. The butterfly who helps him offers lots of suggestions as to where he can find his mummy, but to no avail because, as it turns out, baby monkeys look just like their mummies, unlike baby butterflies. The illustrations add an important visual elucidation of this confusion.

In addition to Lane's (1980) taxonomy there are graphic and wordless picture books. In these books pictures relate to the narrative in a different way: the narrative is the illustration.

In Monique Felix's wordless book (2003) *Mouse Books: The Boat*, a little mouse scampers over the book and chews away the corner to reveal the ocean. He makes a paper boat as the ocean comes tumbling in and he sails away. The story is told in part through the mouse's beautifully expressive face. Similarly, in Shirley Hughes' wordless book *Up Up Up* (1991), a little girl discovers to her delight that she can fly. She sets off on a series of airborne adventures around the area where she lives, much to the consternation of the watching grown-ups.

The Arrival by Shaun Tan (2007) is another wordless graphic novel for older children that seems to tell the story of an immigrant arriving on Ellis Island. But this new country is like no place ever seen before. Giant crockery dominates the landscape, trolleys fly and people keep strange animal hybrids for pets. And yet the people in this alien landscape are familiar. This is a substantial book with detailed pictures using muted shades of brown and cream. There is an immediate complexity in the pictures which requires attention and focus to begin to make meaning from the text.

Why use picture books?

Pictures in books provide a visual dimension to a narrative. Through their expressive power they add depth and meaning to the books, providing an aesthetic experience alongside the literary experience of the narrative. The potential of this belies the assumptions that picture books are somehow simple, or only for very young children who cannot yet read. Picture books have the potential to work on many levels and in many ways that enhance and deepen the experience of the book. Picture books provide a rich source for children's imagination and creativity. They have the potential to invoke pleasure, inspire fantasy, stimulate curiosity, develop empathy and personal understanding and explore the art of story telling. At their most simple, picture books contain a narrative in pictures. These images are accessible to very young children and provide a focus for interaction with others. However, picture books can also contain highly sophisticated images that enable children to engage with them at different levels and in different ways. The Booktrust evokes an effective image of picture books as self-contained art galleries which children can visit over and over again, finding new ideas and resonances each time that they return to them.

In the case study below Rebecca used the idea of pop-up art galleries to engage children with picture books. As you read the case study, notice the ways in which she generated and maintained interest in the books, and the ways in which she got children to focus on the pictures and to develop their ideas about the images.

Case Study

Pop-up picture book galleries

Rebecca explained to the children that on any one day, and as a surprise, the popup art gallery would appear somewhere around school. The children then had the rest of that day to populate the space with their current favourite picture book. The gallery would then be open to other children in the school for one day only before it disappeared again.

The children in her class therefore had to have their ideas ready for the gallery because at any point it might appear. They had to know which book they were going to display and have

$\longrightarrow$

brief notes ready to attach to the book to explain to the visitors what they loved about the story and illustrations.

In preparation for this she worked with the children on understanding the illustrator's craft so that they had a framework for looking closely and explaining aspects of the illustration in their gallery notes alongside the narrative.

It was a huge success. The children in her class became more engaged in books and illustration, and it created a buzz around school about where, when and what would pop up.

Rebecca continued the idea in school for a number of weeks but stopped when interest was still high, with a 'wait-and-see' promise that the gallery would reappear later in the year, and the children needed to be ready.

Rebecca's pop-up picture book galleries focused children's attention on pictures in books. The format of having to produce a brief explanation of their chosen book meant that they had to engage with the craft of illustration and the relationship between the text and the pictures. Additionally, it created a 'buzz' about picture books and maintained this through the pop-up aspect of the activity. Finishing the project while interest was still high also maintained interest through the expectation and anticipation of further projects.

Curriculum Links

As well as engaging children in books and stories, this activity clearly has strong links to the visual arts: viewing, exploring and expressing ideas about pictures. It could also be used as a starting point for exploring different ways of representing ideas in different countries, cultures and over time. This has strong links to aspects of the humanities.

Meaning-making and picture books

Pictures in picture books engage with both linguistic and visual modes of learning. Communicating and making meaning of what we see, hear and experience happens in a number of different ways – these are referred to as modes. There are six identified modes of meaning-making: linguistic meaning; visual meaning; audio meaning; gestural meaning; spatial meaning; and multimodal meaning (a combination of two or more of the other modes) (Cope and Kalantzis, 2000). Picture books that combine words and pictures to communicate the story create meaning through linguistic and visual modes. Wordless, graphic texts communicate meaning visually. These modes of meaning-making continue through our lives; it is not just young children who make sense of the world in different ways.

Think about how easy it is for us, as adults, to find our way somewhere that we haven't been before when we have a map, satellite navigation device or diagram to give us a visual representation of the journey. It is perhaps even easier with a satellite device, when we have visual and auditory information, because in this instance we are making meaning using different modes, which offers us more ways of understanding where we are going. This understanding provides a powerful argument for using picture books with children and young people of all ages and stages. *Michael Rosen's Sad Book* (Rosen and Blake, 2004) exemplifies the power of picture books for older children and adults. In the book Michael Rosen explores his thoughts and experiences following the death of his son. It is illustrated by Quentin Blake, who evocatively interprets Rosen's words: joyfully when Rosen remembers playing goalkeeper 'saves' on the sofa with his son when he was young, and hauntingly in a series of pictures that fade to grey as a day moves on and Rosen explains *there's a sad place inside me because things aren't the same.* The final two pages are similarly highly evocative and deeply moving. There is the juxtaposition of two contrasting pictures, one of a big family birthday gathering with candles, tens of candles on cakes of all shapes and sizes, and then a final picture, no words, one candle and a man sitting alone looking at a framed photograph. The depth and complexity of the subject matter in the book belie the apparent simplicity of the illustrations. These illustrations, in combination with few words, make this a powerful book.

Research Focus

Kress (1997) Multimodal meaning-making

Kress was interested in the way that children symbolically represent what they know before they can write it down. He argues that long before children come to writing they use a range of symbolic ways to represent what they know, what they can do and what they are thinking.

Children's earliest experiences of using symbols to communicate meaning (a thumb-up for good, a box for a helmet) change and develop as they grow and learn and they begin to communicate meanings in a wider variety of ways using toys, materials and equipment: they build, they draw, they model, they engage in craft activities and role play. In these ways children come to understand, to make and represent meaning, and to communicate ideas, thoughts, imaginings and experiences in symbolic ways.

Kress (1997) argues that children have this greater scope to create meaning in different modes because they are not restricted by adult conceptualisations about what are appropriate or correct ways. They are not constrained by having to represent ideas, thoughts and experiences through language, spoken, written or read. Children focus on what best fits the purpose and what is available for use. This results in different ways of meaning-making using different modes.

The complexity of looking

When we look at picture books we see the pictures. We look and, consciously or not, we strive to understand the meaning of the illustrations, either alongside the narrative or as the narrative in wordless books. We assume that the pictures have meaning in the context of the book and that they are orientated towards elucidating a story. This is the case with all types of picture books. Our assumption is that, in some way, the pictures relate to, and offer us, a narrative, and we as readers seek out that meaning in what we perceive. Nodelman describes this relationship thus:

> *Illustrators who understand their craft use all aspects of visual imagery to convey meaning; and the meaning-conscious mind-set required to appreciate such pictures fully, is always conscious of, and in search of possible meanings.*

(1988, p.20)

This is true for children of all ages when they are looking at pictures. Young children will seek out meaning in their way, to discover and make sense of the text. Older children will similarly perceive and seek out meaning from books with the pictures adding depth to the meaning and the experience.

However, looking at pictures is not necessarily the straightforward process that it perhaps first seems. Understanding this relationship between pictures, text and narrative requires skill in comprehending and making meaning of visual imagery. As Nodelman (1988, p.20) notes, pictures are a subtle and complex form of communication; they imply a viewer with a mastery of certain skills and much knowledge. This accords with understandings from cognitive psychology that argue that perception is in the brain, not the eye, and that understandings are deeply embedded in what we bring to a situation. In pictures this includes socially and culturally constructed understandings about the form and the content of pictures and about the focus and ways of looking when we interact with pictures. Barthes (1985 cited in Nodelman, 1988) concurs. In his semiotic theory he argues that all images have a denoted message and a connoted message. The denoted message is the literal meaning, the depiction of reality, and the connoted message is the meaning suggested by the depiction. Interpretation of the meaning relies on a process of perceiving and recognising an image and then creating meaning from this by drawing on social, historical and cultural knowledge that we have. *The Arrival* by Shaun Tan (2007) plays around with our understandings and assumptions and illustrates this point beautifully. Tan confounds the knowledge that we bring to the text. Many aspects of the book are recognisable and familiar. However, the landscape contains giant crockery, strange hybrid animals, foods and instruments. So, despite the depiction of familiar places, people, actions and events, the landscape remains strange. The use of particular illustrative techniques is an integral part of the experience of the text.

Activity

Imagine an alphabet book for very young children which has, on each page, a letter and a picture of something beginning with that letter.

What would typically be on the pages for the letters 'a' 'c' 'k' 'o' 'r' 'y'? How are these items depicted on the page? Think about colour, shape, size, etc.

Now reflect on your choices.

Why have you chosen these images?

Think carefully about:

- the social and culturally embedded assumptions about which items to name and depict;
- the assumptions about appropriate artwork for very young children in these books.

Where is this 'grammar' of books for young children from? Think about both the content and the form of what you imagined. Why this content? Why this form? What are you assuming? Identify the social and cultural understandings evident in your assumptions.

Understanding and making meaning from pictures can therefore be seen to have many dimensions and we need to understand both form and content, and the intersecting relationship between them, to construct meaning from artwork. Looking at pictures is not a neutral act. Indeed Bryson (1988 cited in Nodelman, 1988) argues that no image is automatically understandable. It relies on perceiving and interpreting what we see and these processes are deeply embedded within a social and cultural context.

The activity above provides a straightforward example of this. Many of us will have chosen similar items for the alphabet book and described similar depictions of the items – so, apple for 'a', kite or kangaroo for 'k', orange for 'o', imagined and described in boldly coloured, simple line drawings. This isn't just a coincidence. It is a feature of our experience and understanding of books for young children. These experiences are embedded in the social and cultural context in which we have grown and learned, a context in which we have experienced books for young children and internalised socially and culturally determined patterns of content and form. So you perhaps won't be surprised to know that many alphabet books published in New Zealand often depict a kiwi bird for the letter 'k'.

Research Focus

Picture books and philosophy for children

In their book *Picture books, Pedagogy and Philosophy*, Haynes and Murris (2012) describe how they used existing picture books for children as a starting point for philosophy for children. They demonstrate how pictures in books can be interpreted in multi-layered ways, and they report on their own projects in supporting children to ask, and respond to, probing and powerful questions evoked by the pictures in books. They see that picture books open up spaces for thinking, arguing that the aesthetic properties enhance the power with which ideas and emotions are communicated.

With their multiple narratives, ambiguity and contradictions, picturebooks are emotionally and intellectually demanding texts for children and adults alike. The reader is pulled into different directions of meaning-making through the conjunction of images and/or text.

(Haynes, 2011)

Recognising and knowing how to understand visual imagery in relation to a narrative in picture books is primarily a matter of immersion in books within a specific culture. The experience of living in an environment where there are pictures and books automatically provides most children with that immersion and allows them to begin to understand and make meaning of visual imagery.

Activity

It is suggested that the ability to perceive and interpret pictures relies on an immersion in picture books within a specific culture.

- How do we ensure that children are offered the opportunity to engage with picture books? Think about access to the books, time to immerse themselves in the books, time to discuss their ideas, and time to develop and/or represent their thoughts and ideas.
- How do we ensure that these are relevant to children's understanding and continue to challenge them as their understandings become more sophisticated?
- What professional knowledge do you need as a teacher to ensure that you can provide these opportunities?

We can also actively engage children in attending to what they see, and focusing and thinking carefully about pictures to support this process of meaning-making and so deepen their experience of engaging with picture books. The case study below shows how a year group team and their trainees used picture books to stimulate creative writing. Notice how the pictures offered a framework for the children's ideas while also allowing them freedom to be creative in interpreting the images.

Case Study

Making meaning from pictures in books

The year group team decided to use pictures in books as a resource to stimulate creative writing with their Year 4 classes.

As preparation for this work all the teachers and their trainees spent some time drawing children's attention to the illustrations in picture books and discussing the relationship between the text and pictures, and the significance of the style of the illustrations.

The team collected a range of picture books, with different types of illustrations, that they considered interesting and engaging for the children in their classes, and that they anticipated the children were not familiar with. They removed the text from the pictures and represented them in cartoon strip form.

In a series of planned lessons the children chose a set of illustrations and developed a story to accompany them. The children then compared the story that they had written with others who had used the same set of illustrations. This led to some fascinating conversations about what the images meant and how individual children had interpreted them using their own experiences, knowledge and imaginings.

The teachers and trainees in this case study provided children with a powerful visual stimulus for their creative writing. Pictures are subtle and complex forms of communication and allowing children the freedom to interpret the pictures enabled them not only to be creative, but also to explore creativity itself through seeing how other children interpreted the images differently.

Curriculum Links

As well as enabling children to be creative, the series of lessons offered the teacher a framework for teaching transcription and composition, and it provided the opportunity for the children to engage in and develop skills of speaking and listening. The use of the pictures provided a meaningful and enjoyable context for this learning. The creative aspect of the lessons, both the interpretation of the pictures and imagining of the story, has clear links to the arts: imagining and creating. The stories that were written, and the children's comparison of the differences in their interpretations of the pictures, may also open up opportunities for discussion and exploration of aspects of Personal, Social and Health Education (PSHE).

Ways of looking at picture books

If, as Nodelman (1988) claims, pictures are subtle complex forms of communication, it seems likely that they have the potential for different types and levels of engagement as we look and seek to understand the images presented. The Booktrust identify five different ways of looking which are linked to the ways in which children, as they grow and learn, engage more fully with symbolic images. They describe how, as children develop cognitively, they increasingly begin to understand the meanings of images that are removed from real things. Thus children can begin to create meanings for images that are increasingly more fantastical, wittier, richer with information and more paradoxical. However, these ways of looking are not hierarchical in the sense that they replace one another. Being able to see rich and complex meanings in images doesn't preclude the possibility of looking at pictures for pleasure. Older children (and adults) are able to see images in different ways and with different levels of understanding; indeed we may engage with a picture in all the different ways at the same time.

Way of looking at pictures	Stage of development
1. Looking for pleasure	Sensory and concrete learning
2. Inspiring fantasy	Imaginative and fantasy
3. Stimulating curiosity	Broadening horizons
4. Understanding others	Developing empathy and personal understanding
5. Exploring the making of art and stories	Higher cognitive thinking

1. Initially, young children will look at images for pleasure – to seek out familiar things, to make links between objects, events and language, and to enjoy the sensory pleasure of engaging with images.

2. From the age of three children begin to engage with, and enjoy, imagining characters, places, stories, people and events. Picture books have enormous potential to stimulate children's imagination and engage them in creative ideas and thinking.

3. Picture books can be likened to pictures in galleries and as such can stimulate curiosity. Pictures can act as a provocation to a range of questions. As children develop cognitively and begin to seek to understand and make meaning in their world, pictures can be part of children's fascination with who?, what?, why? and how?

4. Empathy enables children to understand other people. Stories told in pictures and texts enable children to explore this emotional landscape in a safe way. Pictures have an immediacy that text lacks, that enables us to tune into feelings and experiences. They encourage us to imagine 'what if?', and to engage with feelings and situations beyond

ourselves. As children grow and learn, picture books can support their developing awareness of self and others.

5. Older children are able to use their cognitive skills to analyse and interpret pictures both for their meaning and to understand how abstract ideas are embedded in narrative and illustration. They are able to understand how metaphorical images are used and created and how pictures can have multiple meanings. They are able to engage with abstract ideas and concepts embedded in images in picture books.

(adapted from Booktrust, www.booktrust.org.uk/books/children/
illustrators/picture-book-resources/)

One of the most important aspects of this taxonomy is that it demonstrates that picture books are a wonderful resource for children and young people of all ages and, as aforementioned, that we need to move away from the commonly held assumption that books with pictures are only for very young children and develop our understanding and the resources to encourage and enable older children to experience all that picture books have to offer.

Activity

Find a picture from Shaun Tan's (2000) book *The Lost Thing*.

Choose a picture and look closely at it.

- Enjoy the picture – look at it for the pleasure of looking. Admire Tan's artistry. Notice what engages you. Notice your thinking.
- Be aware of the ideas it provokes. What makes you curious? Where do these thoughts lead?
- Notice what you are thinking about the people and creatures. What questions do you want or need to answer? What intrigues you?
- How do you interpret the images in *The Lost Thing?* What do they mean to you?
- What do you think Tan intended in creating this world?
- How does Tan create the world? What are the images, the metaphors, the ideas that are in the picture and have meaning for you?

Notice how all the different ways of looking at a picture can be intertwined: how it is possible to look separately in different ways, to move back and forth between different ways of looking, and to look at many levels simultaneously.

1. How could you use this understanding of ways of looking with children?
2. How could you offer experiences that enabled children to engage with pictures in different ways?

Layers of meaning in picture books – reflecting diversity in society in illustrations

This chapter aims to elucidate how important pictures are in creating meaning in texts. In addition to meaning-making from the text, drawing on social and cultural references of representation, there is another layer of understanding and meaning in pictures in the way in which illustrators choose to represent society. Our society is made up of people of different sex and gender, race, religious affiliation, with different patterns of family life, and within all these different groups, there are people with a disability. Books undoubtedly have a role to play in the perception of society in which we live. McCabe, et al. (2011) in their research into gender and children's books argue that children's books are culturally important as they are *a powerful means through which children learn their cultural heritage* (Bettelheim, 1977). They argue that:

> ... *children's books provide messages about right and wrong, the beautiful and the hideous, what is attainable and what is out of bounds – in sum, a society's ideals and directions. Simply put, children's books are a celebration, reaffirmation, and dominant blueprint of shared cultural values, meanings, and expectations.*

> (p.199)

This *powerful means* by which children learn about the society in which they are growing and learning includes the illustrations in picture books and graphic texts. This raises the question of how different groups of people are, or perhaps should be, represented in the pictures in books. What role do pictures have in reflecting diversity within society? What role do they have in moulding perceptions of different groups in society? You can read more about stories and poems that address issues in Chapter 8.

Research Focus

Two daddy tigers and a baby tiger: promoting understandings about same gender parented families using picture books (Kelly, 2012)

This research explores teachers' interpretations of children's responses to a selection of picture books featuring same-sex parented families.

The research is underpinned by the assumption that children's understandings of and practices towards diversity are constituted within the various discourses that are available to them in their daily lives.

The teachers in the study introduced children to discourses of 'otherness' through the use of picture books. Ten selected picture books featuring same-gendered parents (including anthropomorphised penguins) were read to children alongside other books in the kindergarten. The teachers and researchers kept logs detailing what had been read, the children's

→

responses to the books and noticeable connections or associations made in language, conversation and play. This was followed by semi-structured interviews with the teachers.

Kelly concluded that the children's responses demonstrated that they were open to the possibilities of non-traditional families and notes that:

> making social diversity discourses available through using inclusive resources proactively does not have to be difficult, dangerous or controversial. Sapp's (2010:33) proposition is supported whereby 'early learning around difference can begin and spaces can open up in the classroom that acknowledge multiple sexualities and diverse family structures.'
>
> (2012, p.298)

Additionally, and in contrast to the children's response, she found that the teachers appeared hesitant to ask probing questions or fully engage with the children's thinking or their own to explore understandings in this area.

There has certainly been a change over time in how society is represented in pictures in books (McCabe, et al., 2011; Keith, 2001) Even the briefest analysis of the pictures in young children's books will demonstrate the move towards representing a breadth of different aspects of our culture. In particular, race, gender, religious affiliation, and certain patterns of family life (for example, single-parent families) are more widely represented. Also represented, but to a lesser degree, are disability and certain other patterns of family life, for example single fathers and same-sex parents. Within this it is interesting to observe how different illustrators and authors choose to reflect diversity in society differently. Some illustrators choose to reflect society, depicting diversity as part of the fabric of life. For example, in Lauren Child's Charlie and Lola stories, Lola's best friend is of African-Caribbean origin, although this is only evident in the illustrations. Other writers and illustrators more obviously aim to shape it by challenging assumptions and traditional and accepted patterns within society. For example, *The Paper Bag Princess* (Munsch and Martchenko, 2009) turns the traditional narrative of the beautiful princess awaiting rescue on its head. In this story a princess, wearing a paper bag, rescues a prince. The final delightful twist in the storyline, reflected in illustrations, challenges assumptions about beauty and about gender roles in traditional prince and princess stories.

Activity

Think about the illustrations in picture books.

Imagine you are choosing a collection of books for your classroom.

- What would you be looking for in terms of the depiction of society in the illustrations?
- Why would you make these choices?
- What do you think is the role of picture books in looking at these issues?

Research Focus

Choosing books that depict people with disabilities

Blaska (2004) has developed an Images and Encounters Profile to assist people in choosing children's books. Blaska reviewed 500 award-winning and highly recommended books for children from birth to eight, which were published between 1987 and 1991, for the inclusion and depiction of people with disabilities. The study focused on the storyline, language and illustrations.

Of the reviewed books ten (two per cent) included people with disabilities in the storyline or illustrations. Within those ten books, people with disabilities were integral to the storyline in six of them. They concluded that the limited presence of people with disabilities identified a need for more stories that represent the diversity of society, which includes people with varying abilities.

While more books with characters with disabilities are published today, the percentage is still small when compared to the total number of children's picture books published each year (Blaska, 2004).

The profile identifies ten criteria to assist in choosing children's books. Although the profile refers to all aspects of the book, most of them can be applied to an analysis of the illustrations. The criteria are:

- promotes empathy not pity;
- depicts acceptance not ridicule;
- emphasises success rather than, or in addition to, failure;
- promotes positive images of people with disabilities or illnesses;
- assists children in gaining an accurate understanding of the disability or illness;
- demonstrates respect for people with disability or illness;
- promotes attitude of 'one of us' not 'one of them';
- uses language that stresses person first, disability second, i.e. John who has Down's syndrome;
- describes the disability or person with disability realistically;
- illustrates characters in a realistic manner.

The illustrator's craft

It really goes without saying that picture books require an illustrator, and a look at even a small number of picture books demonstrates the enormous range of illustrative styles within children's books. It is interesting to note the immediacy of the impact of the illustrator's craft on our perception of a book. We often select books and pull them off a shelf purely because the front cover 'appeals' to us. Clearly, what appeals to us is a very subjective thing, and we choose different texts accordingly, but it is the illustrations as much as the title that provide this immediate connection with the text.

Doonan (1993) argues that everything we see in picture books is affective, that it sets the brain ticking and sometimes the heart knocking. This affect is created through the illustrator's craft and their use of techniques and materials in very specific ways, for example illustrator Jane Ray's use of vibrant colour, often including gold, and a particular stylised representation of people; Shirley Hughes' sketch-like illustrations in her books that give a comforting, homely feel to her stories of the everyday lives of young children; Helen Cooper's detailed, vivid and slightly surreal depictions of the landscapes in which her stories take place.

Illustrators use and manipulate different aspects of design in their work to create the desired effects. Marantz (1997 cited in Doonan, 1993) identifies the design aspects of these as composition, shape and line, size and scale, perspective and colour (see below).

These elements of design come together in different ways to form an illustrator's style. Different illustrators therefore have different styles; indeed many become known for their particular style of illustration. For example, and in addition to the illustrators named above, Quentin Blake, Lauren Child, John Burningham, Axel Scheffler, Ludwig Bemelmans, Nick Sharret and Jan Pienkowski all have different and quite distinctive illustrative styles.

Elements of design in art	
Composition	This refers to how the picture and its parts are arranged on the page. It can be a balanced or symmetrical arrangement which tends to settle the viewer; or it may be asymmetrical which, conversely, can be unsettling to the viewer.
Shapes and line	Solid shapes or shapes formed by lines making up a picture. Pointed shapes are generally less restful than rounded ones. Rectangular objects parallel to the ground suggest solidity. Diagonal lines draw the eye upwards or downwards. They are less restful than parallel lines at the bottom of a picture. Lines that go up and down at the sides of pictures give a feeling of height and expansiveness. Lines tend to lead the eye to what the artist feels is important. The lines themselves can be clear or fuzzy, thick or thin, nervous and busy (scribble-type lines) or straight and calm.
Size and scale	The size and scale of the shapes in a picture tell the viewer how these objects relate to one another. Large objects dominate smaller ones and appear, at least initially, to be more important in the composition.
Perspective	The perspective in a picture, or lack of perspective, affects the viewer's point of view. In a traditional Western perspective things will appear larger if closer to the viewer. However, if the artist is working within another tradition other rules on perspective may apply. The point of view is the point from which the illustrator allows us to view the scene. This could be face on, or from above or below, or through a smaller space such as a window, door or peephole. Changing the point of view has an impact on the viewer.
Colour	The impact of the illustrator's choice of colour in a picture is profound. Illustrators make decisions not only about colour but also about shade and tone. Although the effect of colour on us can be subjective there are some conventional associations in Western culture – for example, red is associated with warmth and with danger. Yellows and oranges are generally cheerful colours. Blues are more restful, calm colours. Black indicates night, dark, silence and fear.

(based on Marantz, 1992)

Activity

Choose some illustrated books. The list above may help.

- Identify the ways in which each illustrator uses the aspects of design outlined above to create their particular style.
- What do you think are the most effective elements of their style?
- What impact does the style have on you? Why do you think this is so?
- How well do you think the style reflects the text and/or narrative?
- How does looking at these illustrators' work support your professional knowledge and understanding?
- How could you use this knowledge in the classroom?

Illustrators can make wide-ranging choices about materials and techniques when they illustrate books. These purposeful choices are made to create a particular effect and thus invoke an affective response in the viewer. So, in picture books with words and pictures, illustrators, bringing their individual style to the work, will work closely with the author (or the narrative when they are both author and illustrator of a text) to interpret the narrative and create a dynamic between the words and the pictures. This is evident in Shirley Hughes' work. *Alfie Gives a Hand* (Hughes, 1983) is a picture book for young children in which Alfie finds he can manage without his special blanket at Bernard's tea party. Hughes' style of sketchy line-drawn pictures is used throughout, depicting familiar places and events at a children's party. Some of the pictures are colourful, evoking the cheerful world of children's play; others use pastel shades creating a cosier feel to the page. In contrast, *The Lion and the Unicorn* by Hughes (1998) has a much darker feel. The story is one of war, the evacuation of a young boy and his friendship with an injured soldier. The illustrations are recognisably Hughes in her use of line and depiction of children's everyday domestic lives. However, in contrast to *Alfie*, the illustrations in *The Lion and the Unicorn* use deep shades of greys, oranges and blues to create a feeling of darkness and fear. She also uses perspective to emphasis Lenny's plight: he is depicted as a small boy in a vast landscape. This depiction highlights how small Lenny is both physically, in a big house in the open countryside, and metaphorically, a child in a world war. In both these texts there is a dynamic relationship between the words and the pictures. It is through the combination of author's words and the artistry of the illustrations that we fully experience the narrative.

The case study below demonstrates how children can be encouraged to focus on illustrations in books. Notice how the teacher encouraged children to look at and form opinions about illustrations, and how she used this process to learn about the children's knowledge and understanding.

Case Study

Actively engaging children in looking at pictures in books

Helen, a Year 3 class teacher, wanted to encourage the use of illustration in story telling. As a starting point to this she wanted the children to begin to look carefully at the illustrations in books.

To encourage this Helen put some labels on some shelves in the library area in the classroom: words such as dreamy, vibrant, detailed, dark, real, imagined. To begin with the class discussed what the words meant and looked at some examples of illustrations and decided which category fitted them best. They discussed how the artist had used shape, size, colour, scale, perspective, materials, techniques and composition to create the images in the books and discussed why these techniques had been used in the context of the narrative.

Over the following weeks the children were encouraged to look carefully at the pictures as they read books and to reorder the books on shelves according to the quality of the illustrations.

Helen noticed that the children themselves developed this further by selecting books from the shelves and looking carefully to decide whether they agreed with the other children's view. They also asked to add words to describe texts that they felt didn't match any of the categories offered.

The interest in the illustrations enabled Helen to observe children's understandings of, and responses to, books. It supported children's cognitive development as they sought to understand the pictures and their relationship to the text. She was also surprised by how engagement with the pictures enabled the children to demonstrate their own wider knowledge, thoughts and feelings, and seek to understand the motives, thoughts and feelings of others.

As with the other case studies in this chapter, the activities provided by the teacher encouraged children to engage with pictures in books, enhancing their language, familiarising them with a range of books and stories, and exploring the relationship between text and illustration. In addition to this, the teacher's observation of the children's discussion enabled her to observe other aspects of their knowledge and understanding.

Curriculum Links

This activity supports a number of aspects of the English curriculum. Children are able to participate in discussion about books and explain and discuss their understanding of the text and pictures. They also have the opportunity to form opinions about books, and to ask questions and offer explanations when considering other children's opinions about the books. The process of listening to different opinions in a considered way is also an important aspect of PSHE.

The task of focusing on the pictures and making aesthetic judgements about the craft of illustration would also support children's development in the creative arts.

Research Focus

Children reading picture books

Arizipe and Styles' (2016) text reports findings from an extension to a study that they conducted in 1999. The authors revisited the project *Children reading picture books* for a number of reasons: research undertaken in the intervening years; the emergence of new thinking around visual literacies; and the growth of ways in which children can engage with picture books, including through the use of technology.

In the text the authors revisit their findings from their initial study, listing them as:

- *children as young as 4 were very good at analysing the visual features of texts;*

- *most children were deeply engaged by the texts and keen to discuss the moral, social, spiritual and environmental issues they raised;*

- *analysing visual text, and the relationship between word and image, made demands on higher order reading skills (inference, viewpoint, etc.);*

- *as well as learning through looking, we had clear evidence of children learning through talking, and the importance of enabling questions was underlined;*

- *there were many similarities between the responses of children in schools with completely different catchment areas;*

- *the younger children's drawings often showed understandings they were unable to articulate;*

- *our findings confirmed our original belief that careful looking and constructive dialogue enables children (including those who are very young or do not speak English fluently or do not read print confidently) to make worthwhile judgments about pictures which are often profound, complex and richly interconnected with other ideas or symbolic systems;*

- *the children in our study learned effectively because they found the activity they engaged in to be worthwhile;*

- *children can become more visually literate and operate at a much higher level if they are taught how to look.*

(p.180)

Arizipe and Styles (2016) then go on to outline a wide range of research and relevant theory that has developed since their original research, including case studies from postgraduate enquiry into children and picture books. They conclude that the research evidence is very positive,

... once again, the first thing to come through for many researchers was the excitement and pleasure of engaging with picturebooks and the emotional bonds forged with the texts.

(p.180)

In their final chapter Arizipe and Styles (2016) focus on pedagogical approaches to using picture books with children. They note that it will require a commitment from teachers and practitioners to developing knowledge about picture books and adopting pedagogical practices that enable children to access all that they have to offer. In achieving this they stress the importance of:

- *using well-crafted picturebooks that have the potential to "teach" readers both literary and literacy skills as the reader/viewer is encouraged to engage deeply and this can lead to critical thinking and meaningful learning;*

- *having time to look closely at images and do re-readings;*

- *valuing the intertextual knowledge and visual literacy practices that children bring to their meaning-making from outside the school context;*

- *providing meta-language to discuss the visual features of picturebooks as well as some reference to how pictures and text interact;*

- *asking about and discussing cultural references in picturebooks;*

- *encouraging in-depth interpretation and understanding through talk and collaborative discussion.*

(p.180)

Conclusion

The quality and breadth of picture books now available for children has been one of the most significant developments in children's literature over recent years. Alongside the development of picture books for very young children, what has also emerged are picture books which are capable of engaging older children. These books, which are often challenging and rich in meaning, provide an excellent provocation to learning in the classroom.

Learning Outcomes Review

You should now understand what is meant by picture books and the value of using them with children of all ages. You should be aware of some of the complexity of looking at pictures and the different ways in which we can look and appreciate picture books and graphic texts. You should be able to describe aspects of the illustrator's craft and recognise these in the different illustrative styles. This, alongside ideas in the case studies, should enable you to consider how you can use picture books and graphic texts in the classroom.

Self-assessment questions

Choose a picture book.

1. What is the relationship between the pictures and the narrative?
2. What social and cultural understandings do you bring to understanding the book?
3. How may the pictures support children's meaning-making from the text?
4. Describe the illustrative style. What is the effect of the illustrator's choice of materials and techniques? What are the affective aspects of the book?
5. Identify ways in which this book could be used as part of your teaching.

Further Reading

Bang, M. (2000) *Picture This. How Pictures Work.* San Francisco: Chronicle Books.

Lewis, D. (2001) *Reading Contemporary Picturebooks. Picturing Text.* London: RoutledgeFalmer.

Maybin, J. and Watson, N. (eds) (2009) *Children's Literature Approaches and Territories. Section 5 Words and Pictures.* Buckingham: Open University Press.

Sipe, L. (2011) The Art of the Picture Book, in Wolf, S., Coats, K., Enisco, P. and Jenkins, C. (eds.) *Handbook of Research on Children's and Young Adult Literature.* London: Routledge.

References

Almond, D. and Dunbar, P. (2007) *My Dad's a Birdman.* London: Walker Books.

Arizipe, E. and Styles, M. (2016) *Children Reading Picturebooks: Interpreting Visual Texts*, 2nd edition. London: Routledge.

Blake, Q. (1997) *Mrs Armitage and the Big Wave.* London: Red Fox.

Blaska, J. (2004) Children's literature that includes characters with disabilities or illnesses. *Disability Studies Quarterly*, 24(1). Available at: http://dsq-sds.org/issue/view/38 (accessed 12.04.16).

Child, L. (2012) *Who's Afraid of the Big Bad Book?* London: Orchard Books.

Cooper, H. (1998) *Pumpkin Soup.* London: Doubleday.

Cope, B. and Kalantzis, M. (2000) *Multiliteracies: Literacy Learning and the Design of Social Futures.* London: Routledge.

Donaldson, J. and Scheffler, A. (2000) *Monkey Puzzle.* London: Macmillan Children's Books.

Doonan, J. (1993) *Looking at Pictures in Picture Books.* Stroud: The Thimble Press.

Felix, M. (2003) *The Boat (Mouse Books).* US: Creative Company.

Haynes, J. (2011) Feeling the pea beneath the mattresses: philosophising with children as imaginative, critical practice. Paper in progress. ESRC Seminar at Birkbeck College, University of London, 21 October 2011.

Haynes, J. and Murris, K. (2012) *Picture Books, Pedagogy and Philosophy.* London: Routledge.

Hughes, S. (1983) *Alfie Gives a Hand.* London: Red Fox.

Hughes, S. (1991) *Up Up Up.* London: Red Fox.

Hughes, S. (1998) *The Lion and the Unicorn.* London: Red Fox.

Keith, L. (2001) *Take Up Thy Bed and Walk, Death, Disability and Cure in Classic Fiction for Girls.* London: The Women's Press.

Kelly, J. (2012) Two daddy tigers and a baby tiger: Promoting understandings about same gender parented families using picture books. *Early Years: An International Journal of Research and Development,* 32(3): 288–300.

Kress, G.R. (1997) *Before Writing: Rethinking the Paths to Literacy.* London: Routledge.

Lane, S. (1980) *The Art of Maurice Sendak.* London: Bodley Head.

Marantz, S. (1992) *Picture Books for Looking and Learning. Awaking Visual Perceptions Through the Art of Children's Books.* Phoenix, Arizona: Oryx Press.

McCabe, J., Fairchild, E., Grauerholz, L., Pescosolido, B.A. and Tope, D. (2011) Gender in twentieth century children's books. Patterns of disparity in titles and central characters. *Gender and Society,* 25(2): 197–226. Available at: http://gas.sagepub.com/content/25/2/197.full.pdf (accessed 12.04.16).

Munsch, R. and Martchenko, M. (2009) *The Paper Bag Princess.* Annick Press.

Nodelman, P. (1988) *Words about Pictures. The Narrative Art of Children's Picture Books.* London: University of Georgia Press.

Rosen, M. and Blake, Q. (2004) *Michael Rosen's Sad Book.* London: Walker Books.

Tan, S. (2000) *The Lost Thing.* Melbourne: Lothian Books.

Tan, S. (2007) *The Arrival.* London: Hodder.

Weisner, D. (1992) *June 29th 1999.* Boston, MA: Houghton Mifflin Harcourt.

Weisner, D. (2006) *Flotsam.* Boston, MA: Houghton Mifflin Harcourt.

Whybrow, I. and Reeve, R. (2005) *Hey I Love You!* London: Pan Children's.

6 Stories and poems from and about different cultures

Learning Outcomes

By reading this chapter you will have:

- considered the range of children's literature available which relates to different cultures;
- explored ways of widening children's knowledge and understanding of different cultures through literature.

Introduction

Mona Siddiqui, a well-known academic commentator on Islam, said on the BBC's *Desert Island Discs* in October 2012, *celebrating diversity is creating difference*, and this is always a potential problem for teachers to bear in mind. Why should we present children with the experience of children growing up in very different worlds from their own? Many children whose family is from a different cultural or religious background from that surrounding them in a modern British school already feel a gap between home and school – do we risk widening that gap by choosing to study a book or story which underlines these differences?

On the other hand, can we help fill the gap by sharing stories which show that people have the same feelings and reactions whatever their surroundings? Can children from different backgrounds become closer together, and learn to see each other as individuals, by considering together how they would react in situations whose circumstances may be very unfamiliar to some?

These two points of view should always be borne in mind when we choose a story to use in the classroom. But the overwhelming reason for choosing any text should always be whether it is a good story and well told – if these two elements are right, the children will engage with it no matter what the cultural background.

> *Selecting good multicultural children's books begins with the same criteria as those for selecting any good children's books – the literary elements of plot, characterization, setting, style, theme and point of view must be interwoven to provide an interesting story. In addition, good multicultural children's books will challenge stereotypes and promote a realistic glimpse into the lives of diverse groups of people. By providing children with*

accurate and positive representations of the many cultural groups that make up the community, society and the world in which they live, books can help children learn to identify stereotypes and biases when they encounter them.

(Partners Against Hate, 2003)

Of course, the 'other culture' most prevalent in children's literature has become so much a part of everyday life that many children no longer see it as 'different': the literature of the USA. So many popular books and series are set in the States that young readers can frequently become fully involved without even realising that the setting is not British. Beverly Cleary's *Ramona* series, for instance, which narrates the family and school life of Ramona Quimby from the age of six, contains very little which would not be easily identifiable for a British child – much more familiar, for instance, in many details than Mairi Hedderwick's totally British *Katie Morag* books, gentle pastoral stories set on a fictional Scottish island closely based on the real Isle of Coll. So, should we consider North American literature as part of a shared culture? And conversely, should we include fiction from within our own broad community which nonetheless offers a completely different life experience from that of the children in our classroom? In the case study below you will see that a study of North American fiction can offer interesting insights into variations in vocabulary usage on different sides of the Atlantic Ocean.

Case Study

One language – two lexicons

Carrie, a School Direct trainee, had discovered during a spelling lesson focused on words from the Years 5–6 spelling list in the National Curriculum with her Year 6 class that several children suggested that *neighbour* could be spelled *neighbor* and *programme* as *program*, and said that they had seen the words spelled in that way in their story books and in spellcheckers. Carrie discussed some of the differences between US and UK spelling and said that she would find a selection of words with different spellings in UK and US English in time for the next lesson, and asked that children do the same.

Not only did children produce lists of alternative spellings, but some, after discussions with their parents, also brought in lists of alternative names for everyday items. Spelling alterna-tives included other words which are spelled *-our* in UK English and *-or* in US English, many of which end with *-re* in the UK but *-er* in US (*center, fiber, theater*), many words which have a double consonant in UK English and a single in US (*canceled, quarreled, traveled*), as well as *grey* and *gray*, *pyjamas* and *pajamas*, and *sledge* and *sled*.

Everyday items were numerous and included: for cars – hood and bonnet, trunk and boot, petrol and gas; in the street – pavement and sidewalk, junction and intersection; and for food – crisps and chips, chips and fries, biscuit and cookie.

→

Children were also very entertained by finding that a smartly dressed American man walks though the street in his vest and pants.

Carrie decided that there was a great opportunity to link the children's enthusiasm for exploring vocabulary differences to their reading and provided a selection of stories with US origins for groups to read and to note vocabulary differences. She also asked the children to note any they found while watching television at home.

This case study, which evolved from comments from children in a spelling lesson, demonstrates the potential for exploring language through literature. Carrie commented afterwards that she would explore possibilities for similar activities related to Australian English in the future, and perhaps look at other origins of words in English such as India and the Middle East.

Curriculum Links

This kind of vocabulary study might also emanate from the children's literature of French-, German- and Spanish-speaking countries where these are the modern foreign languages studied in a school. However, US English is so much a part of children's cultural experience through television, film, music and children's literature that a study of spellings and vocabulary might be considered an essential part of an English curriculum.

The history of multicultural children's literature

Stories from other cultures have always been part of our range of familiar children's literature in the form of Greek and Norse myths, and the stories of the Arabian Nights' Entertainment, which we offer without any need for explanation. These, however, can be accepted just as fantasy stories, as set in the world of the imagination. The many different cultural origins of familiar traditional stories are discussed in Chapter 7, and do not fall strictly within the remit of what is generally meant by 'multicultural' fiction here. Traditional tales are, to a large extent, set in their own world and children do not expect to find aspects of their own physical lives reflected here.

In the early years of the twentieth century, and right up until the 1960s and 1970s, schools and libraries usually offered a generous selection of books telling stories of children in other lands, designed to educate children about foreign cultures through fiction. The best-known of these were probably the 26 books in Lucy Fitch Perkins' 'Twins' series (*The Dutch Twins*, *The Eskimo Twins*, and many others). These appeared over two decades from 1914 to 1937, and in many cases represented ways of life which were already passing, although they were not generally presented as such. For instance, *The Eskimo Twins* (1914) is summarised on the Twins Homepage in the following terms:

> *Menie (the boy) and Monnie (the girl) are two fun-loving, roly-poly little kids living in Northern Alaska. Their father is the greatest hunter in the village, and in fact at the beginning of the story proves his prowess by killing a polar bear. This bear was discovered by the twins and their friend Koko while they were off coasting. However, as Monnie is a girl, the boys take all the credit for finding the bear and force Monnie to pull the sled with the bear's skin back to the village. The twins have many adventures, such as fishing with their father, getting lost while hunting, and frolicking in the sun on 'the summer day', but throughout the book is a subtle message of misogyny. However, this does not ruin the tale of two adorable little Eskimo children living at the edge of the world.*
>
> (www.angelfire.com/az/ladybecca/twins.html)

In the modern classroom, however, this will no longer do.

Hazel Rochman (1993) in her book *Against Borders* writes:

> *A good book can help to break down {barriers}. Books can make a difference in dispelling prejudice and building community: not with role models and literal recipes, not with noble messages about the human family, but with enthralling stories that make us imagine the lives of others. A good story lets you know people as individuals in all their particularity and conflict; and once you see someone as a person – flawed, complex, striving – then you've reached beyond stereotype. Stories, writing them, telling them, sharing them, transforming them, enrich us and connect us and help us know each other.*
>
> (p.19)

Any book or text selected for use in the classroom will be chosen to enrich the children's lives by engaging them in a story. The characters and the storyline must engage the children, and whatever the setting, if they are to understand and involve themselves with all the story has to offer, they must be helped to understand the world in which the characters live. A book may have illustrations which take the children to an unfamiliar situation, may show us lives in which there are different rhythms or priorities from our own, or may explain cultural features we had not known, through the eyes of an outsider. A 'good book' in the multicultural genre will both show children from backgrounds which are not those of the majority, something which is familiar and close to them, and also increase the sensitivity of others to the diversity of life and family patterns.

We should also, when considering such books, be aware of their provenance. Is the writer sharing their own experience, or writing from an outsider's viewpoint? Lissa Paul (cited in Maybin and Watson, 2009, pp. 84–5) cites the imaginary example of the Disney marketing department in 1995 creating the profile of their latest heroine Pocahontas – ticking all the boxes by being feminist, environmentally aware and from an ethnic minority group as well. Their later heroine, the Chinese princess Mulan in 1998, can be seen to be in much the same mould. It is easy to see these not so much as genuine multicultural essays but rather as attempts to engage as wide a consumer base as possible by dressing up all-American heroines in fancy guise. For this reason, it is important, when choosing the texts we plan to share with our classes, to choose ones as far as possible which are written from first-hand experience by writers whose own lives have contained the elements they are writing about. An outsider can see and describe the sights, customs or lives of another group of people, but will not necessarily understand the significance or the feelings of those involved.

White, Christian, middle- or upper-class children still dominate the world of fiction, but for more than 100 years they were virtually all that was to be seen – any kind of foreigner was likely to be stupid, comic or criminal, and any adventure set abroad would contain as little interaction with those who actually lived there as possible. In other school books, too, notably reading schemes, this same culture showed. Sheila McCullough's *Village with Three Corners* reading scheme, in the 1970s, broke new ground by introducing Ram, Sita and Gopal to a very English village setting. Any casual reader of the books in our classrooms would still concede, however, that there is still a long way to go before every child feels equally 'mainstream' in our schools.

One children's fantasy from 1899 which has earned itself a particular, but in many ways unfair, reputation as racist, tells the story of a little boy whose smart new clothes are all stolen from him by naughty tigers. He outwits the tigers by running round and round a tree so very fast that the tigers chasing him melt away into butter. He then takes the butter home and his mother uses it to make delicious pancakes. A silly story, of course, a fantasy – but one beloved by children for 50 years or so, until the title *Little Black Sambo* was deemed offensive both because of the use of the word Black and the choice of name, Sambo, so often used as a derogatory term. The fate of the book since then has been interesting: original copies sell for high prices at book fairs because of their curiosity value; the full text and facsimiles are easily available on the internet; and versions in which the hero is variously Japanese, Polish and Indian are all successful in other countries. The fate of Little Black Sambo gives an important perspective on the importance of even a casually chosen name or word in anything we say or use in our classrooms. (Incidentally, the author, Helen Bannerman, was a Scotswoman who lived for 32 years in Southern India – the children in her books are Indian or Tamil.)

Virginia Kroll's (1993) *Masai and I* tells the story of a girl, Linda, who learns at school about the Masai nation in Africa and their lives and begins to wonder about how different her own life would be if she were a member of the Masai. Nancy Carpenter's illustrations show beautifully how her ideas develop and she sees comparisons and contrasts, coming to understand that other people's worlds contain similarities with and differences from our own. In Ann Grifalconi's (1989) *The Village of Round and Square Houses*, a folk legend from Cameroon is retold through the eyes of a young girl. Again the illustrations play an important part in creating the world of the story and showing the context without every point being underlined in the text. The book is a good one for showing that people living in different cultural environments *are just as human as we are, some good, and some not so, with needs, thoughts and feelings* (Russell, 2010, p.1).

Bernard Ashley's (1995) *Cleversticks* celebrates diversity through exploring a situation familiar to most children – that of finding that 'everyone is special'. Ling Sung, who has just started school, feels that he is the only one with no especial gift or talent, until he finds that he is the only person in his class who can use chopsticks – not even his teacher can manage it successfully. This understated story does not go into details about where Ling Sung is from, or why he has this talent, and so opens the way for classroom discussions and activities. To find an ability that makes one special, whether it is writing one's name or tying one's shoelaces, is an empowering thing for a child, and this story gives a gentle multicultural aspect to this universal experience.

In the case study below, you will see how a trainee teacher faces a dilemma when choosing texts for a topic on stories and poems from different cultures.

Case Study

Finding stories and poems which depict different cultures

Zoe, a second-year trainee teacher, was asked to work with her Year 2 class on texts from different cultures in a rural school with an overwhelmingly white British population. Her class teacher explained that the cultures represented could be any which Zoe chose and that a key outcome for the topic should be to expand children's understanding of how people lived in places very different from their own. The topic was to be followed by a study of contrasting environments in geography.

Zoe decided that she would look for texts which were written by people from the cultural settings in which the writing was set. Initially, she found it difficult to find many books which met her criterion, but after discussions with fellow trainees and her English tutor, she came up with three pieces to use as central.

The first was the poem *Blessing* by Imtiaz Dharker which appeared in *Postcard from God* (2001). This poem describes vividly the event of a burst water-pipe in a settlement where water is a precious commodity, and how the children want to play in the water as all the adults are scrambling to save it in anything they can find:

The skin cracks like a pod.

There never is enough water.

→

The poet grew up in a Pakistani family in Scotland, but eloped to Bombay and lived there as an adult, and so understands both the importance of water to the Indian community she describes and the contrast with a life where clean water is always readily available. Zoe asked the class to look at how the water is described and consider why the poet used precious metals for comparison. This led onto creative writing in which the children described something (for example, snowflakes) by using similes, without saying what they were describing.

The class used various instruments such as woodblocks, bongos and rainsticks to create their own water music. They also looked at which countries or parts of the world might suffer from this kind of problem, which led to watching a WaterAid charity video, and to the class putting on a special event in support of this charity.

The second text Zoe chose was *The Swirling Hijaab* by Na'ima bint Robert and Nilesh Mistry (2002). This story, with lots of bright illustrations, is about a little girl playing with her mother's *hijaab* (the veil worn by some Muslim women). The story follows the girl's imagination and shows how she can turn her mother's scarf into lots of different things. The experience of making one item into lots of different 'dressing-up' accessories was a familiar one enjoyed by the children, and many more ideas were suggested in discussion.

The obvious cross-curricular link here was with religious education, as the story gave a good introduction to some elements of the Muslim faith and culture. Why is it important for some Muslim women to wear a *hijaab*? What does it mean to them? The ritual of daily prayers and fasting is introduced in the story, and this was compared and contrasted with the children's own family observances. The *hijaab*, seen by some non-Muslims as an alien or mysterious object, becomes simply a familiar item in life like any other scarf, and perhaps becomes less strange and alarming to those children who are not used to it.

The religious element in this story led to discussion on festivals and special days in different cultures, and Zoe then introduced the final poem she had chosen, *Diwali* by Debjani Chatterjee (2000, p.149). This short poem, whose author grew up in Delhi, speaks of the celebration of the Diwali festival in a Hindu household. The children picked out details which were similar to their familiar Christmas celebrations (such as twinkling lamps, cheery greetings, welcoming visitors) and investigated unfamiliar details to learn more about the Hindu celebration (Rangoli art, incense, the goddess Lakshmi). They then learnt about the Muslim festival of Eid, and other winter celebrations in different cultures, and looked at maps and atlases to see where these days were celebrated around the world.

The children then created their own Rangoli art patterns and lanterns to decorate the classroom, and eventually the mother and grandmother of a boy in the class whose family celebrate Diwali each year were invited in to help the children try making and tasting some of the traditional sweetmeats.

The case study demonstrates the potential of poetry and stories to inspire a range of classroom activities which will broaden children's understanding of different cultures.

Curriculum Links

There are obvious links in the case study to religious education, as well as opportunities to increase children's awareness of different cultures and traditions. In addition, maps might be studied to find areas where there are large populations of Hindus or Muslims and to find places where droughts occur frequently.

Themes in multicultural children's literature

Much of the research and commentary which has been done into the importance of multicultural literature in the classroom has come from the United States, where the emphasis tends to be on the experience of children of African-American backgrounds and those with roots in the Latin American nations. In the British schoolroom we are more likely, perhaps, to be concerned with the needs of British-Asian families and, increasingly, those of Eastern European origins. Kate Russell, Senior Adviser for Geography for Staffordshire, has compiled a very comprehensive list of books and stories available in the UK, divided by regions and countries, which is available on the internet (www.sln.org.uk/geography/Documents/primary/Some%20Story%20and%20non-fiction%20books.pdf) and could be of great use in selecting a story to use with your class.

Most stories which are set in another cultural environment are carefully researched for accuracy these days. We have all met older stories and fables in which, for instance, lions and tigers live together in the jungle, or polar bears and penguins happily share icebergs. These situations occur in books for small children and can be accepted as fantasy in the same spirit as the idea of a tiger who comes to tea. As children grow older, though, books can become an important medium for learning to understand about crops and animals in different countries, and could lead to awareness of such issues as 'airmiles' and different local economies. In Eileen Browne's *Handa's Surprise*, Handa is carrying a basket of fruit on her head as she walks to her friend Akeyo's house in an undefined African setting. As she travels, the fruit is gradually stolen by different animals and finally replaced by a crop of tangerines knocked from a tree by a goat. Discussion of where all the various fruits and animals mentioned could have come from could form an interesting focus for class research. Children could investigate whether all could be available in a single area, for example.

A very different economic focus from the familiar Western one is also found in Steve Brace's *From Beans to Batteries*, in which Aldomaro, who lives in the mountains of Peru, has a problem to cope with when his precious radio batteries run out and he can no longer listen to the daily radio doctor's broadcast. The story tells how he and his sister pick some beans, the only resource available to them, and then go on a three-hour journey to sell these in the market to raise money to buy replacement batteries. In a world where consumerism and the ready availability of all we want is so taken for granted, this book gives a counterpoint which will be completely novel to most children.

Lisa Bruce's (1995; 1996) Jazeera stories tell of a family's migration from the Indian sub-continent to the UK and the central character's return to visit her family's roots in India for holidays – a situation familiar to many in our classrooms, and which can help to show the importance of such links to other children who may not have this feature in their lives. Theresa Heine's (2004) *Elephant Dance* deals with a similar theme, this time presenting aspects of Indian culture through the voice of a visiting grandfather who tells Ravi and Anjali tales of life in his home. The language uses imaginative metaphors and similes to evoke the feeling of Indian life: the sun is a ferocious tiger; the wind stamps and snorts like a wild horse; monsoon rains are as silver as bangles and the ensuing rainbow is compared to the colours of bright silk sari.

As readers grow up, they will find a huge range of literature set in other countries or areas, alongside more and more books which describe the issues of those moving between life in modern Britain and a family history with elements of other lives. Social realist fiction such as Beverley Naidoo's *The Other Side of Truth* (2000) whose protagonists are two Nigerian refugee children, or explorations of racial issues such as Malorie Blackman's *Noughts and Crosses* series, can provide sympathetic and provocative starts for exploration of many issues related to multicultural identity.

Conclusion

At a primary level, it is important to make children aware of the almost infinite range of difference in lives and individuals, and that they come to an appreciation that all are of value and have an important contribution to make.

> *Book collections for children should serve as 'mirrors' that reflect the children and families in the school as well as 'windows' that help children explore the true diversity of our world. Books can also teach children to understand and challenge bias and bullying and to promote social action in order to combat injustice.*
>
> (www.adl.org/education-outreach/books-matter/#.VxC2Q_krLIU)

It is our job as teachers to make sure that every child can find him- or herself in the reading we share with them.

Learning Outcomes Review

You should now have considered the range of children's literature available which relates to different cultures and explored ways of widening children's knowledge and understanding of different cultures through literature.

Self-assessment question

1 What do you consider to be the value of finding stories and poems about different cultures which are written by people who have experienced those cultures first-hand?

Further Reading

Partners Against Hate – an interesting US site which presents ideas and suggestions for inclusive reading: www.partnersagainsthate.org/educators/books.html

Neat Solutions – another useful booklist site: www.neatsolutions.com/books/multicultural.html

References

Ashley, B. (1995) *Cleversticks*. London: HarperCollins Children's Books.

Brace, S. (2008) *From Beans to Batteries*. Swindon: Child's Play International.

Browne, E. (2006) *Handa's Surprise*. London: Walker Books.

Bruce, L. (1995) *Jazeera's Journey*. London, Methuen.

Bruce, L. (1996) *Jazeera in the Sun*, London, Methuen.

Chatterjee, D. (2000) Diwali, in Cookson, P. (ed.) *The Works*. London: Macmillan.

Dharker, I. (2001) *Postcards from God*. Newcastle: Bloodaxe Books. (This poem is also widely available on the internet.)

Grifalconi, A. (1989) *The Village of Round and Square Houses*. London: Pan Macmillan.

Heine, T. (2004) *Elephant Dance*. London: Barefoot Books.

Kroll, V. (1993) *Masai and I*. London: Hamish Hamilton.

Maybin, J. and Watson, N. (eds) (2009) *Children's Literature Approaches and Territories. Section 5 Words and Pictures*. Buckingham: Open University Press.

Naidoo, B. (2000) *The Other Side of Truth*. London: Puffin.

Partners against Hate (2003) *The Importance of Multicultural Children's Books.* Available at: www.partnersagainsthate.org/educators/books.html (accessed 12.04.16).

Robert, N. and Mistry, N (2002) *The Swirling Hijaab.* London: Mantra Lingua.

Rochman, H. (1993) *Against Borders: Promoting Books for a Multicultural World.* Chicago: American Library Association.

Russell, K. (2010) *Some Geographical Story and Non-fiction Books.* QLS Staffordshire.

7 Traditional stories and fairy tales

Learning Outcomes

By reading this chapter you will:

- be aware of the strong tradition of fairy stories which exists around the world;
- understand the significance of fairy stories and traditional tales for cultural heritage;
- be able to consider ways of developing interesting and stimulating classroom activities based upon traditional tales.

Introduction

If you want them to be more intelligent, read them more fairy tales.

(Albert Einstein)

Nearly all children meet very early in their acquaintance with fiction some of the traditional tales which pass from generation to generation: Cinderella, Snow White, Red Riding Hood, Hansel and Gretel, The Three Bears, The Ugly Duckling and many others. Any bookshop or library will offer multiple versions, from the simplest retellings to subtle psychological interpretations. It is fair to say that many such stories are embedded in the national consciousness. Think how often the press refers to a Cinderella story or an ugly duckling, or we come across phrases such as 'huffing and puffing' or 'the goose that lays the golden eggs' without even thinking twice about their origins.

Interest in such stories has never faded among adults any more than among children – understandable, as in most cases the original folk stories were intended for and handed on by an adult audience. As recently as 2012, the authors Philip Pullman and Marina Warner (1994) brought out new works discussing and retelling traditional tales, and there was major excitement about the discovery of a previously unpublished story by Hans Christian Andersen, *The Tallow Candle*, thought to be the first he wrote (Flood, 2012).

Although the origins of these stories vary widely, from the oriental tales collected in the Arabian Nights and the ancient German and Russian folk tales collected by Arthur Ransome (2005) and the brothers Grimm, to the imaginings of Hans Christian Andersen, by way of most of the countries of Europe, there are certain features they can be said to have loosely in common. Firstly, in nearly every case there is a poor or disadvantaged central character – often orphaned – who will end up rich, successful and happy. (Although a few of Andersen's stories have tragic endings, these are not by and large the stories best loved or known by children.) Secondly, there is an element of magic or the supernatural which justifies the term 'fairy story'. Thirdly, they take place in a timeless world, somewhere in the distant past, which has elements of everyday life but is no recognised country or society. And, of course, virtue will be rewarded and wrongdoing will always be found out and punished. It is very rare to find any of the traditional and best-known stories with a sad ending – although some of Andersen's work (for instance, *The Little Tin Soldier* or *The Little Mermaid*) certainly 'ends in tears'. In addition to these markers, the stories are traditionally framed in the telling by *Once upon a time* and *happily ever after*, confirming for the reader exactly what world he or she is in.

The origins of traditional tales

Many stories have very ancient roots; there are Indian and Arabian collections from as early as the sixth century, and the legends of the Greek and Norse gods and of King Arthur can be seen to fit into the same general family. From the mid-seventeenth century, there came to be a more widespread interest in collecting and retelling the stories in printed collections and presenting them as suitable for children, as much for moral instruction as entertainment. In the nineteenth century, more and more writers turned their attention to the fairy story. Some, like Andrew Lang, collected and retold stories from across the world (starting with *The Blue Fairy Book* in 1889) and others added to the genre with their own work (for example, Oscar Wilde, whose collection *The Happy Prince* appeared in 1890).

Research Focus

Although we tend to use the term 'fairy stories' for traditional tales, the stories do not always include supernatural elements. Carpenter and Prichard (1995, p.177) maintain that we acquired the term 'fairy stories' from an English translation of the French *contes des fées*, which was adopted as a description of such stories in the late seventeenth century. In seventeenth-century France, literary salons were set up by aristocratic women where people would *show their wit and eloquence by inventing wondrous tales* (Zipes, 2009, p28). The stories, which were often published, notably by Charles Perrault, were often adapted from those the aristocrats had heard from their governesses and servants. The stories were not, however, originally written for children, although simplified versions were eventually printed and distributed throughout France by pedlars.

Carpenter and Prichard (1995) inform us that the earliest recorded analogue of Cinderella can be found in a ninth-century Chinese book of folk tales. Marina Warner (2012) has discussed parallels from many cultures, including the ancient Egyptian story of Rhodopis from the first century BC, in which a passing bird drops the shoe into the prince's lap and he sets out to find the owner. An ancient Chinese version is interesting, when one considers the major cultural importance of tiny feet in old imperial China. Indeed, the tale has similarities with many others from different cultures, including, as you will see in the case study below, a tale which is well known in India. When you are reading the case study, think about how you could help children to identify common themes in traditional tales by comparing other stories. The case study below shows how a trainee teacher shared a story she had learned as a child with her class and asked them to compare it with one with which they were familiar.

Case Study

Rama and Sita, and Cinderella

Surindar, a PGCE trainee, wanted to introduce her Year 1 class to fairy tales from around the world. She chose the Rama and Sita story from India and Cinderella from Europe. The class discussed the fact that they both had elements common to many fairy tales, including a magical element, animals and talking mirrors, and people being transformed. There was also the element of the main character being the youngest of sisters, and being beautiful and caring.

With her class, Surindar discussed other features of fairy tales including:

- events often happening in groups of three;

- bad people often getting their just deserts;

- and a problem or some sort of conflict being resolved, thus leaving the story to end in a happily ever after solution (or so it would seem).

Surindar chose tales which the children knew very well – Cinderella – and a tale that was newly introduced to them – Rama and Sita. Surindar read and told the stories and discussed them with the children. Then, using pictures to help children to remember the tales, she and the children placed the characters in different categories, as below.

Category	Cinderella	Rama and Sita
Characters	Prince Cinderella Two stepsisters The queen	Prince Rama Princess Sita Three queens King
Tale	Prince and Cinderella in love	Rama and Sita in love
Good/very helpful	Fairy Godmother	Lakshman

→

Category	Cinderella	Rama and Sita
Bad/not helpful	Stepmother	Ravan
Talking or helpful animal	Mice	Monkeys
How animals help	Cinderella seeks the help of the mice to get her to the ball	Rama seeks the help of the talking and flying monkeys to find Sita
The problem	The Prince needs to find Cinderella to then marry her	The prince needs to rescue Sita from Ravan who has kidnapped her
Moral of the story	Treat people the way you want to be treated and then more good comes out of it than evil Adherence to truth and the need to honour one's word Good always wins over evil	

The class found that the two fairy tales had many similarities and, as one child suggested, seem as if they could have been written by the same author for different children around the world.

Curriculum Links

Activities such as that devised by Surindar will help you to address key elements of the English curriculum. The National Curriculum (DfE, 2013) requires children in Year 1 to become *very familiar with key stories, fairy stories and traditional tales* (p.21) and this theme continues in Years 2, 3 and 4:

- becoming increasingly familiar with a wider range of stories, fairy stories and traditional tales;
- recognising simple recurring literary language in stories and poetry (Y2);
- increasing their familiarity with a wide range of books, including fairy stories, myths and legends;
- identifying recurring themes and elements in different stories and poetry (for example, good triumphing over evil, magical devices) (Y3–4).

Research Focus

Cinderella

Betsey Hearne (2011) observes that the story of Cinderella is one of the most widely distributed fairy tales in the world. It permeates popular culture from jokes to skipping rhymes and is the basis for many books, films and musicals.

$\longrightarrow$

Films such as *Pretty Woman* are based on it. Literature as diverse as Shakespeare's play *King Lear*, Charlotte Bronte's *Jane Eyre* and George Bernard Shaw's play *Pygmalion* have reflected Cinderella themes. The Broadway musical *My Fair Lady* based on *Pygmalion* was a smash hit, and the subsequent film starring Audrey Hepburn and Rex Harrison won Academy Awards for best picture, best actor and best director (Hearne, 2011, p.212).

Hearne observes that in folklore parlance Cinderella is known as 'The Persecuted Heroine'. This story has a very basic pattern of a young person (usually female) whose mother or father is dead, and who is being persecuted by the remaining parent, stepparent, sibling or stepsibling. She or he undergoes a series of tests of fidelity, endurance or courage, receives magic help, is eventually identified as the true hero/heroine despite initial disguise, wins the prince or princess and lives happily ever after. Hearne identifies a number of different versions of Cinderella tales from around the world.

- The Chinese orphan Yeh-shien receives, like many Cinderellas, help from an animal – a fish, who is killed by her jealous stepmother but whose bones provide magical assistance.

- The German orphan Aschenputtel's dead mother helps her by means of a hazel tree that grows on her grave and in which the doves roost and warn the prince of the stepsisters' deceit, and pluck out their eyes at the end of the tale.

- The dying mother of the Russian girl Vasilisa offers her a doll which, if she gives it food and drink, will advise her on what to do in the tests that she will have to endure.

- The Japanese orphan Benizara proves her worth by writing an exquisite poem.

- In a story from the Republic of Georgia, the little rag girl makes herself known by sticking pins into the king's bottom through the basket where her stepmother has hidden her.

The Cinderella most commonly known today is Perrault's, on which Walt Disney based his 1950s film. In Hearne's view this version of Cinderella portrays the weakest heroine. She observes that different oral traditions, such as those listed above, reveal braver Cinderellas, perhaps reflecting how the oral variations reveal contrasting value systems.

Judy Sierra (1992) has found and recorded a collection of 25 versions of Cinderella from around the world. In most of these stories the main character is an active heroine who draws strength from a spiritual connection with her mother, even after her death. True power comes from the mother's love, and the daughter's strength and physical beauty are a manifestation of inner goodness. The prince is the reward for this, not the reason. In contrast to these powerful and connected heroines, Hearne (2011) examines the Disney version of Cinderella and is scathing in her analysis:

> *In contrast to these many brave Cinderellas of folklore tradition, Disney's ubiquitous film and book spin-offs feature a sentimental pawn, with a heroine less in a state of suffering than in a state of insufferable cheeriness. The first twenty minutes of the seventy-six minute production are about cute birds and mice … our American obsession with excess, tends to bury folktales' powerful simplicity. Gus, Lucifer, Bruno and*

$\longrightarrow$

> company become main characters: the king and minister provide slapstick distraction
> from conflict. The fairy godmother's power is diminished by her absent minded befud-
> dled demeanour. Cinderella does not have to seek her out, stay loyal to her, remain
> steadfast or otherwise prove herself. What she has to do is GIVE UP. That's the moment –
> when she throws herself on the garden bench sobbing that dreams are no use – when
> the fairy godmother finally shows up and fixes everything. Bibbity, Bobbity, Boo.
>
> (p.212)

Underlying themes

The world of the fairy story is, then, a courtly world of kingdoms and castles, princes and
princesses, animals which talk and have human characteristics, and wishes that come true – all
elements which appeal to the imagination of young children. At the same time, many of the
stories contain a moral or an embedded message that gives a truth about life. For example:

- plain and gawky children can grow up to be elegant (The Ugly Duckling);

- relationships can be problematic with step-relations (Cinderella, Snow-White, Hansel and
  Gretel);

- time spent doing a job properly is worthwhile (The Three Little Pigs).

There are many other simple truisms. Philip Pullman, who recently retold a selection of
the stories of the Brothers Grimm (2012a), has analysed many of the features common in
the genre: speed of time passing, absence of extraneous detail and description, recurrence
of 'lucky numbers' of characters (seven dwarves, 12 dancing princesses, three bears, 'seven
at one blow' for Jack the Giant-killer, etc.) and above all, unambiguously one-dimensional
characters. The wicked have no subtle motivation or scruples of conscience; the good
are never seriously tempted to compromise their standards. As Pullman put it in an
interview in the *Guardian* (2012b): *The tremors and whispers of human awareness, the whispers
of memory, the promptings of half-understood regret or doubt or desire that are so much part of the
subject matter of the modern novel are absent entirely.* Quick-wittedness and native cunning are
character assets which will win rewards; lying and deception are acceptable when they are
for a good end; princesses are good and beautiful, and marriage is the desirable conclusion
for any princess.

Marcus Crouch has commented that *each new generation has to meet the traditional tales of the
past, and for each new interpreters are needed* (Crouch, 1962, p.67), and certainly an evolution is
visible in the common versions of the familiar stories over time. Many stories – and it is worth
remembering again here that originally they were told not just for children – had in their
early forms extremely violent and bloodthirsty endings featuring retribution for the villains,
which would certainly not be acceptable today. Modern children are more likely to be offered,
for instance, a wolf running away in agony than being boiled alive by the three little pigs.

The Little Mermaid offers perhaps the supreme example of 'softening up': in the Disney cartoon version (1989), which many modern children know as the definitive story, the mermaid is allowed a redemption and eventually sails away happily with her prince, once it has been realised that he is her true love. In Andersen's original, in which the prince marries his human bride, the mermaid cannot bring herself to save herself by killing him, and she is doomed to become a disembodied spirit: perhaps a little too harsh for today's generation.

Fairy stories have been subjected to analysis and retellings by Freudians, feminists, Marxists, politicians, structuralists and every other school of literary and psychological theory, and yet the basic stories carry on undefeated. Retellings from 'politically correct' points of view, stories based in and around the traditional tales (for example, Catherine Storr's *Polly and the Wolf* stories, written in the 1950s) rely on a knowledge of the original versions in order to be appreciated. Joan Aiken has written a wide range of original fairy stories, from those based in a traditional setting – 'The Third Wish' (in *More Than You Bargained For*, 1955) has an old woodcutter granted three wishes by a bad-tempered goblin, but uses them wisely – to the completely modern – Matilda in *All You've Ever Wanted* (Aiken, 1953) has a fairy godmother whose birthday card verses always come literally true, with disastrous and wildly comic results.

Research Focus

The emergence of fairy stories as recreation for children in the nineteenth century

Until the mid-eighteenth century most authors who wrote fairy stories for children in Europe emphasised moral issues and what Zipes (2009) refers to as *the Protestant ethic*. Zipes maintains that:

> This ethic highlighted the values of industriousness, honesty, cleanliness, diligence, virtuousness – and male supremacy. The fairy tale was intended to play a major role in the socialization process.

> (2009, p.31)

However, Zipes describes the way in which in the later nineteenth century fairy tales were parodied and authors such as Dickens (*The Magic Fishbone*, 1868), Thackeray (*The Rose and the Ring*, 1855), Carroll (*Alice's Adventures in Wonderland*, 1865) and Wilde (*The Happy Prince*, 1888) *began to experiment with the fairy tale in a manner that would make young readers question the world around them* (p.32).

This movement spread to America where fairy tales written for a different population began to emerge in the late nineteenth century, even including Native American fairy tales in *The Indian Fairy Book* in 1869. By 1900, Frank L. Baum had produced *The Wizard of Oz* using the structure of the European fairy tale to describe Dorothy's adventures away from Kansas. Baum wrote fourteen Oz books and used them to comment on politics and culture. Zipes asserts that Baum *set the stage for other fairy tale novels and series such as those by JRR Tolkien, CS Lewis, TH White and Michael Ende* (p.32).

Activity

Consider how fairy tales have become part of our cultural heritage. Think of examples of phrases and ideas which we use in everyday life which emanate from fairy tales, e.g. *once upon a time*, *long long ago*, *live happily ever after*, *rags to riches*.

Curriculum Links

As you will see from the National Curriculum (DfE, 2013), fairy stories and traditional tales are very much part of the literature which children should encounter at primary school. This can provide a range of opportunities for children to draw upon their existing knowledge and to develop their understanding of the nature of stories, as the case study below illustrates.

Case Study

John, a PGCE student, was asked to plan a series of lessons for a Year 4 class based on a theme of fairy stories. He decided to begin by asking the class to show what they already knew about fairy stories, and so provided pairs of children with KWL grids: simple three-column grids in which the columns are headed *What I already know*, *What I would like to know, and What I have learned*.

John gave children around ten minutes to make brief notes in the first column and then asked them to share what they knew with other people on their tables. He then drew the class together and created a class KWL grid on screen, drawing upon children's ideas. As children mentioned things they knew, he noted them in the first column. These included:

- people used to pass them on from grandparents to parents to children;

- the Grimm brothers wrote lots of them in books;

- you can see films of fairy stories;

- usually the baddies get killed or eaten at the end;

- some fairy stories are made into pantomimes.

After writing some of the children's ideas on screen, John asked them to discuss them in groups to see if they could add more information or if they disagreed with anything. He then added

→

further ideas to the grid and asked children what they would like to know about fairy stories. A list was made on screen in the second column, which included the following.

- Where do we get fairy stories from in the first place?

- Are they told in other countries?

- Why are the endings sometimes different in different versions?

John had prepared a collection of fairy tales from around the world and had also located several suitable websites which children could use. In the next lesson, he asked children to work in pairs to find out more using both books and the internet. These activities developed over a two-week period and at the end of each session John looked at the KWL grid with the children and added items to the third column: *What I have learned*. Sometimes this led to disputes and discussions as children disagreed about origins of tales, story endings and so forth. Such disagreements were turned into challenges by John, who invited children to look more widely for evidence.

The programme of lessons concluded with four groups writing and performing their own versions of fairy tales in assembly, and a fifth providing a commentary and historical perspective on the growth of fairy tales.

Activity

- How could you develop a series of lessons which drew upon what children already knew about traditional tales and developed their knowledge and understanding?
- Which stories would you use?
- What kind of activity would the lessons lead towards?
- How could you make use of different versions of stories, including films?

Curriculum Links

Besides helping children to explore the nature of traditional stories, activities such as those in the case study develop children's ability to look at ways in which events can be interpreted differently in subjects such as history and religious education. There is scope here to go on to look at an historical event and for children to use the internet to examine different versions and to draw conclusions about them. Anna's case study later in this chapter illustrates this further.

How do we acquire our knowledge of traditional tales?

Zipes (2009) maintains that:

> ... *it is not an exaggeration to say that most children, if not adults, learn about the classical fairy tale as well as the classics in children's literature through Disney films, books, videos and other ephemera.*

> (p.38)

However, Zipes asserts that multimedia versions of fairy tales *have not diminished the effect of the fairy tale as an oral and literary genre that can be regarded as the most dominant in the field of children's literature* (p.38). Indeed, Zipes asserts that the new media provide new possibilities and argues that fairy tales are now part of school curricula and are read to children by parents, teachers and librarians as well as being used by therapists, social workers and psychologists to analyse psychological problems in children and adults.

The exploration of different versions of fairy tales provides rich opportunities for classroom activities. You have already seen how Surindar's class contrasted two stories with a similar theme. In the case study below, Anna looks at the same story but explores different interpretations with her class.

Case Study

Anna, a School Direct trainee, wanted her Year 5 children to write in role and chose fairy stories as an ideal theme because most children were familiar with some of them. She decided to focus on the story of Cinderella and provided each of the five tables in her class with two different versions of the story, so that the class would experience ten different interpretations of the tale. The stories included versions from Andersen, Dahl and from politically correct fairy stories, as well as versions found in the school library and on the internet.

She asked children to choose a character from the story and to make notes about that person's characteristics. Each table had to have a Cinderella, two ugly sisters, a prince, Cinderella's father and stepmother. When the children had shared their notes about their characters' characteristics with the people in their group, Anna rearranged the groups so that there was a table for each character and the children could come together and share their ideas for, say, the prince's characteristics.

Anna then read three versions of the story to the children and asked them each to choose one version, or one of the ones they had read in their groups, and to imagine how they would feel and react as a character in the story. A series of activities then followed over a two-week period including:

→

- children writing letters to friends telling them about their situation and their feelings and what they intended to do next;

- hot-seating, in which children answered questions in role as their character;

- writing parts of the story in the first person as if they were one of the characters;

- improvised dramatisations of the story followed by performances for a Year 3 class.

At the end of the programme, Anna developed the theme of interpreting a character and putting oneself into an unfamiliar role during PSHE lessons. She also encouraged children to look at different interpretations of stories and events in a subsequent history topic on Victorians, reminding them about how they did something similar when looking at fairy tales.

Activity

Choose another well-known fairy tale and consider how you could develop a series of interesting lessons in which children explore different versions.

Curriculum Links

A study of traditional tales from around the world lends itself to links with both history and geography topics. Children could investigate how people lived in the times when versions of stories are set. Were there kings and queens, princesses and princes whose behaviour influenced storytellers? How did royalty live and how did this compare with those less fortunate? What would a palace or castle have been like to live in? What was a peasant cottage like to live in?

For geography, a map of Europe or the world could be provided and children could be asked to locate places where different versions of tales can be found and put flags or markers there.

The language of fairy tales

Knowles and Malmkjaer (1996) discussed the use of language in fairy tales, arguing that this tends to be simple and easy to follow. Similes are used to link the magical world to the everyday world.

Can you think of some?

Adjectives tend to be the most basic and *in the case of gradable adjectives* (hot – warm – cool – cold) *often at the ends of the scales in question*. Simple and common adjectives also tend to feature, with red being commonly used rather than crimson, vermilion or scarlet; and handsome rather than attractive or good-looking.

Knowles and Malmkjaer conclude that the simple language makes the stories easy to follow, *even though the stories told in them are fantastic.* They assert that:

> *For this reason, partly, the genre appealed to those writers of the nineteenth century who wished at once to instruct, entertain and develop the imaginations of the children of the Industrial Revolution.*

(p.163)

Conclusion

By this point you are probably thinking again about the relevance and importance of the stories you may have thought of as slightly old-fashioned and only for the youngest children. The tradition of these tales is all around us in modern culture. The assumption is made in the press and in films like Pixar's *Shrek* series that all the characters will be familiar to a worldwide audience. The obsession with princesses which extends from little girls dressing up to a fascination with real royal families, and is frequently seen in car signs proclaiming 'Little Princess on Board', has its origins in the world of fairy stories.

Traditional tales and fairy stories are central to the cultural heritage of people around the world and merit a place in the curriculum in schools. There is great scope for learning about other cultures by reading their stories and by comparing them with our own. What is very clear is that while tales may be part of countries' cultures they also cross international borders and are reinterpreted and developed as they do so.

Learning Outcomes Review

In this chapter you have read about the strong tradition of fairy stories which exists around the world. You should now understand the significance of fairy stories and traditional tales for cultural heritage, recognising how phrases, characters and plots have come to be part of everyday conversation. You should also be able to consider ways of developing interesting and stimulating classroom activities based upon traditional tales.

Self-assessment question

1   What are the key features of fairy tales? Think about character, setting, plot and language.

Further Reading

For alternative versions of traditional tales, each of the following has wide appeal for both adults and children:

Dahl, R. (2001) *Revolting Rhymes*. London: Puffin.

The stories are told in verse and are full of humour. Dahl decides that some characters clearly do not deserve the heroic status so often afforded them and provides different endings. Goldilocks, for example, is branded a thief and a vandal and is eaten by the bears whose food she has stolen and whose house she has damaged.

Garner, J.F. (1994) *Politically Correct Bedtime Stories: Modern Tales for Our Life and Times*. New Jersey: John Wiley & Sons Inc.

These delightfully funny tales take political correctness to its extremes. An opening passage from Little Red Riding Hood gives a flavour. Red Riding Hood is asked by her mother to take fresh fruit and mineral water to her grandmother *not because this was womyn's {sic} work, mind you, but because the deed was generous and helped engender a feeling of community.*

Scieszka, J. (1992) *The Stinky Cheese Man and Other Fairly Stupid Tales*. New York: Viking Press.

Scieszka parodies traditional tales and makes links between them, as well as blending tales together and creating new ones, as in *Cinderumplestiltskin* and *The Tortoise and the Hair.*

References

Aiken, J. (1953) *All You've Ever Wanted*. London: Puffin.

Aiken, J. (1955) *More Than You Bargained For*. London: Puffin.

Carpenter, H. and Prichard, M. (1995) *The Oxford Companion to Children's Literature*. Oxford: Oxford University Press.

Crouch, M. (1962) *Treasure Seekers and Borrowers*. London: The Library Association.

DfE (2013) *The National Curriculum in England Key: Stages 1 and 2 Framework Document*. London: DfE. Available at: www.gov.uk/government/uploads/system/uploads/attachment_data/file/335133/PRIMARY_national_curriculum_220714.pdf

Flood, A. (2012) Hans Christian Andersen's first fairytale found. *Guardian*, 13 Dec.

Hearne, B. (2011) Folklore in children's literature. Contents and discontents, in Wolf, S., Coats, K., Enciso, P. and Jenkis, C. (eds) *Handbook of Research on Children's and Young Adult Literature*. London: Routledge. pp209–22.

Knowles, M. and Malmkjaer, K. (1996) *Language and Control in Children's Literature*. London: Routledge.

Pullman, P. (2012a) *Grimm Tales for Young and Old.* London: Penguin Classics.

Pullman, P. (2012b) The challenge of retelling Grimm's fairy tales. The *Guardian*, 21 Sep.

Ransome, A. (2005) *Old Peter's Russian Tales.* Gutenberg e-books (first published 1923).

Sierra, J. (ed.) (1992) *Cinderella.* The Oryx Multicultural Folktale Series. Phoenix, AZ: Oryx Press.

Warner, M. (1994) *Stranger Magic: Charmed States and The Arabian Nights From the Beast to the Blonde: On Fairy Tales and Their Tellers.* London: Vintage.

Warner, M. (2012) *Grimm Thoughts.* Broadcast on BBC Radio 4, December 2012.

Zipes, J. (2009) Origins: Fairy tales and folk tales, in Maybin, J. and Watson, M. (eds) *Children's Literature: Approaches and Territories.* Milton Keynes: Open University Press. pp26–39.

8 Fiction which addresses issues

Learning Outcomes

By reading this chapter you will:

- consider the impact that fiction has on our understanding of issues;
- understand how Victorian and early twentieth-century fiction deals with issues;
- understand how this changed over time;
- consider the treatment of contemporary issues in fiction;
- reflect on some of the wider questions to consider when reading and using fiction to explore issues in the classroom.

Introduction

When you read a book, you are discovering that you are not alone in the world.

(Morpurgo, 2012)

A genre which has risen greatly in popularity in the past twenty years or so is the fiction whose theme is children coping with difficult situations. The idea in itself is not new: Victorian and early twentieth-century fiction has many children coping with difficulties. This earlier literature tended to focus on disability and treat the matter and the people involved in ways that would now be considered unacceptable, but reflected social and cultural understanding of Victorian and early twentieth-century life. In contrast, more current literature deals with a wider range of issues, which are framed within current social and cultural understandings.

The impact of literature on our understanding

There is an assumption made that books will have an impact on the reader, and those of us who are readers sense this. We know that we enjoy reading; we sense that reading enriches our lives; we know that reading can be a flow activity (see Chapter 4); and we know that reading broadens our horizons. So, how can we explain this? How does it happen? What are our understandings of how books influence us as readers? This is a particularly apt question to ask of the aspects of books that potentially shape our perspective on life through the way that they deal with issues.

An interesting theory is the link between fiction and theory of mind. Theory of mind refers to our understanding of mental states – desire, knowledge, belief – which enables us to predict other people's behaviour. Theory of mind is the basis of social cognition, which is at the heart of our ability to function in a social world. Developmental evidence (Astington and Edward, 2010) suggests that theory of mind is learned. In the absence of certain developmental and learning disabilities, and given an appropriate set of experiences, theory of mind develops in a child's first five years of life. In the earliest stages of development children learn to:

- realise intentionality in others;

- recognise that others have different needs and desires from their own;

- understand how things look from others' perspectives.

This development continues through children's pre-school years, as children begin to understand that our minds don't simply mirror reality but that we actively construct representations of reality. Also, that these representations change with new experiences or information, and that they differ from person to person. Language is hugely significant in this process. Children need to understand and be able to use words that express internal mental states, words such as *know, think, mean, forget, guess, want,* and *need.*

So, at its simplest, we can hypothesise that fiction for young children can have a two-fold effect. It alerts children to the inner life of others and, chosen carefully, enriches children's language in ways that enable them to build understandings of others and develop the language to talk about internal states within themselves and others. Once theory of mind is established, and given appropriate opportunities, children's development continues towards greater sophistication and complexity in their understanding of self and others. Fiction books have a powerful role to play in this development, enabling children to access experiences and the inner lives of others. Oatley (2008) develops this notion in his theory of the impact of fiction on our psyche. He offers us an analogy of a flight simulator. Just as the flight simulator simulates flight, fiction, he argues, simulates our social world. It acts as a set of simulations of the *what-ifs of social life* (Oatley, 2008, p.1032). He argues that it stands to reason that there is a limit to what we, as an individual, can experience. Fiction can open up our experiences. As Proust (cited in Oatley, 2008) explains, the novelist:

> *sets loose in us all possible happiness and all possible unhappiness, just a few of which we would spend years of our lives coming to know.*

(p.1031)

Research Focus

The mind's flight simulator (Oatley, 2008)

Oatley's (2008) hypothesis, supported by a range of research studies, is that fiction acts as a kind of simulation that runs on minds. Fiction is simulation in two ways. Firstly, regarding theory of mind, in our everyday lives we use aspects of our understanding about ourselves to infer what others may be thinking or feeling. In fiction, the author offers us cues

⟶

about our own theory of mind processes so that we can use these simulative faculties for the fictional characters.

Secondly, regarding 'complexes', Oatley (2008, p.1030) argues that when we want to understand a complex process it is useful to run a simulation – for example, computer simulations of traffic flow or the spread of disease in populations. The social world, he argues, is similarly complex, and authors of fiction write simulations that explore the complexity by following a trajectory of possibilities in the social world.

He offers an example of this regarding the character of Iago in *Othello*.

The usual interpretation of Shakespeare's *Othello* is that its principal character, Iago, is a psychopath, an embodiment of evil from whom one should shrink in horror. Oatley (2008) argues that the play can be read just as plausibly, and for psychologists perhaps more interestingly, with Iago being a career soldier rather than a career criminal.

Iago is a non-commissioned officer, Othello's loyal and long-serving third in command. When the opportunity arises for the appointment of Othello's second in command Iago is passed over for an outsider, someone of higher social standing but without combat experience. This is in contrast to Iago's experience and proven military skill. This causes Iago to experience profound resentment. Oatley (2008) argues that in this Shakespeare offers us the opportunity to enter a simulation and experience this trajectory of a very difficult emotion. He argues that in doing this we may begin to recognise some of the implications of resentment in ourselves.

The case study below provides an example of how books can be used as a starting point for exploring different aspects of children's lives. It is important to notice how Sophie becomes aware of some of the more subtle aspects of this approach and realises that she will need to reflect on her own understandings of same-sex parents before using books to explore this issue in the classroom.

Case Study

Using fiction to explore same-sex families

Sophie, a third-year student, on her pre-placement days in a Year 3 class, was talking with the teacher about the children in the group. She had asked the teacher to identify individual children's abilities and needs so that she could start to consider this in her ideas and plans for the following term. The teacher identified a child in the class who lived in a same-sex family; she had two mummies. While this hadn't been an issue previously, the teacher had recently noticed that the other children were becoming interested in why she had two mummies and had started to ask questions. The teacher felt that it was important that she was proactive in supporting all the children's understanding of different families. However, she was also aware of the fact that it had the potential to be a sensitive topic with others. The teacher said that she intended to open up some discussions in PSHE about different families, using fiction

→

books as the starting point. She encouraged Sophie to start collecting books and considering how she could open up discussions about families from the texts.

She was able to find books that had different families in them. This included books where the family structure wasn't the focus of the book and those where it was. She was also able to find a few books that focused specifically on same-sex families: *And Tango Makes Three* (Richardson, et al., 2007), in which two male penguins become parents; *Mommy, Mama and Me* (Newman and Thompson, 2009), which traces a typical day in the life a of a toddler with two mummies; and *King and King* (De Haan and Nijland, 2002), a play on the traditional fairy tale of the prince being required to marry. He searches for, and marries, another king.

Additionally, Sophie sought advice and information on ways to discuss the issue of same-sex families, in particular ways to approach the issue of same-sex families. She found a journal article 'Two daddy tigers and a baby tiger' (Kelly, 2012) that explored promoting understandings about same-sex parented families using picture books. This was helpful in encouraging her to examine her own ideas and how this may affect her approach in the classroom. She realised that she would need to think very carefully about her own attitudes and how these may be reflected in her teaching, if she was to use the fiction books effectively to explore the issues of similarities and differences in families.

Curriculum Link

There are clear opportunities here for work in PSHE. An increasing number of children come from families which comprise different groupings from what was once regarded as conventional. Discussions will need to be managed sensitively and perhaps in a generalised way rather than focusing on individuals' own situations. It is advisable to seek advice and support on how to approach these issues in a school. There may be staff, or other professionals, whose experience or expertise you can draw on and it is important to consider your own views and attitudes and how these may affect what you do. Additionally, a school may have a particular way of approaching certain issues, which you would need to take into account.

So, if we accept that fiction can have an impact on how we view the world, how does children's literature reflect certain issues in society? How has this changed over time? And what are the implications of this for the choices we make about the books we use with children and the implications of these choices for teaching?

Victorian and early twentieth-century fiction

Victorian and early twentieth-century fiction is littered with children who are crippled (and this was nearly always the term used – no politically correct reference to being 'otherwise abled' for the Victorians), bereaved of a parent, or coping with poverty or adverse circumstances. These situations were usually resolved one way or another before the end of the book – the crippled child was either cured, for example Clara in Johanna Spyri's *Heidi* (1880) or Colin in Frances Hodgson Burnett's *The Secret Garden*, (1911) or became so weak and pure that he or she died a peaceful and Christian death, for example *Jackanapes* (Ewing, 2012) or *At The Back of the North Wind* (MacDonald, 2009). Family fortunes could be restored, as in E. Nesbit's *The Railway Children* (1906), in which Father is proved to have been framed and he returns from his imprisonment to take his family back to comfortable gentility. Crusty old adults can be reformed by a child's influence, for example Burnett's *Little Lord Fauntleroy* (1886).

Perhaps the most realistic of these early stories is E. Nesbit's *The Story of the Treasure Seekers* (1904), which tells of the efforts of a motherless family of children to restore the family fortunes. The story is narrated by the eldest, Oswald, who says near the beginning *Our mother is dead, and if you think we don't care because I don't tell you much about her, you only show that you do not understand people at all*. The adventures in this book are realistic, exciting and humorous, and realistically unsuccessful – but even so, a rich uncle turns up at the end and takes the whole family to live in his mansion in Blackheath.

In Frances Hodgson Burnett's still popular and frequently filmed *A Little Princess* (1905), the heroine becomes a skivvy (the lowest rank of housemaid) living in the garret of the school where she was once the prize pupil; but when her fortunes are restored she is whisked off to a life of lavish luxury again. In another still read classic of the time, Jean Webster's *Daddy-Long-Legs* (1912), Judy is plucked apparently at random from an orphanage by a rich and mysterious benefactor and sent to college; she eventually meets and marries her sponsor. Any reader brought up on this kind of diet would assume that the miraculous happy ending was life's usual fare.

Activity

Recall some of the characters from books you know from this period. It may be worth returning to them and reminding yourself of the ways in which people are referred to, including the language used.

Consider other texts in which physical characteristics are considered to denote particular character traits, for example, Captain Hook, Long John Silver.

- What is notable about the texts? How do they reflect the social and cultural understandings of the time in which they were written?
- How have these understandings changed?
- What are the implications of this for using these books with children in primary schools?

Moving on

Children with 'problems' largely disappeared from popular fiction for several decades. Orphans still cropped up regularly, but they were generally sent to live with benevolent relations. Good examples of this include Tolly in Lucy Boston's *Children of Green Knowe* series (1954–76), or the Fossil children in Noel Streatfeild's *Ballet Shoes* (1936). Fallen fortunes and the discovery of the long-lost treasure or a hidden will were recurrent themes, but there was seldom any sense of the characters suffering in any way beyond living in physically straitened circumstances. Eve Garnett made a celebrated effort with *The Family from One End Street* (1937) to counter the relentless middle-classness of the current children's fiction, though her work has later been derided as patronising and promoting a stereotype view of those she sought to champion. For example:

> *So long as he had his job, and his family were well and happy, and he could smoke his pipe and work in his garden, see his mates at the Working Men's Club once or twice a week, dream about his Pig, and have a good Blow Out on Bank Holidays, {Mr. Ruggles} wanted nothing more.*

> (Garnett, 1937)

Physical weakness or disability is also largely absent from stories written for children in the first half of the twentieth century. A character might perhaps wear glasses, but if this is the case it will generally be to indicate that this person, though somewhat 'nerdy', is the brainbox who will come up with the cunning plan or spot the vital clue, which will bring about the happy ending. Of the fiction which is still read from this time between what is often regarded as the two golden ages of children's literature (see Chapter 10), the only well-known example of a character with a disability is Mary, the older sister in Laura Ingalls Wilder's *Little House* series, who is blind. Mary's blindness is unusual in fiction, in that it is simply a fact, like Pa's fiddle-playing, and not used to make any kind of moral point. In this, these books are well ahead of their time. The early books tell of the childhood of the author, Laura, in the Midwest as her father's pioneering spirit moves the family from the Big Woods of Wisconsin across into Indian Territory and later to settle in the new Dakota Territory. The simple routine of their days, and the detailed descriptions of, for instance, how Pa builds a log cabin, combined with the realistic personalities of the small girls, give the stories a lasting charm. It is from the fourth book of the series (*By the Shores of Silver Lake*), however, which opens when the family is recovering from a bout of fever which has left Mary blind, that the relationship between the girls becomes more interesting. Laura, the younger, is now the dominant one and the 'eyes' of her older sister. Mary, the 'big girl' who has always been looked up to, envied for her blonde hair and a model of good behaviour, has become dependent.

Activity

Disability and learning needs in children's literature

Think of characters in books that have a disability or learning need. Notice how they, and their need or disability, are portrayed. You may notice that it is part of the fabric of life, like Mary in the *Little House* series, or used as an example to all of redemption or 'spirit', like Colin in *The Secret Garden*, or to denote character traits such as geeky or evil, such as Captain Hook, or in some more current literature, that it is the main focus of the book, such as *Sleepovers* (Wilson, 2001).

- What other representations can you find?
- What are the implications of this for our, and children's, perception and understanding of people with disability or learning needs?
- How would you use this knowledge to shape your provision and practice in school?

The 1960s, 1970s and beyond

The1960s and1970s saw the arrival of much more awareness of physical disabilities in writing for children, as well as acknowledgement of many other problems children may face which had hardly been mentioned in earlier texts. There was a proliferation both of books in which a previously active child has to adjust to a new situation after a life-changing accident, and of those which have been called 'second-fiddle books' (Thomson, 1992 cited in Keith, 2001) in which an able-bodied child has his or her attitudes and perceptions challenged or changed by becoming acquainted with someone who is 'different'. The term 'second-fiddle books' was coined by Pat Thomson ('Disability in modern children's fiction', *Books for Keeps*, July 1982) to describe books in which the disabled character exists only to promote the personal development of the main, able-bodied character.

> *Samantha becomes a better person through having known someone in a wheelchair. Bully for Samantha, but what about the person in the wheelchair?*

(Thomson, 1992 cited in Keith, 2001, p.24)

In Judy Blume's *Deenie* (1973), a 13-year-old girl is diagnosed with scoliosis (curvature of the spine), and as she adjusts her life to this knowledge and to wearing a body brace, she becomes friendly with a girl she had always avoided in school because of her severe eczema. In *Welcome Home, Jellybean* (Marlene Fanta Shyer, 1978), the narrator Neil tells of his mother's decision to bring his sister, who has severe learning difficulties, home from the residential institution where she has spent her early childhood. This brings about major changes in the household as all the family react to the change in their lives.

Research Focus

The portrayal of disability in fiction

Lois Keith (2001) explores issues of the portrayal of disability in texts in her book *Take up thy bed and walk: death, disability and cure in classic fiction for girls*. In addition to tracing the pattern of representation of people with disability she makes the following thought-provoking observations about the nature of the representation.

- Writers attempting to portray disabled characters with conviction and to make readers aware of some of the 'problems' that they face have often been limited by their own narrow views and lack any real understanding of what it is to be disabled. This has resulted in some rather joyless books with confusing messages.

- Books often have startling inaccuracies, for example characters who lose a leg in an accident are somehow up and walking on their own very quickly.

- Although the death of a major character remains unusual in books for children and young people, where the character is disabled it is more frequent. Keith questions this, asking whether these stories really do reflect reality – in which some children with disabilities do have life threatening conditions – or whether it is the inability of the writer to imagine a happy, full life as a grown up disabled person.

- The phenomenon of 'second-fiddle books' (Thomson, 1992 cited in Keith, 2001): the ongoing tendency for books with disabled characters to be 'problem' books and the 'infuriating genre' (Keith, 2001) of books in which the disabled character exists only to promote the personal development of the main able-bodied character – they exist to bring out the good in others.

- Even books that avoid the sentimentality and pitfalls evident in other books fall short, for example with negative references (including self-references) to a person's disability, hints that characters are likely to die young so the future doesn't have to be considered, and apparently miraculous cures.

- Characters in books who become disabled during the course of the book, rather than from birth, are often a champion of some sort, physically active or especially beautiful (or all of the above) prior to becoming disabled. This technique is used to heighten the fall. Religious faith and greater awareness of physical and psychological issues means that the miracle cure is no longer possible but even these texts seem to need to end with at least a partial cure.

In view of these observations, Keith offers us two texts that she describes as rare examples of how books dealing with impairment and disability can be honest without being tragic, observing that they are serious and funny, personal and political: *Blabber Mouth* (Gleitzman, 1992), and *Sticky Beak* (Gleitzman, 1995). Keith concludes that comparisons are often made between the contribution of disabled writers to literature and of black writers, who have, over the past decade, brought not only a new subject matter to children's literature, but a new way of writing about black people's experience. Whether it is black history and the experience of racism, or black family life, the writers provide knowledge and insight as well as a literary experience quite different from previous books. Similarly, she argues, disabled writers need to have their voice heard. However, she also cautions that, just as black writers are not writing solely to inform and educate, so the growing body of disabled writers want to be read by all kinds of readers, and concludes:

> ... it is to be hoped that, like black writers, disabled writers will write from a different perspective, less prone to stereotypes of tragedy and despair; less full of 'problems' and 'issues' with no solution; and less blaming of the disabled person as if no social factors were involved. There is a wealth of experience and history to draw on and disabled writers will certainly do this differently.

(Keith, 2001, p.236)

Judy Blume was probably the first writer to become well known for her open approach to issues which had not previously been widely discussed in children's fiction. Many of her novels were aimed at older teenage readers, but such titles as *Blubber*, which describes bullying from the point of view of both the bully and the victim, *Iggie's House* (1970), which is concerned with racism, and *It's Not the End of the World* (1972), in which Karen faces her parents' divorce, are suitable for younger readers. *Are You There, God? It's Me, Margaret* (1970), which combines anxiety about religion with the pre-teen girl's concern over the growing-up issues of pre-teenage girls, has become a classic in the genre. However, as the girls' areas of interest include getting their first bras and starting their periods, the book is perhaps more one to recommend selectively for private reading than to risk in the classroom.

Research Focus

Teachers' criteria for rejecting works of children's literature
Wollman-Bonilla (1998)

Following a negative response that teachers had to Wollman-Bonilla's choice of a book to use with children, she was interested to find out how teachers choose books that deal with different issues, in particular the criteria they use for rejecting certain texts as not suitable for use in the classroom. Wollman-Bonilla began from the assumption that all children's books reflect a socio-cultural perspective – a set of values and beliefs – and that teachers will tune into and choose those that reflect their perspective. She was interested in what teachers explicitly label as inappropriate for classroom use and why.

It is important to note that the research was conducted in America and so particular socio-cultural perspectives may be evident in the study which, if repeated here in the UK, may differ.

$\longrightarrow$

Wollman-Bonilla selected texts that she regularly read in the classroom. The teachers assessed them as either appropriate or inappropriate for elementary grade aged children (Key Stages 1 and 2). Outcomes showed that teachers regarded texts as inappropriate for three main reasons.

1.   It might frighten or corrupt children by introducing things they don't or shouldn't know about, for example homelessness, death, that the world is a cruel place and discrimination. This seemed to arise from a desire to protect children's assumed innocence.

2.   It fails to represent dominant social values. For example, one teacher commented that, 'I wouldn't read this book because it models improper English.' Other teachers were concerned about books that included families living with financial hardship; they viewed them as negative and depressing. Others expressed concern about books that seemed to challenge the idea that hard work is the key to success.

3.   It identifies racism or sexism as a social problem. Some teachers thought that books that challenge or reverse traditional gender roles could be controversial and lead to misunderstandings. Some reacted negatively towards the characters in non-traditional roles, such as a feisty girl and boys playing with dolls. And, with regard to race, teachers preferred to articulate a view of race as 'we are all the same' rather than highlight difference and therefore rejected books that appeared to identify black children as different, regarding them as racist.

Texts read aloud regularly by researcher			
Texts regularly rejected by teachers		Texts regularly accepted by teachers	
Book	Theme	Book	Theme
Amazing Grace (Hoffman, 1991)	Overcoming racism and sexism	Cloudy with a Chance of Meatballs (Barrett, 1978)	Weather and food fantasy
Bridge to Terabithia (Patterson, 1977)	Friendship, death	The Frog Prince Continued (Scieszka, 1991)	Fairy tale spoof
Fly Away Home (Bunting, 1991)	Homelessness, hope	The Lorax (Dr Seuss, 1971)	Environmental responsibility
Honey I Love and other love poems (Greenfield, 1978)	Child's experiences in black community Black history	Love You Forever (Munsch, 1986)	Parent–child bond
Nettie's Trip South (Turner,1987)	The injustice of slavery Racism	Owl Moon (Yolen, 1987)	Appreciation of nature Family rituals
The Paper Bag Princess (Munsch, 1980)	Gender stereotypes challenged	Roxaboxen (McLerran, 1991)	Imaginary play Passage of time

$\longrightarrow$

Texts read aloud regularly by researcher			
Texts regularly rejected by teachers		**Texts regularly accepted by teachers**	
Book	*Theme*	*Book*	*Theme*
Roll of Thunder Hear my Cry (Taylor, 1976)	Racism Black history	*Song and Dance Man* (Ackerman, 1988)	Children's relationship with grandfather
Smokey Night (Bunting, 1994)	Urban violence Racism	*The Relatives Came* (Rylant, 1985)	Relatives' visit
Tar Beach (Ringgold, 1991)	Urban life Overcoming poverty and racism	*Volcano* (Lauber, 1986)	Volcanic eruptions
William's Doll (Zolotow, 1972)	Gender stereotypes challenged	*Wilfred, Gordon, McDonald Partridge* (Fox, 1984)	Child's relationship with elderly Memory

The potential minefields of discussing race and religion in the classroom are more usually approached by writers for older children. Writers such as Peter Dickinson, Jean Ure and Malorie Blackman have all produced thought-provoking and intelligent novels, but ones whose scope and style may be well beyond suitability for a primary classroom.

Judy Blume's *Iggie's House*, mentioned earlier, is unusual in tackling a neighbourhood's prejudice against the arrival of a black family through the eyes of a ten-year-old. An interesting earlier example of the same situation is found in the work of Edward Eager, an American writer of the 1950s and 1960s. In *The Well-Wishers* (1960), his protagonists first hear in church *that he had heard of a family that was about to move into the neighbourhood ... some people apparently didn't want this family to move in.* The minister invites his congregation to sign a petition supporting the new arrivals, in the face of a petition against them from other quarters. Naturally the children's side wins eventually.

> *When Deborah saw the family, she realised for the first time why it was that the Smugs had tried to prevent them moving in. Her voice rang out loud and clear. 'Oh', she said, 'Is that all it was? 'Yes', I told her, 'that's all it was.'... 'How silly' said Deborah.*
>
> (Eager, 1960, p.150)

Race and colour are never mentioned here, but the message is there to be picked up for discussion if wanted. Interestingly, and unusually in books for young children, the *Amazing Grace* series addresses issues of race and gender. *Amazing Grace* (Hoffman, 2007) was a ground-breaking book when it was first published as it openly addressed racial and gender stereotyping in a book for very young children. In *Amazing Grace* (Hoffman, 2007), Grace longs to play Peter Pan in her school play but her classmates say that Peter is a boy and he isn't black. Grace's Ma and Nana intervene to tell her that she can be anything she wants to be if she puts her mind to it.

Divorce and family break-up is probably the most common problem situation faced by children today, and here the current queen of the genre is probably Jacqueline Wilson, with her titles such as *The Suitcase Kid* (1992), *The Bed and Breakfast Star* (1994), *Double Act* (1995) and the Tracy Beaker books (1991–2006), all of which have been widely acclaimed. Her characters face unexpected and difficult situations with imagination and humour, and she nearly always uses an unsophisticated first-person narration which makes the stories appealing and involving for younger readers.

Anne Fine, an ex-Children's Laureate, has also dealt sensitively with a wide range of 'problem' situations, not all of them easily categorised. *Bill's New Frock* (1989) gives an interesting starting-point for the topic of gender attitudes – younger readers tend to take for granted that Bill has actually become a girl overnight, while older ones would consider just that it is everyone's perspective on him which has changed. At the superficial level this is a very funny story, which would merit its use in the younger years' classroom on this ground alone. Considered more deeply, it could make older children think more about their own sexist attitudes and assumptions. *Up on Cloud Nine* (2002) is again a clever and very funny story, a character study of a boy, Stolly, through the eyes of his best friend Ian, while Stolly himself is in a hospital bed in a coma after his latest mishap. The book, while never didactic, touches on issues from depression and family relationships to the rarely mentioned question of boys expressing emotions and being honest about their feelings. In *The Tulip Touch* (1996), the narrator Natalie tells the story of her years of friendship with Tulip, whose dysfunctional family background and deeply disturbed attitudes attract her to cheerful, normal Natalie with her secure and warm family, while Natalie is fascinated by Tulip's wild imagination and inventions. The closeness of their friendship is challenged when Natalie wants to break away, and Tulip becomes more dangerous. The fact that Tulip's background is only hinted at, never described in detail, and that we are never told how her life evolves after the scope of the book, makes this outstanding story resonate in the memory long after reading it.

Books also provide a way of opening up children's understanding (and discussion when appropriate) about issues that have recently become, or are in the process of becoming, more visible in society. This includes refugees and asylum seekers, and transgender. Clearly, as with all such books, these can be used to address specific issues that arise, or are part of the school community, or they may just be books in a classroom or school library that are there to reflect the diversity within our society.

Are You a Boy or Are You a Girl? (Savage and Fisher, 2015) deals with the issue of non-binary gender in a picture book that is accessible for younger children. Tiny, the main character, chooses not to define as a boy or a girl, enjoying a wide range of activities, games and interests. However, when Tiny moves to a different school some other children struggle to understand this and Tiny is faced with some problems when trying to make friends. Similarly, *My Princess Boy* (Kilodavis and DeSimone, 2011), a book about a boy who loves to dress up as a princess and dance, challenges notions of binary gender identity and explores what this means for this boy and his family as they face misunderstanding and prejudice.

Seeking Refugee is a series of picture books that tell stories about children who have left their home country to seek refuge from wars, famine and persecution. There are five books in the series and each one, originally produced as an animation, tells an individual child's story: their ordeal, their feelings and their hopes. For older children Benjamin Zephaniah's (2001) *Refugee Boy* explores the experience of being a refugee in England. It tells the story of Alem, a boy who came to England with his father ostensibly for a holiday, but is left here, in an act of love by his family as they believe he will be safer in London than Ethiopia. The book tells the sometimes heart-breaking, sometimes joyful story of what it is to be a child refugee in England.

The case study which follows looks at another contemporary issue: families that are affected by parental absences through involvement in the many overseas conflicts in which countries engage.

Case Study

Using fiction to support children from military families

A primary school situated near an airbase began to take a number of children whose parents were in the armed services. Many of the children had parents who were deployed overseas on active service. The school were aware that this was a difficult time for the children and families involved and were keen to do what they could to support the children.

As a staff group they looked at the evidence and advice on the needs of these children. This led to some significant reassessment of their practices, some of which were quite challenging to the staff. For example, the Foundation Stage staff found that they had to reassess their approach to children making guns and role playing fighting. Despite their previous reservations about gun play, they recognised that this was a significant part of these children's lives and, as with other experiences that are evident in children's play, this reflected their need to role play their lived experiences.

Additionally, as part of the assessment of their provision, the staff looked at the fiction books in the school. They found they had no fiction books that reflected or explored life for these children and their families. They also had no fiction books that dealt with issues of sadness, anger or loss.

The staff were able to source and buy a small number of specific books for the younger children: *I Miss You* (Andrews, 2007), *My Daddy's Going Away* (MacGregor, 2010) and *Night Catch*

$\longrightarrow$

(Ehrmantraut, 2008). Additionally, they purchased some books that explored issues of sadness, anger and loss, books such as Molly Bang's (2008) *When Sophie Gets Angry* and *Michael Rosen's Sad Book* (Rosen and Blake, 2011).

The staff also identified a series of books by Margot Sutherland, a psychologist, who has written these fiction books to help children with difficult feelings. These included *The Frog who Longed For the Moon to Smile* (2003a), a book about yearning, *The Niffloo Called Nevermind* (2003b), that deals with the issue of bottling up feelings, and *The Day The Sea Went Out and Never Came Back* (2003c), about loss.

However, much to their dismay, the fiction books on offer in the UK that included or dealt specifically with the issues of children with parents in the armed services were extremely limited, particularly for the older children. So, in response, they began to explore the potential of doing a project with the children at Key Stage 2 and their parents to write some stories with a view to producing books for use in the school. Their starting point for this was to explore the best way to approach this work with the children and families. This included discussions in school, meeting with other professionals and people from the military, and reading Sutherland's (2001) book *Using Story Telling as a Therapeutic Tool with Children*.

Curriculum Links

It is highly likely, even if you do not teach in a school close to a military base, that some of the children you teach will be affected by their parents' involvement in military action. There may be scope to discuss this within PSHE, but great care needs to be exercised and staff need to develop strategies across the school, especially when some children may suffer bereavements or their parents may be affected in other ways by their experiences. It is vital that you seek advice from within the school, and perhaps from other professionals, to inform your work with children around sensitive issues.

Conclusion

It might be felt that all fiction tends to present readers with issues to consider and to challenge their thinking. However, the growing popularity of stories and poems which address issues such as divorce, gender stereotyping and race provides a more overt focus on topics which often have real significance for young readers. Whether these books are shared with children by their teachers or simply provide reading matter which engages children, it is likely that they will throw up questions which will challenge the thinking of both children and their teachers.

Learning Outcomes Review

You should now have considered how children's fiction that deals with issues impacts on the reader. You should be able to identify how Victorian and early twentieth-century fiction dealt with issues and how this has changed over time. You should be aware of some of the contemporary issues dealt with in children's fiction, including an awareness of issues that are still not easy to find in children's books. Through the research identified, the activities and case studies, you should have developed an understanding of some of the wider implications of reading and using fiction to explore issues in the classroom.

Self-assessment questions

Choose one of the books identified in the chapter and read it carefully.

1   What are the issues raised?
2   How are they raised?
3   What, if anything, would you need to consider about the presentation of the issue or the language used in the text?
4   What age range would you consider the book appropriate for? Why?
5   How could you incorporate use of the book in your teaching?
6   What aspect of the issue would you have to be sensitive to? Why? How would you achieve this?

Further Reading

Fine, A. (1996) *The Tulip Touch*, London: Puffin.

The usually well-behaved Natalie, from a secure family background, develops a close friendship with Tulip, whose notoriously bad behaviour means she is both unpopular and often in trouble. The book explores the girls' relationship as they get into a series of difficult situations.

Sachar, L. (1998) *Holes*. New York: Farrar.

Stanley Yelnats is sent to Camp Green Lake after being wrongly convicted of a crime. Here, along with the other inmates, he spends his days digging holes in the desert under the watchful eyes of the warden. The story is both gripping and occasionally frightening and raises issues about crime and punishment.

Wilson, J. (2001) *Sleepovers*. London: Doubleday.

Daisy's sister, Lily, has special needs and Daisy worries about how her new friends will react to her when they come to her house for a sleepover.

References

Andrews, B. (2007) *I Miss You.* New York: Prometheus Books.

Astington, J. and Edward, M. (2010) The development of theory of mind in early childhood. *Encyclopaedia on Early Childhood Development.* Available at: www.child-encyclopedia.com/sites/default/files/textes-experts/en/588/the-development-of-theory-of-mind-in-early-childhood.pdf (accessed 12.04.16).

Bang, M. (2008) *When Sophie Gets Angry – Really, Really Angry.* London. Scholastic Books.

Burnett, F.H. (2009) *The Secret Garden.* Oxford: OUP.

De Haan, L. and Nijland, S. (2002) *King and King.* Berkeley, CA: Tricycle Press.

Eager, E. (1960) *The Well-Wishers.* New York: Houghton Mifflin Harcourt.

Ehrmantraut, B. (2008) *Night Catch.* Aberdeen: Bubble Gum Press.

Ewing, J.H.G. (2012) *Jackanapes.* Hamburg: Tredition Classics.

Fine, A. (1989) *Bill's New Frock.* London: Methuen.

Garnett, E. (1937) *The Family from One End Street.* London: Frederick Muller.

Gleitzman, M. (1992) *Blabber Mouth.* London: Macmillan.

Gleitzman, M. (1995) *Sticky Beak.* London: Macmillan.

Hoffman, A. (2007) *Amazing Grace.* London: Frances Lincoln Children's Books.

Keith, L. (2001) *Take Up Thy Bed and Walk.* London: Routledge.

Kilodavis, C. and DeSimone, S. (2011) *My Princess Boy.* London: Aladdin.

MacDonald, G. (2009) *At the Back of the North Wind.* Radford: Wilder Publications.

MacGregor, C. (2010) *My Daddy's Going Away.* London: Random House.

Morpurgo, M. (2012) *Parkinson Masterclass.* Sky Arts, 24 December 2012.

Newman, L. and Thompson, C. (2009) *Mommy, Mama and Me.* Berkeley, CA: Tricycle Press.

Oatley, K. (2008) *The Mind's Flight Simulator.* Available at: www.thepsychologist.org.uk/archive/archive_home.cfm?volumeID=21&editionID=167&ArticleID=1441 (accessed 12.04.16).

Richardson, J., Parnell, P. and Cole, H. (2007) *And Tango Makes Three.* London: Simon and Schuster.

Rosen, M. and Blake, Q. (2004) *Michael Rosen's Sad Book.* London: Walker Books.

Savage, S. and Fisher, F. (2015) *Are You a Boy or Are You a Girl.* London: TQUAL books.

Spyri, J. (2009) *Heidi.* Oxford: OUP.

Sutherland, M. (2001) *Using Story Telling as a Therapeutic Tool With Children.* Milton Keynes: Speechmark Publishing Ltd.

Sutherland, M. and Armstrong, N. (2003a) *The Day the Sea Went Out and Never Came Back.* Milton Keynes: Speechmark Publishing Ltd.

Sutherland, M. and Armstrong, N. (2003b) *The Niffloo Called Nevermind.* Milton Keynes: Speechmark Publishing Ltd.

Sutherland, M. and Armstrong N. (2003c) *The Frog Who Longed For the Moon to Smile.* Milton Keynes: Speechmark Publishing Ltd.

Thompson, P. (1982) Disability in modern children's fiction. *Books for Keeps*, 75(2): 1–5. Available at: http://booksforkeeps.co.uk/issue/75/childrens-books/articles/other-articles/disability-in-modern-childrens-fiction (accessed 12.04.16).

Keith, L. (2001) *Take Up Thy Bed and Walk.* London: Routledge.

Wilson, J. (2001) *Sleepovers.* London: Doubleday.

Wollman-Bonilla, J. (1998) Outrageous viewpoints: Teachers' criteria for rejecting works of children's literature. *Language Arts*, 75(4): 287–95.

Zephaniah, B. (2001) *Refugee Boy.* Bloomsbury. London.

9 Fantasy and magic

Learning Outcomes
....

By reading this chapter you will:

- explore the genre of fantasy and magic;
- consider classroom activities related to the genre;
- have an increased awareness of the range of texts available.

Introduction

The whole area of fiction which can be variously classed as fantasy, magic or science fiction covers a vast territory: the whole realm of 'what-if?' ideas. A very loose definition might be 'stories which explore the possibilities of some kind of paranormal or technical development which is not currently a part of everyday life'. But who would choose to read a story described like that?

The instant reaction to the idea that magic and science fiction can be grouped together may be surprise or disagreement, but in fact the two types have more in common than may appear at first sight. A boy grows up in a bleak and largely hostile environment, then at the age of about eleven he starts a journey from which he discovers his true identity and parentage, and eventually becomes powerful and wise. It's Harry Potter; it's also *Star Wars*, Ursula Le Guin's *A Wizard of Earthsea,* E. Nesbit's *Harding's Luck* and many others.

The books often acknowledged as the first of the golden ages of children's fiction (see Chapter 10 'Classic fiction') – Lewis Carroll's *Alice's Adventures in Wonderland* (1865) and Charles Kingsley's *The Water Babies* (1862–63) – are both fantasies which introduce the reader to whole new magical worlds of possibilities, although neither is completely free of the moralising which characterised the majority of the Victorian child's reading diet. (These books are discussed at greater length in Chapter 10.) After these, many authors followed the lines of fantasy, addressing questions and ideas which every child must surely have enjoyed at some time. What if animals could talk and lead social lives like people? What if toys came alive and had secret lives of their own? Or if there were whole races of people sharing the world with us, unseen? What if our wishes could come true? What if magical charms, as seen in old fairy stories, turned up in everyday life? What if magic were just a subject we could learn like maths and geography? And, moving into modern times, what if we were visited by someone from another planet? What if one had the powers of teleportation or mindreading?

There are so many examples of children's fiction answering all of the above questions that it would seem unnecessary as well as impossible to make a list; everyone will have personal favourites, and perhaps will always feel the sense of magic most strongly in the books first loved in their own childhoods. Some stories have been given new life, if made-over, by film and television adaptations (for instance Mary Norton's (1952–59) *The Borrowers*; Christianna Brand's (2005) wonderful *Nurse Matilda* series, filmed in a watered-down form as *Nanny McPhee*; or Nesbit's (1902) *Five Children and It* – the latter also benefiting from Jacqueline Wilson's 2012 sequel, *Four Children and It*). Many of the classics from the early twentieth century have never been out of print and can be timelessly met by a new generation; new examples appear every year.

Activity

Consider some of the fantastic ideas which feature in stories. Can you name a story for each of the features below?

- What if animals could talk and lead social lives like people?
- What if toys came alive and had secret lives of their own?
- What if our wishes could come true?
- What if magical charms, as seen in old fairy stories, turned up in everyday life?
- What if magic were just a subject we could learn like maths and geography?
- What if we were visited by someone from another planet?

Themes in fantasy and magic literature

Such books as David Almond's *Skellig* (1998) or Andrew Norriss's *Aquila* (2001), both of which won the Whitbread Prize, further blur the distinction between magic and science. *Skellig* is set very much in the modern everyday world, in which ten-year-old Michael finds a strange man in the garage – who or what Skellig is is never spelled out or explained – maybe an angel, maybe some strange remnant of another race? *Aquila,* which also ran as a successful series on children's television in the 1990s, tells of the discovery by two boys on a geography field trip of what seems at first to be an ancient Roman relic but turns out to be a vehicle from the future, technologically advanced and also equipped with such devices as an invisibility shield, which gives it an air of magic.

A strong theme, of which writers never seem to tire, is the idea of being grown-up – a perennial fascination for children. The first book to explore this idea was probably F. Anstey's *Vice Versa* (1882), in which a father and son change bodies; the theme has been used by, among others, E. Nesbit (*Five Children and It,* 1902), Edward Eager (*Seven-Day Magic,* 1962), Mary

Rodgers *(Freaky Friday,* 1972) and Hunter Davies, *(Flossie Teacake's Fur Coat,* 1984), as well as many films such as Tom Hanks' *Big* (1998). The humour of the situation in nearly all of these is seeing the child protagonist retaining his own personality and interests while coping with an adult's life and business – a ten-year-old enjoying a driving lesson, for instance, in *Flossie Teacake's Fur Coat*, or a toddler in disguise as a portly gentleman, bouncing around on a train journey singing songs and making loud comments about his fellow-travellers *(Seven Day Magic)*. Only in the Nesbit story does the baby's mind change as his body ages, and the beloved little brother become a supercilious young man who fails to recognise his siblings.

In the case study below a trainee teacher explores being grown up with her class as part of a project on fantasy literature.

Case Study

Amy, a PGCE student, was planning a writing activity for her Year 4 class based on the theme of being grown up. She looked at the text types resources created by the National Strategies and found useful guidance and knowledge for writers of fantasy stories.

- *Choose adjectives carefully to describe the places and things in the story.*

- *Use similes to help the reader imagine what you are describing more clearly. (The glass castle was as big as a football field and as tall as a skyscraper. Its clear walls sparkled like blocks of ice in the sun.)*

- *Don't make everything so fantastic that it is unbelievable.*

- *Make what happens as interesting and detailed as the setting where it happens. Don't get so involved in creating amazing places and characters that you forget to tell a good story about what happens to them.*

(DCSF, 2008a)

Amy decided that she would introduce the children to the theme through reading an episode from *Flossie Teacake's Fur Coat* in which eight-year-old Flossie becomes 18-year-old Floz when she puts on her sister Bella's old fur coat. Although Floz is then able to work as a waitress, go to sixth-form college, have a driving lesson and even go to the pub, she continues to think and act like an eight-year-old. Amy chose the book partly because she had enjoyed it as a child, but also because the adventures can be read as single, complete episodes.

She began by asking her class what kinds of things they would like to do if they were suddenly 18. She had anticipated that there might be some suggestions which she would not wish to pursue, and before asking children to discuss in pairs and note some ideas on miniwhiteboards, she asked them to make sure that their suggestions were ones which they would be happy for their usual teacher to hear. The children came up with a range of ideas including flying a plane, being a footballer, a teacher and a rock star.

→

Amy then introduced the children to Flossie and read an episode in which Flossie becomes a waitress. The children loved the story and laughed loudly several times. Amy then asked them what they liked about the story and what Hunter Davies, the author, had done to make it so enjoyable. The children especially enjoyed the fact that they could relate to Flossie and her frustrations at not being allowed to do things she wanted to do. They liked the fact that through magic she was able to experience things they would not be permitted to do.

Children were asked to work together to create short stories, which could be about Flossie or a character they invented, but they had to devise a means by which their characters changed age and experienced unfamiliar things. Amy had been a little concerned about what some of these might be, but was pleasantly reassured by the choices children made.

Curriculum Links

By using a theme of growing up as the basis for fantasy reading and writing we create opportunities for children to reflect upon the ways in which they change and in which others behave towards them. There are opportunities for discussions in PSHE, as well as research in history projects, perhaps involving children talking to parents, carers and grandparents about changes which have taken place during their lifetimes.

Activity

Consider how you could plan for activities on another common fantasy theme. You could, for example, look at gender change and use Anne Fine's (1989) *Bill's New Frock* as a starting point.

Time travel

Another recurrent aspect of fantasy, both magical and scientific, is time travel. Once again, although the fantasies of H.G. Wells and Jules Verne were already well known, it was E. Nesbit who first achieved widespread success in this area in children's literature. With books such as *The Story of the Amulet* (1906) and *The House of Arden* (1908), where children go into the past to seek something which is lost in the modern world, and *Harding's Luck* (1909), in which the hero moves to and fro between a grim modern life, in which he is a crippled orphan, and a sixteenth-century life, in which he eventually decides to stay as the strong son of loving parents, she suggests a whole realm of different realities and parallel worlds. The idea has also been developed by Alison Uttley: *A Traveller in Time* (1939) tells of Penelope's shifts between her aunt's farm in the twentieth and the sixteenth centuries. Many of Penelope

Lively's children's stories deal in a witty way with relationships with the past – *The Revenge of Samuel Stokes* (1981), for instance, has a modern housing estate haunted by the architect of the eighteenth-century park which lay beneath it. In Penelope Farmer's *Charlotte Sometimes* (1969), a new girl at boarding school regularly exchanges bodies and lives with a pupil at the school in the time of the Great War. Lucy M. Boston's *Green Knowe* stories, written between 1954 and 1976, tell of a lonely child's gradual development of friendships with the generations of children who have lived in the old house before him.

Overlapping realities

A sense of shared place and overlapping realities of time are common themes in such stories. One of the best-known modern classics in this area must be *Tom's Midnight Garden* by Philippa Pearce (1958), in which the magical adventures are linked with speculations about the nature of time as Tom tries to understand what is happening to him in his night-time visits to a garden. The garden seems to move at random backwards and forwards in time, and in Tom's daytime life it no longer exists behind the old house, but he regularly meets and plays with a girl called Hatty there, who also grows older and younger unpredictably from one night to another. Near the end of the book, Hatty says, *Nothing stands still, except in our memory* – a metaphysical comment which is both simple enough for children and complex enough for adult readers. Margery Fisher comments:

> *The author, wisely, attempts no explanation …*
>
> *Authors who try an elaborate analysis, or who lay down rules for a journey into Time, hold up the action of the story and only succeed in bewildering the reader.*

> (1961, p.124)

A more technical style of fantasy is represented by the writings of, for example, Nicholas Fisk. Familiar objects such as animated and responsive toys, or situations such as playing video games, are given an unearthly twist and placed in a futuristic context. Tim Kennemore, Jan Mark, Jean Ure and Joan Aiken have all written highly effective collections of short stories in this genre, many of which could be provocative stimuli for imaginative work in the classroom. Some caution, however, would be needed in the selection, as the distinction between fantasy and the supernatural, and even child-size horror, is blurred, and some of the ideas in such stories could upset children and offend parents.

Activity

Consider if there are any children's stories which include fantasy and supernatural themes which you would avoid using in the classroom. Discuss your views with a colleague.

At first glance it seems almost a truism that these books represent escapism, and are designed to stretch the imagination and add a dimension of excitement to everyday life. However, from the earliest examples there has almost invariably been some kind of moral lesson involved. Mrs Doasyouwouldbedoneby and Mrs Bedonebyasyoudid, in *The Water Babies* (Kingsley, 2008), teach Tom the lesson that *the soul makes the body* as he gradually learns to 'be clean'. The magic creatures who are frequently the guides to new worlds often appear very moral (the Psammead in *Five Children and It* is fond of lecturing the children on their manners; the cuckoo in Mrs Molesworth's (1927) *The Cuckoo Clock* speaks like a stern tutor or governess; the Mouldiwarp in *The House of Arden* tells the children that they can have no magic unless they have not quarrelled for the previous three days.) Ursula Le Guin's *A Wizard of Earthsea* (1968) has to learn, slowly and cautiously, that *To light a candle is to cast a shadow* – in other words, every deed has two sides to be considered.

Research Focus

The Harry Potter phenomenon

Gupta (2009) describes the extraordinary phenomenon of the Harry Potter books, which were translated into more than 60 languages, made into films, generated fan websites, computer games and *a vast range of Harry Potter-branded commodities (picture books, postcards, posters, playing cards, cups, t-shirts etc.); textbooks and curricula at various levels excavated the books; an immense amount of mass media and academic writing was devoted to them* (p.339).

Indeed, at the School of Education at Durham University a popular undergraduate module is Harry Potter and the Age of Illusion, whose aims are:

- to place the phenomenon that is Harry Potter in its social, cultural and educational context and understand some of the reasons for its popularity;

- to consider the relevance of Harry Potter to the education system in the twenty-first century;

- to understand twenty-first century education in the light that the Harry Potter series, and other educational fiction, casts on it;

- to make explicit connections between Harry Potter and citizenship education.

It is clear that fantasy and magic are as popular as ever and this is illustrated by the Potter phenomenon reaching China where Gupta notes:

… where children's books usually have a print run of 10,000, the first three Harry Potter™ translations had first print runs of 200,000 each. The enormous success of Harry Potter™ in China is marked by the increasing print runs for subsequent books in translation: the fourth (Goblet of Fire) had a first print run of 400,000, the fifth and sixth (Order of the Phoenix and Half-Blood Prince) of 800,000, and the final book of 1 million.

(2009, p.341)

→

Gupta describes discussions at a workshop at Peking University on 'Harry Potter in China' and comments that:

> it was generally agreed that the Harry Potter phenomenon in China was an aspect of China's emerging place in the world stage as an economic and cultural force. It was observed that the phenomenon was both impelled by and has generated a greater sense of connectedness with the world, and a widely shared feeling that China has an active global role to undertake in the future.

(2009, p.346)

One wonders if J.K. Rowling had any notion that her stories might have such impact when she began to write them in an Edinburgh café.

A key feature of many fantasy stories is the choice of device which authors use to effect a transformation in the characters or in the settings of their stories. In the case study below, a trainee teacher devises an inventive method of exploring these.

Case Study

Yousef, a PGCE trainee, wanted to look at magical devices with his Year 4 class and decided to focus on a range of popular stories in which a change was effected to settings or characters.

He began by asking the children about different devices which they knew about from stories they had read or heard, including those from TV dramas and films. At first, the children found it difficult to think of many ideas.

Rather than asking children to write stories straight away, Yousef encouraged them to explore a range of fantasy and magic tales by showing them how they could make simple board games which involved dice and counters and magic cards. He created an example in which the players had to throw dice and move their counters on a 100-square board, similar to snakes and ladders but without the serpents and ladders, which had 15 squares labelled 'magic'. If a player landed on one, they had to take a magic card, read it and then move backwards or forwards a stated number of squares according to whether the magic was good or evil. Children were asked to work in groups of three or four to come up with ideas for the magic cards and to create a board game with instructions for other groups to play. They could use established ideas, providing they included the name of the story they came from, or they could make up their own.

Yousef provided a selection of fantasy and magic story books and a list of examples of ways in which characters moved from one world to another:

- *Harry Potter:* platform $9\frac{3}{4}$;

- *The Lion, the Witch and the Wardrobe:* a wardrobe;

→

- *The Voyage of the Dawn Treader*: a painting;

- *Peter Pan*: magical flight;

- *Charlotte Sometimes*: sleeping in a certain bed;

- *Flossie Teacake*: wearing a fur coat;

- *Alice*: drinking from a bottle.

The activity went well and children enthusiastically created many ideas for spells and portals to take characters to other worlds or other ages, or to bring good or bad fortune. Examples produced by the children included the following.

- *You find a secret trapdoor and open it. Inside you find a jungle full of wild animals. Go back six spaces.*

- *You are given a magic sweet. When you suck it you become invisible and no one can see you moving. Go on ten spaces.*

- *You meet an old wizard who offers you a magic potion. Take another Magic card to see what happens when you drink it.*

In subsequent lessons, Yousef asked children to choose a magic card in pairs and to write a few paragraphs about what happened to them or the characters they chose after they followed the magic card's instructions.

Curriculum Links

The work Yousef's class engaged in offers opportunities for children to look closely at familiar stories and to learn about less familiar ones. Through this exploration they can develop ideas for their own writing and for drama activities. The work also lends itself to co-operative learning and many speaking and listening activities.

In addition, the National Curriculum Years 3–4 programme of study (DfE, 2013) states that pupils should increase:

- *their familiarity with a wide range of books, including fairy stories, myths and legends.*

(p.35)

They should also be able to identify themes and conventions in a wide range of books. These might include elements such as good triumphing over evil or understanding some of the magical devices used by authors.

In some areas of fantasy fiction, particularly in the earliest books, the magic world is eventually shown to be some form of heavenly afterlife, which the child eventually attains by dying.

George Macdonald's *At the Back of the North Wind* (1871) is a classic example, with its ending: *A lovely figure, as white and almost as clear as alabaster, was lying on the bed … They thought he was dead. I knew that he had gone to the back of the North Wind.* Even as recently as 1956, in the final book of C.S. Lewis's (1951–56) *Chronicles of Narnia* series, death is still seen to be a desirable ending for the characters, as this is how they achieve eternal life in the world which equates to the Christian idea of Heaven. Much has been written about the overt and hidden Christian symbolism and messages of the seven books in this series. They are wonderfully exciting stories, with humour, good characterisation and many ingenious nods to the classic tales of Homer and Virgil which were Lewis's passion, but the ending in which all the visitors from this world are found to have been killed in a train crash so that they can enjoy Narnian heaven for ever is one which many readers have found less than satisfactory on many levels. Indeed, Philip Pullman's *His Dark Materials* trilogy was in part intended as a direct counter to this overtly Christian message: *I hate the* Narnia *books, and I hate them with a deep and bitter passion* (cited in Gooderham, 2003).

More rewarding in many ways, because more subtle and thought provoking, is the conclusion to Arthur Calder-Marshall's *The Fair to Middling* (1960). In this book, the orphans of the Winterbottome Home, all of whom have some disability, are offered through strange adventures the chance to become normal; all, in different ways, make the decision to accept what they are and work towards understanding their situation better.

Research Focus

High and low fantasy

Gamble and Yates (2002) describe two types of fantasy: high and low. In low fantasy *non-rational happenings occur in the rational world* (p.102), as, for example, in Dahl's *The Magic Finger*, in which a girl has the power to use her finger to make things happen, or in *Matilda*, where the heroine has kinetic powers which enable her to make things move. In both examples, the world in which the story is set is familiar and recognisable to the reader.

In high fantasy, events take place in an alternative world which might be entered *through a portal from the primary world* (p.103), as in Lewis' *Narnia* series, or the alternative world might be a world within a world which only special people can enter, such as Hogwarts in the Harry Potter series. The alternative world might also be one in which it is assumed that the primary world does not exist, for example Middle-Earth in Tolkien's (1998) *The Hobbit* and *Lord of the Rings*.

In the case study below you will see that there are opportunities to make links between fantasy worlds and their representations in maps. Consider how you could develop children's understanding of cartography while encouraging them to develop their knowledge of fantasy worlds.

Case Study

Imogen, a PGCE trainee, decided to combine work in geography on maps with a study of fantasy and other genres of fiction. She made a collection of stories which include maps and which would be familiar to her Year 6 class, either through having read the books or seen the film versions. She found the following and created copies to show to the children. (Please take note of copyright laws when copying texts.)

Adams, R. (1972) *Watership Down*. London: Rex Collings.

Grahame, K. (1958) *The Wind in the Willows*. London: Methuen (first published 1908).

Jansson, T. (1950) *Finn Family Moomintroll* (trans. Elizabeth Portch). London: Ernest Benn.

Milne, A.A. (1926) *Winnie-the-Pooh*. London: Methuen.

Pullman, P. (2003) *Lyra's Oxford*. London: Fickling.

Tolkien, J.R.R. (1937) *The Hobbit*. London: George Allen & Unwin.

Having shown the maps to her class and discussed them, Imogen asked children to work in pairs to create maps for their favourite stories. She modelled this by talking with them about a story they had recently read as a class, Kenneth Grahame's (1958) *The Wind in the Willows*.

Curriculum Links

An interesting follow-up to this activity could be to explore early maps. These often resemble some of those which authors of fantasy fiction create. Comparing different types of maps, from ordnance survey to relief maps to maps which accompany stories, can help develop children's awareness of different ways in which features can be represented.

Activity

Consider some of the stories which you know (the list at the end of the chapter will help you) and decide whether they represent high or low fantasy.

Conclusion

The many areas in which fiction can extend beyond the real, then, have been used by authors to present for children ideas about religion, philosophy, history and even maths and physics – an example here being Russell Stannard's (1989) *Uncle Albert* trilogy, an entertaining foray into fiction by a distinguished particle physicist. But the most important contribution fantasy stories make, surely, is the confirmation for the reader that the world of reading is always one of infinite possibility.

Learning Outcomes Review

You should now have an increased awareness of the fantasy and magic genre and the range of texts available, and have considered classroom activities related to the genre.

Self-assessment questions

1   What do you understand by the terms high and low fantasy?
2   Are there any aspects of magic and fantasy fiction which you would avoid?

Further Reading

Joan Aiken – see the Chapter 7 on traditional tales for a wider discussion of this author's short magic stories. Her 'Hanoverian sequence' of novels, set in a fictional version of the nineteenth century, contain mystic and magical elements as well.

Nicholas Fisk – science fiction stories such as *Trillions, Sweets From a Stranger* and *Grinny*, in which ideas such as teleportation, animated toys and artificial intelligence are explored. Perhaps an interesting starting point for discussing when magic becomes science fiction.

Tim Kennemore – In her witty book of short stories, *Here Tomorrow, Gone Today* the writer sets some in a recognisable but slightly futuristic world in which, for example, extreme old age becomes the latest look of choice among teenagers.

Robinson, C.N. (2003) Good and evil in popular children's fantasy fiction: How archetypes become stereotypes that cultivate the next generation of *Sun* readers. *English in Education,* 37(2): 29–36.

Jean Ure – as well as many good novels for older children, this author has written some ghost stories for younger readers which are exciting but neither sad nor scary. Try *A Twist in Time* (Walker Books, 2000) or *The Girl in the Blue Tunic* (Scholastic, 1997).

References

Almond, D. (1998) *Skellig.* London: Hodder.

Anstey, F. (2008) *Vice Versa.* Gutenberg e-book (first published 1882).

Boston, L.M. (1954–72) *Green Knowe* series. London: Faber and Faber.

Brand, C. (2005) *Nurse Matilda – the Collected Tales.* London: Bloomsbury (first published 1964–70).

Calder-Marshall, A. (1960) *The Fair to Middling.* London: Puffin.

Carroll, L. (1998) *Alice's Adventures in Wonderland.* London: Macmillan (first published 1865).

Davies, H. (1984) *Flossie Teacake's Fur Coat.* London: Puffin.

DCSF (2008) The National Strategies *Primary Support for Writing, Fiction.* 00468-2008DWO-EN-12.

DfE (2013) *The National Curriculum in England: Key Stages 1 and 2 Framework Document.* London: DfE. Available at: www.gov.uk/government/uploads/system/uploads/attachment_data/file/335133/PRIMARY_national_curriculum_220714.pdf (accessed 12.04.16).

Eager, E. (1962) *Seven-Day Magic.* New York: Harcourt Brace Young.

Farmer, P. (1969) *Charlotte Sometimes.* London: Puffin.

Fisher, M. (1961) *Intent on Reading.* London: Brockhampton Press.

Gamble, N. and Yates, S. (2002) *Exploring Children s Literature.* London: Paul Chapman.

Gooderham, D. (2003) Fantasizing It As It Is: Religious Language in Philip Pullman's Trilogy, His Dark Materials. *Children's Literature,* 31: 155–75.

Grahame, K. (1958) *The Wind in the Willows.* London: Methuen.

Gupta, S. (2009) Harry Potter goes to China, in Maybin, J. and Watson, N. (eds) *Children's Literature: Approaches and Territories.* London: Palgrave Macmillan. pp.338–52.

Kingsley, C. (2008) *The Water Babies.* Gutenberg e-book (first published 1862–83).

Le Guin, U. (1968) *A Wizard of Earthsea.* London: Puffin.

Lewis, C.S. (1951–56) *Chronicles of Narnia.* London: Bodley Head.

Lively, P. (1981) *The Revenge of Samuel Stokes.* London: Heinemann.

Macdonald, G. (1871) *At the Back of the North Wind.* London: Ward Lock.

Molesworth, Mrs (1927) *The Cuckoo Clock.* London: Macmillan (first published 1877).

Nesbit, E. (1902) *Five Children and It.* London: T. Fisher Unwin.

Nesbit, E. (1905) *The Story of the Amulet.* London: T. Fisher Unwin.

Nesbit, E. (1908) *The House of Arden.* London: T. Fisher Unwin.

Nesbit, E. (1909) *Harding's Luck.* London: T. Fisher Unwin.

Norriss, A. (2001) *Aquila.* London: Puffin.

Norton, M. (1952–59) *The Borrowers* series. London: Puffin.

Pearce, P. (1958) *Tom's Midnight Garden.* Oxford: Oxford University Press.

Rodgers, M. (1972) *Freaky Friday.* New York: Harper Collins.

Rowling, J.K. (1998–2009) *Harry Potter* series. London: Bloomsbury.

Stannard, R. (1989) *The Time and Space of Uncle Albert.* London: Faber & Faber.

Tolkien, J.R.R. (1998) *The Hobbit.* London: Collins (first published 1937).

Tolkien, J.R.R. (1998) *Lord of the Rings.* London: Collins (first published 1954–55).

Uttley, A. (1939) *A Traveller in Time.* London: Puffin.

Wilson, J. (2012) *Four Children and It.* London: Puffin.

10 Classic fiction

Learning Outcomes

By reading this chapter you will:

- consider what is meant by classic children's literature;
- identify some texts regarded as classic children's literature;
- consider how we define a classic;
- think about why we read classic books with children;
- understand and critique the 'golden age' of children's books;
- reflect on the issue of modern classics;
- consider how we can introduce adult classics to children.

Introduction

Pieces of eight! Curiouser and curiouser! Do you believe in fairies? Do these words make you *smile like a Cheshire Cat,* or feel that it's *time for a Little Something?* Or would you rather just be *messing about on the river?*

If any of these phrases rings a bell with you, then you probably already realise the extent to which the books which have been shared by generations of children have become embedded in the English we use every day. Many such examples are used frequently without our even realising it; perhaps, then, it is worth introducing a new generation to this literature to give them the sense of recognition, *so that's where* that *comes from.* However, in a survey by the British Library, reported in the *Times Educational Supplement* (Bloom, 2014), 82 per cent of teachers said that they had seen children struggling to identify with classic authors such as Dickens, Austen and Charlotte Brontë. The survey of 520 teachers also concluded that 76 per cent of the teachers believe that the children find it difficult to think of the authors as real people with real lives. In the same article, entitled 'Why Classic Authors are Dead to Pupils', Bethan Marshall, a lecturer in English education commented that: *They think they're completely irrelevant. Authors now seem more real than those who wrote hundreds of years ago.* So, clearly, there is much for us to do in schools if we wish to engage and maintain children's interest and enjoyment of classic fiction.

Activity

Which of these books can you identify?

1. Which author included the characters Tweedledum and Tweedledee in a book?
2. In which land did Gulliver find that the people were very small?
3. Who wrote stories in which his son had friends including a bear and a tiger?
4. What were Timmy, George, Julian, Anne and Dick known as collectively?
5. In which story does Augustus Gloop appear and what personality trait does he display?
6. Near to the end of which book does a female character scream, 'Oh! My Daddy, my Daddy!'
7. Whose driving in *The Wind in the Willows* leads to trouble with the law?
8. In which story does the Darling family appear?
9. In which story does the central character meet a scarecrow, a lion and a tin man?

Answers at the end of the chapter.

Ask any group of readers what they would count as the classic books of children's literature, and there will generally be some consensus over the titles included. Informal research suggests that Lewis Carroll's (1998) *Alice* books are always among the first to be mentioned, followed by A.A. Milne's (1924; 1926; 1927; 1928) *Winnie the Pooh* books, Grahame's (1994) *The Wind in the Willows* and Stevenson's (1994) *Treasure Island*. Women nearly always include Alcott's (1994) *Little Women* (and often Coolidge's (1872) *What Katy Did*), though men seem largely unaware of these books, and the 'boys' books' which were popular at the end of the nineteenth century have by and large not stood the test of time so well and are now read only as period pieces; Ballantyne's *The Coral Island,* for instance, or Jeffries' *Bevis,* both blockbusters in their day, have been more or less ignored for generations. E. Nesbit's (1995) *The Railway Children* is usually in the list, due perhaps to the lasting popularity of its filmed versions, and Frances Hodgson Burnett's (1994) *The Secret Garden,* with the same author's *A Little Princess* (1996) greatly loved by girls, and the work most popular for its author in its day, *Little Lord Fauntleroy* (1886), completely ignored.

The case study below shows how a book considered to be a classic children's text can be used across the curriculum. Notice how the book is the starting point for a wide range of learning in a number of different curriculum areas, and how it offers a context for the children's learning.

Case Study

Using a classic as a starting point for classwork

In the school in which Rani, a third-year student, was going to do her final placement all children read a book each term. Time in each day was given to reading and each class chose and read a text. The book that her class had read the previous term, and thoroughly enjoyed, was *The Secret Garden*, and the class teacher wanted to build on this interest and engagement. They decided to use this for some cross-curricular work.

The children identified aspects of the book that had delighted or intrigued them and were given the opportunity to follow this through as a sustained piece of work over a number of weeks. They were encouraged to keep returning to the text to focus their work. Topics that the children chose to do included:

- growing roses;

- investigating the lives of British families in India in the late nineteenth century;

- creating portraits of the characters;

- investigating cholera;

- finding out about the landscape, flora and fauna of North Yorkshire;

- investigating the wildlife of the Yorkshire moors;

- finding out about antecedents to titled families;

- understanding the architecture of stately homes;

- baking 'Mrs Sowerby' buns;

- creating 3D 'shoebox' representations of the secret garden;

- investigating the life of servants in houses like Misselthwaite.

The children were able to choose how they represented their learning. This included 2D and 3D artwork, presentations through PowerPoint and posters, photographs, displays, computer animations, books, roses to admire and buns to eat. They also read parts of *The Painted Garden* by Noel Streatfeild, a novel in which the central character, awkward ten-year-old Jane, is given the part of Mary in a Hollywood production of *The Secret Garden*; the contrast between the child actors and the parts they are playing gives the story a great deal of human interest. The work culminated in a day in which the children presented all that they had done to one another. The day included 'Mrs Sowerby' buns. Finally, the children watched the film of the book and were delighted to compare what they now knew and had imagined with the filmmaker's interpretations of Burnett's work.

The text in this case study was used as a stimulus for work across a range of curriculum areas. The text provided the initial impetus and coherence between the different aspects of learning as children pursued their own interests and ideas. The presentation of their learning focused the children's efforts on both the content and how best to communicate their learning, and it enabled learning across the curriculum for all the children. Finally, watching the film offered an opportunity for the children to reflect on what they had learned.

Curriculum Links

A number of subject areas were covered in this cross-curricular work. The case study demonstrates one way of planning and teaching, one in which the work is highly contextualised and the children have a significant degree of ownership over how they engage with, and represent, their learning.

Why read classic books?

It has been said that *the great function of literature is to extend one's sympathy* – like travel, it broadens the mind. Reading the classic stories of the past opens the window for imaginative children into whole new worlds which they can only profit from knowing. So what have these works, and others of their time which are still read for pleasure, in common? Can any book which is still known and read 100 years or more after it was written be called classic simply because of its longevity?

The literary canon

Classic books often form part of the literary canon. In an educational context the literary canon usually refers to the specification of named texts that are in the syllabus of a school or university. The literary canon can be understood in a number of ways: an official literary canon sets down the texts which must be taught and becomes part of the statutory curriculum; a de facto literary canon is one that emerges from practice and may not have official status but, nevertheless, is clearly observable in what is taught in schools; in a compromise between the two there is a range of identified texts from which teachers can choose what to study (Fleming, 2007). In all these cases, somebody somewhere is making a decision about what is included and what is not included.

While perhaps this is not such a significant issue in the primary school where teachers have more freedom to choose texts, it is worth reflecting on which books we choose to use in the classroom and the implications of these choices.

Traditional reasons for choosing classic texts (or texts from the literary canon) have been associated with:

- notions of quality – selection of texts by authors considered to be 'the best';
- texts that are considered to have particular cultural significance;
- texts which are considered to have particular historical significance;
- texts which have a social significance.

These texts have thus acquired a certain status in society, and therefore reading and knowing about them has an associated social, cultural and educational status. Those who argue for inclusion of classic texts in schools argue that all children should have the right to engagement with these texts. It is considered that these texts are part of a child's entitlement to the cultural capital (forms of knowledge, skill, education and other advantages that give people status in society) of the society in which they are growing and learning. One aspect of the argument for these texts to be part of the school curriculum is based on issues of equality and social inclusion. It is argued that, whereas some children will have access to a range of texts in the home, including classic texts, other children will not have the same opportunities. Therefore, schools should provide these opportunities.

These arguments for a literary canon do, however, give rise to questions about what should be included. What is 'the best' literature, and which books have cultural, social and historical significance within any given society? There have been fierce criticisms of traditional notions of a literary canon by post-colonial (a set of theories that critique the cultural legacy of colonial rule) and feminist theorists. These theorists have questioned the dominance of texts written by white, middle-class men. Others have critiqued the relevance of many classic texts, arguing that more contemporary literature has greater resonance for children. Some also argue that the canon is based on an unquestioning reverence and acceptance for certain texts rather than a critical and questioning approach. A more recent critique with the emergence of new technologies is that the literary canon only engages with the written text and not other forms of literacy and texts now available in different forms (Fleming, 2007).

Many questions remain: Should there be an official literary canon? Should teachers be able to choose any texts to teach in school? Should children have an entitlement to the literary canon? If there is a literary canon, who should define it? What should be included? How much of it should be statutory? These things are not necessarily mutually exclusive. There will always be likely to be at least a de facto literary canon, as there is likely to be some consensus between teachers about what should be taught, and this is likely to include some classic texts. However, these debates remain ongoing and are given fresh impetus each time we debate revisions to the National Curriculum. Perhaps it is because fundamentally the arguments cannot be dissociated from what we as a society believe about the aims and purposes of education. As Eagleton (1983) argues, it is important to see the literary canon as a construct; there is no such thing as a literary canon outside the context in which it is situated.

For us as primary school teachers it is important that we are aware of these debates so that we can make informed choices about the books that we select to have in our classroom and use in our teaching.

Activity

I believe these books are classic because of their unfettered reach of imagination, the nobility and innocence of their child heroes and heroines, and the simple themes of quest, beauty, bravery, and compassion.

(Wharton, n.d.)

When asked we can usually come up with some books that are regarded as classic children's literature. But what defines a classic? Here are some suggestions:

- strong main characters;
- strong setting;
- can be enjoyed at different levels by readers of different ages;
- contains universal human themes including:

  - about the world and the human heart;
  - about moral and aesthetic goodness;

- is *a text that has wide readership that has gained status over time and is considered a standard of its genre* (Randall and Hardman, 2002, p88);
- has a message in the text that readers can reflect on and use as a model for living their lives in certain ways;
- a book that has lasted more than one generation.

Consider Nesbit's (1995) *The Railway Children.*

- Which of these features does it have?
- What else would you add to the list? Why?
- Choose a different book that you regard as a classic. Consider it against the suggestions above, including any that you have added.
- So, what makes a classic?

The golden age of children's books

Many of the books we now think of as children's classics were written in the period between the mid-1860s and the 1920s. This is often referred to as the golden age of children's literature. *The Water Babies* appeared in 1862–63, *Alice's Adventures in Wonderland* in 1865, and *The Light Princess,* the first of George MacDonald's fairy stories, in 1864. Although all of these contain elements which were satirising or making commentary on the education of their day, they were written primarily to entertain the reader rather than to teach him or her how to be a better person. The name is partly taken from Kenneth Grahame's first book, *The Golden Age* (1895), which is a collection of short stories whose central child characters see the adults in their lives as another, remote, species, 'The Olympians'. Whole new worlds for children were invented: the Never Land, Through the Looking Glass, the Enchanted Places, the Secret Garden – the worlds where magic could and did happen. This recognition that children lead an imaginative life of their own which can be quite detached from the adult world around them was one of the new features which distinguished the books of such writers as Lewis Carroll, E. Nesbit (1958; 1902; 1908; 1909; 1995) and Frances Hodgson Burnett, to name but three of the writers from this time whose works are still read and loved. Books were appearing written for the younger reader, with no overt purpose of improving the character; their purpose was to amuse and delight.

The big innovations of the golden age books though, can be summed up as follows.

- Children are acting independently and are in control.

- Parents and adults become background figures.

- Magic can happen.

- Even wrongdoing can turn out right – or at any rate, as a valuable experience.

Some critics consider that the golden age ended with the century, while others suggest that it ended with the First World War in 1914, whose 'reality shock' shook up the whole perception of childhood and innocence. Humphrey Carpenter (1985) defines it as *from Alice to Winnie the Pooh* (1926). Certainly it was over by the end of the twenties, just as the cult of childhood and the fashion for baby parties had ended with the Wall Street Crash and the Depression. The changes it had introduced, though, and many of the books, have remained a lasting legacy.

Humphrey Carpenter (1985), in his study of children's literature, *Secret Gardens,* identified what he sees as the crucial difference between the earliest books for children and those which began to appear from the 1860s onwards – the absence of parents and of overt moral instruction.

> *All children's books are about ideals. Adult fiction sets out to portray the world as it really is; books for children present it as it should be. Child readers come hoping for a certain amount of instruction, but chiefly for stories in which the petty restrictions of life are removed …. Adults, on the other hand, are more likely to want to feed them a set of moral examples.*

> (p.1)

The characters in the stories are still expected to learn something from their experiences – think of Alice having her morals improved by everyone she meets, or Tom in Kingsley's *The Water Babies* meeting Mrs Doasyouwouldbedoneby and Mrs Bedonebyasyoudid – but they are not, on the whole, subjected to punishments or homilies by their parents at the end of each episode. There is certainly still a hidden agenda of moral improvement – the Victorians do not seem, perhaps, to have felt that it would be good for children to read simply for entertainment or in order to exercise their imaginations.

It is also noticeable that the lessons are still distinctly divided by sex – R.M. Ballantyne, for instance, one of the most popular early authors of exotic adventures, wrote in The *Gorilla Hunters* (1862):

> *Boys {should be} inured from childhood to trifling risks and slight dangers of every possible description, such as tumbling into ponds and off trees, etc., in order to strengthen their nervous system ... They ought to practise leaping off heights into deep water. They ought never to hesitate to cross a stream over a narrow unsafe plank for fear of a ducking. They ought never to decline to climb up a tree, to pull fruit merely because there is a possibility of their falling off and breaking their necks. I firmly believe that boys were intended to encounter all kinds of risks, in order to prepare them to meet and grapple with risks and dangers incident to man's career with cool, cautious self-possession ...*

(p.44)

After all, these boys will have a mighty empire to defend and rule when they grow up. Girls, on the other hand, will grow up to be wives and mothers in the Victorian pattern of things, and so must learn to be domestic angels and 'little mothers' to their younger siblings. Even girls who are sparky, feisty and rebellious when we first meet them – Johanna Spyri's (1969) *Heidi*, Susan Coolidge's *Katy*, L.M. Montgomery's *Anne of Green Gables*, or Louisa May Alcott's Jo, for example – are likely to disappoint any Victorian girl reader when they become increasingly docile, domestic and sweet embodiments of Christian virtue through series of sequels.

The case study below shows how children were encouraged to consider how boys and girls are represented in classic and contemporary fiction. Notice how the teacher enabled children to come to their own understanding and to demonstrate their understanding through representing it in performance.

Case Study

Comparing characters in classic and contemporary fiction

The children in the class were given an envelope with the name on it of a character from a book. Inside the envelope were details of sections of a book that they must read to find out about their character. The children were given the task of reading the sections and creating a pen portrait of their character. They had to glean as much as possible about the character from the text.

The class teacher had selected contrasting characters and passages to illustrate the differences between life as a girl or boy in classic fiction and in more contemporary fiction.

→

Once the pen portraits were completed the children were placed in pairs and asked to compile a dialogue that revealed the differences. Some children chose to do them as formal interviews, some as comedy, some as dramatised conversations. One group chose to do a poem in which the differences were revealed in interleaved lines, and one group wrote a rap. The dialogues were then worked into performances, videoed and shown to the whole class.

Reading and comparing the representations of girls and boys in classic and contemporary fiction enabled the children to consider and draw their own conclusions about how things had changed. Using children's literature provided a meaningful content for this learning.

Curriculum Links

Engaging children in considering gender roles and identities across time, and presenting the differences as a dialogue, has the potential for learning in a number of curriculum areas. Issues of gender can be considered in PSHE. An understanding of the roles of men and women in society can contribute to children's historical understanding of how the past is different from the present. Additionally, novels can be considered as a source of information about the past. In English, children have the opportunity to learn and develop a range of knowledge and skills in the National Curriculum (DfE, 2013), including the following:

Comprehension (Years 3–4)

- listening to, discussing and expressing views about a wide range of contemporary and classic poetry, stories and non-fiction at a level beyond that at which they can read independently;
- increasing their familiarity with a wide range of books;
- preparing poems and play scripts to read aloud and to perform, showing understanding through intonation, tone, volume and action;
- participating in discussion about books, taking turns and listening to what others say.

Composition (Years 3–4)

Drafting and writing by:

- composing and rehearsing sentences orally (including dialogue), progressively building a varied and rich vocabulary and an increasing range of sentence structures.

These elements of the curriculum are also part of the programme of study for Years 5–6, building on and enhancing what was learned in Years 3–4.

Creating and performing a dialogue provides an opportunity to learn about drama and performance and this performance element also included the ICT skills of recording and showing the performances.

Research Focus

Critiquing golden age literature

Gubar (2009) in her text *Artful Dodgers: Reconceiving the Golden age of Children's Literature*, argues that:

> There is something odd about the way scholars treat the Golden Age of children's literature. On the one hand, the unprecedented explosion of children's literature ... has been accorded immense respect as the 'Golden Age' moniker indicates ...Yet the same authors who have been given the most credit for making the Golden Age golden have simultaneously been censured for producing escapist literature that failed to engage with the complexities of contemporary life and promoted a static, and highly idealised picture of childhood as a time of primitive simplicity.
>
> (p.vii)

She argues that this critical account underestimates the richness and complexity of golden age literature.

Gubar develops a thesis that the Victorians' representations of children are diverse and dynamic. She draws parallels with the recognition that there is no single interpretation of the 'Romantic Child' in the Romantics movement and, similarly, that the Victorians' view of children and childhood in their literature reflects conflicting conceptualisations. She argues that:

> two concurrent intertwined phenomena – Golden Age children's literature and the cult of the child – must be reconceived to reflect the fact that many of the male and female artists who participated in them were conflicted about how to conceive of children rather than fully committed to an idea of innocence. Moreover, ... the Victorians and Edwardians frequently manifest a high level of critical self-consciousness about the whole problem of representing, writing for, looking at, interacting with, and worshipping children.
>
> (Gubar, 2009, p.viii)

Gubar's reconceptualisation of the cult of the child shows that in their artwork and writing many of the key members of the cult were informed

> not simply (or even mainly) by primitivism but by a habit of extolling the child's innocent simplicity while simultaneously indulging a profound fascination with useful sharpness and precocity.
>
> (2009, p.ix)

This reconceptualisation is used in Gubar's thesis to look again at a number of the writers of golden age children's literature identified in this chapter.

An interesting consideration is the popularity of girls' school stories; throughout this time, and right up until the 1960s, the works of Angela Brazil, Elinor Brent-Dyer (The *Chalet School* series), Dorita Fairlie Bruce *(Dimsie* and *Springdale* series) and many others in the genre reigned supreme among girls as no similar books for boys did. There seems a strong case for arguing that, just as children could only achieve their adventures in a world without parents around to cramp their style, so girls can only attain their full potential in a community without boys. In a girls' school, female characters can be bold, reckless, adventurous, even rule-breakers, in a way which would not have been expected of them in a mixed group of children.

Research Focus

Gender in twentieth-century children's books

The overt distinctions made between expectations of boys and girls in texts regarded as classic fiction are perhaps easy to dismiss as 'of its time'. However, the research outlined below suggests that, while things have changed, they have not perhaps moved as far as we might think.

In their investigation of 'Gender in Twentieth Century Children's Books' McCabe, et al. (2011) analysed the representation of males and females in the titles and central characters of 5,618 children's books published in the twentieth century in the USA.

They found that:

- compared to females, males are represented twice as often in titles and 1.6 times as often as the central character(s);

- in none of the book series investigated are females represented more frequently than males;

- the 1930s–60s exhibit greater disparities than earlier and later periods.

The authors conclude unequivocally that *the disparities we find point to the symbolic annihilation of women and girls in twentieth century children's literature, suggesting to children that these characters are less important than their male counterparts'* (2011, p.218).

Considering characterisation

In her study of the work of E. Nesbit, *Magic and the Magician*, Noel Streatfeild (1958) writes: *One way of gauging the aliveness of a family in a book is to ask yourself: 'Would I know them if they sat opposite to me in a bus?' The answer in the best books is inevitably 'yes'* (p.71). Even though film and television have gained in ubiquity since 1958, this is still an interesting test to apply to the books we love. Most children would probably recognise Harry Potter, even if he didn't look exactly like Daniel Radcliffe. What about Alice, Mary Lennox and Dickon Sowerby from *The Secret Garden*, The March girls from *Little Women*, The Famous Five, or Horrid Henry?

Activity

Many authors don't tell us what their characters look like.

- How do we build a picture of the appearance of characters where authors aren't explicit about it?
- Why do you think some writers choose to create characters in this way?
- What are the implications of this?

TV producers and filmmakers have a powerful influence on characterisation; think of Harry Potter, or the Railway Children, or Johnny Depp's recent interpretation of the Mad Hatter in Alice in Wonderland. They have all been imagined by the creative processes behind the production.

- Find out about how filmmakers, TV producers and actors approach creating well-known characters for film/TV. What do they take into account? Who is involved? What do they see as their responsibility to the text and the author? What are the implications of this when the text is a well-known classic text?

There is a saying that, 'the pictures are better on the radio'.

- Do you think that this also applies to books? Are the characters as imagined more resonant than those created by filmmakers and TV producers?

Modern classics

The term 'modern classic' is frequently used; among others, it has been applied to the work of Philip Pullman, Michael Morpurgo, J.K. Rowling, C.S. Lewis, Malorie Blackman and Eric Carle (*The Very Hungry Caterpillar*). What do we mean by using this term? Does it imply more than that these works are immensely popular with a generation of readers? Are we saying something about the quality of the writing, the durability of the themes, or that they are books that we feel guiltily that we ought to have read even if we haven't?

Activity

- Identify a contemporary book for children that is highly regarded.
- Consider it against the features of a classic text identified earlier in the chapter.
- Do you consider this contemporary text to be a classic? Justify your response.
- Which contemporary books in your opinion are, or will become, classic children's literature? Why?

Moving on to adult classics

Many readers first come to adult classics by way of scenes or sections in them which introduce the main protagonist as a child – Jane Eyre at Lowood, for instance, Pip in *Great Expectations*, or David Copperfield. Although it would probably not be sensible to attempt an entire Dickens or George Eliot novel in the classroom, many children would be engaged by the scene of Maggie Tulliver welcoming her brother home from school (from *The Mill on the Floss*) or Pip meeting the escaped convict in the churchyard – and if such introductions can give children a taste for following these stories at a later date, then few would deny that the introduction was worthwhile. The case study below shows how a classic text can be used with older primary aged children. Notice the reasons why the trainee chose this text, including what he hoped the impact would be for the children's engagement with classic texts, and how he used the text in a developmentally appropriate way with the children.

Case Study

Using adult classics in the primary classroom

As part of a series of English lessons for Year 6, Giles, a second-year student, was asked to develop the children's creative writing. As a provocation to writing he decided to use some YouTube clips of classic fiction. He looked through the many which are available on YouTube and decided to use the graveyard scene from Charles Dickens' *Great Expectations*. There were a number of reasons for this choice.

- It is dramatic and therefore likely to engage the children.

- It has a strong affective content.

- A number of themes are introduced which offer opportunities for the children to develop their own ideas.

- Although there are only two characters in the scene a number of characters are alluded to which again offers opportunities for children to develop their ideas.

- It provided an introduction for the children to what is regarded as excellent literature.

In the initial lesson Giles set the room up by making it dark. After he had introduced the lesson the children went into the darkened room and Giles played the clip. Once it had finished the children were asked to decide whose story they would like to tell. They had the opportunity to discuss their ideas in pairs and he had also prepared a series of prompt cards for children who needed some support with developing their ideas. These included the following.

- Imagine you are the man. Why are you wearing chains? Why are you dressed in those clothes? Why are you so hungry? What are you feeling? What do you think about Pip?

→

- Imagine you are the boy. What happened to your parents? Why are you coming to their graves? What are you feeling as the man grabs you? Who do you think he is? Why has he grabbed you? How will you get away? What about your promise – will you keep it? How will you get the food to bring back?

Following their discussions, the children were given large sheets of paper with a still frame from the clip in the middle. The children recorded their ideas around the still frame as the starting point for the stories that they were going to write. Once finished, the sheets were put up in the room so that the children could look at others' ideas and thoughts before they started writing their stories the following day.

When the series of lessons had finished and the children had written their stories, Giles intended to:

- produce a book of the stories to put in the classroom so that children could read each other's stories;

- tell (and then perhaps read) them the opening of *Great Expectations* to whet their appetite for the book.

In these lessons the trainee chose the text and the extract carefully in anticipation that it would engage the children and encourage interaction. He introduced it in a way that was appropriate for the children and would get them to consider aspects of the text such as setting, plot and character. In these ways he hoped to whet their appetite for this and other classic texts.

Activity

In response to their survey that showed a lack of engagement with classic authors the British Library created a website *Discovering Literature*. Their aim is to engage children and young people with classic Romantic and Victorian texts through access to a range of materials. The website has a wealth of information about the authors and the texts, based on expert interpretation and contemporary research. In addition, the site provides access to a wide range of related items from the British Library and other collections: manuscripts, first editions, illustrations, playbills, relevant newspaper article and advertisements. There are also videos and films about the authors' lives and works as well as teaching resources to use in our endeavours to engage children with classic texts.

Explore the website at: www.bl.uk/romantics-and-victorians

- Choose a text and create a portfolio of information about the author and text. Include videos, films and items from the collections that you think would engage and interest a particular year group.
- How might you adapt this for use with a younger or older year group?

Curriculum Links

Using such a text creates opportunities to develop a range of knowledge and skills in English, including maintaining a positive attitude to reading and understanding through engagement with the text, and opportunities to use, consolidate and develop a range of comprehension, transcription and composition skills.

Additionally, children have the opportunity to consider the past and how things have changed. The text also raises questions that could act as a stimulus to discussion in PSHE.

Using authentic historical texts, though, can pose problems for the teacher. How would you go about introducing children to the following?

- Archaic vocabulary or phrasing – for example, *Reasoning thus, he followed her a few steps, to emerge in another great cavern ... He lowered his torch instantly lest the light should awake them* (*The Princess and the Goblin*, Macdonald, 1872).
- Contemporary social attitudes which are no longer usual or acceptable – Mark Twain's (2008) *Tom Sawyer,* for instance, written in 1875, is full of references to 'niggers', 'halfbreeds' and 'Injuns', which were perfectly acceptable at the time – how do we deal with them today?
- Details of life which are no longer familiar – life with domestic servants, for instance, and attitudes towards them, or naughty children being walloped by parents or teachers: – *when the soot got into his eyes, which it did every day in the week, or when his master beat him, which he did every day in the week –* (*The Water Babies,* Kingsley, 1863).
- And all these examples are from books written expressly for children – the problems can be much greater with 'adult' books.

Would you select an abridged or updated edition of the book? Or would you just show them the video?

Conclusion

Pat Pinsent suggests that:

> *it is worth considering whether or not it is really the best policy to give children 'classics' before they are able to appreciate them properly ... Sometimes it may be necessary to question whether or not children will really be deprived of anything worthwhile if they never meet them. There can be no absolute answer to such questions, and teachers are inevitably aware that if some children do not read these books at school, they will probably never experience them at all, at least as books.*

(Pinsent, 1997, p.40)

and concludes that:

> *the only possible answer is to make the children into critical readers, able to detect and withstand all forms of prejudice, however subtly they are conveyed.*

(p.41)

This is a difficult task for any teacher, but one which is worth striving toward.

Learning Outcomes Review

You should now have considered what we mean by classic children's literature. You should be able to identify some books that are regarded as classics and understand some of the features of a classic text. You should have some understanding of the context of the development of literature for children. You should be developing your views on why and how we can use classic texts in primary classrooms, including modern classics and more adult classic texts.

Self-assessment question

1   Having read the chapter and considered the issues raised about classic children's literature, consider the following.

   • Books regarded as classics for children are dated in their language, social context and social attitudes. Therefore, they have little relevance for children today and so should have no special place within the English curriculum.

Discuss your views with a colleague.

Further Reading

Lurie, A. (2003) *Boys and Girls Forever.* London: Chatto and Windus.

Alison Lurie discusses classics from Oz and Dr Seuss to Narnia and Harry Potter in a user-friendly and always entertaining way, giving details of the authors' backgrounds and an excellent introduction to books which may not all be familiar.

Montgomery, H. and Watson, N. (eds) (2009) *Children's Literature: Classic Texts and Contemporary Trends.* Buckingham: Open University Press.

Spofford, F. (2002) *The Child That Books Built.* London: Faber and Faber.

This is a memoir of the author's own childhood reading, and traces the development of themes in a child's reading as he matures. It is excellent both at recalling the way a loved book can lead the reader into its special atmosphere, and at showing how the books of childhood fit into and illuminate the child's growing understanding of the world.

References

Alcott, L.M. (1994) *Little Women.* London: Puffin (first published 1868).

Ballantyne, R.M. (1858) *The Coral Island.* London: T. Nelson and Son.

Ballantyne, R.M. (2007) *The Gorilla Hunters.* Project Gutenberg e-book (first published 1862).

Bloom, A. (2014) Why classic authors are dead to pupils. Available at: www.tes.com/article. aspx?storycode=6428956 (accessed 12.04.16).

Burnett, F.H. (1886) *Little Lord Fauntleroy.* London: Frederick Warne.

Burnett, F.H. (1994) *The Secret Garden.* London: Penguin (first published 1911).

Burnett, F.H. (1996) *A Little Princess.* London: Penguin (first published 1905).

Carle, E. (1969) *The Very Hungry Caterpillar.* London: Hamish Hamilton.

Carpenter, H. (1985) *Secret Gardens.* London: George Allen and Unwin.

Carpenter, H. and Prichard, M. (1984) *Oxford Guide to Children's Literature.* Oxford: OUP.

Carroll, L. (1998) *Alice's Adventures in Wonderland* (first published 1865) and *Through the Looking Glass* (first published 1871). London: Macmillan.

Coolidge, S. (1872) *What Katy Did.* London: Ward Lock.

DfE (2013) *The National Curriculum in England: Key Stages 1 and 2 Framework Document.* London: DfE. Available at: www.gov.uk/government/uploads/system/uploads/attachment_ data/file/335133/PRIMARY_national_curriculum_220714.pdf (accessed 12.04.16).

Eagleton, T. (1983) *Literary Theory: An Introduction.* London: Basil Blackwell.

Fleming, M.P. (2007) *The Literary Canon: Implications for the Teaching of Language as Subject.* Strasbourg: Council of Europe.

Grahame, K. (1895) *The Golden Age.* London: Bodley Head.

Grahame, K. (1994) *The Wind in the Willows.* London: Penguin (first published 1908).

Gubar, M. (2009) *Artful Dodgers: Reconceiving the Golden Age of Children's Literature.* Oxford. Oxford University Press.

Jeffries, R. (1882) *Bevis: The Story of a Boy.* London: Sampson Low.

Kingsley, C. (1863) *The Water Babies.* London: Ward Lock.

MacDonald, G. (1864) *The Light Princess.* London: Blackie.

MacDonald, G. (1872) *The Princess and the Goblin.* London: Blackie.

McCabe, J., Fairchild, E., Grauerholz, L., Pescosolido, B.A. and Tope, D. (2011) Gender in twentieth century children's books. Patterns of disparity in titles and central characters.

Gender and Society, 25(2): 197–226. Available at: http://gas.sagepub.com/content/25/2/197. full.pdf (accessed 12.04.16).

Milne, A.A. (1924) *When We Were Very Young.* London: Methuen.

Milne, A.A. (1926) *Winnie the Pooh.* London: Methuen.

Milne, A.A (1927) *Now We are Six.* London: Methuen.

Milne, A.A. (1928) *The House at Pooh Corner.* London: Methuen.

Montgomery, L.M. (1994) *Anne of Green Gables.* London: Reader's Digest (first published 1908).

Nesbit, E. (1902) *Five Children and It.* London: T. Fisher Unwin.

Nesbit, E. (1908) *The House of Arden.* London: T. Fisher Unwin.

Nesbit, E. (1909) *Harding's Luck.* London: T. Fisher Unwin.

Nesbit, E. (1958) *The Story of the Treasure Seekers.* London: Puffin (first published 1899).

Nesbit, E. (1995) *The Railway Children,* London: Puffin (first published 1906).

Pinsent, P. (1997) *Children's Literature and the Politics of Equality.* London: David Fulton Publishers.

Randall, E. and Hardman, A. (2002) *A–Z of Key Concepts in Primary English.* Exeter: Learning Matters.

Spyri, J. (1969) *Heidi.* London: Puffin (first published 1871).

Stevenson, R.L. (1994) *Treasure Island.* London: Penguin (first published 1883).

Streatfeild, N. (1949) *The Painted Garden.* London: Puffin.

Streatfeild, N. (1958) *Magic and the Magician: E. Nesbit and Her Children's Books.* London: Ernest Benn.

Twain, M. (2008) *The Adventures of Tom Sawyer.* London: Puffin Classics (first published 1875).

Wharton (n.d.) The golden age classics. Available at: www.rainbowresource.com/pdfs/ products/prod031448_smpl0.pdf_(accessed 12.04.16).

Answers to activity on page 150

1	Lewis Carroll	2	Lilliput	3	AA Milne	4	The Famous Five
5	Charlie and the Chocolate Factory (very greedy)	6	The Railway Children	7	Mr Toad	8	Peter Pan
9	The Wizard of Oz						

11 Everyday fiction

Introduction

Towards the end of one episode of *The Simpsons*, Lisa makes a comment to the effect that whatever has happened, it will all be forgotten and everything will be back to normal at the beginning of the next episode. This is of course a self-referential whimsy to the conventions of a series, but does sum up to some extent the appeal of what is possibly the most widespread of fiction genres: the appeal of the everyday, and the knowledge that there is a well-defined world whose parameters are not subject to change.

Familiar settings

Many successful children's series have been set in worlds where the main interest is in recognition of the familiar and in the personalities and interaction of the characters. For younger children, there are such examples as Shirley Hughes' *Alfie* stories, Dorothy Edwards' (1950–56) *My Naughty Little Sister* series, Leila Berg's (1952) *Little Pete*, Jean and Gareth Adamson's (1960–2000) *Topsy and Tim*, and others, in which such familiar situations as playing in the snow or a day at the shops provide the action and children recognise their own world in the story. Similarly, Lauren Child's (2000–10) *Charlie and Lola* series reflects children's everyday life but with a twist. Charlie and Lola are a brother and sister. Lola, the little sister, is an energetic and wildly imaginative child. Charlie is the sensible older brother who gently and patiently tries to navigate Lola's way through the world. The books deal with the everyday concerns of childhood, wonderfully evoked in some of the books' titles, *I Will Never, Not Ever, Eat a Tomato*; *I Am Not Sleepy and Will Not go to Bed*; *I am Too Absolutely Small for School*; and *I Slightly Want to Go Home.* Percy the park keeper is another children's favourite. In the books Percy is at hand to solve the many, often humorous, scrapes that his friends,

Fox, Badger, Mole, Squirrel and Owl, get into. In *The Owl's Lesson* (Butterworth, 1997) Percy finds a nest on the ground with a baby bird inside. The bird confesses that he can't get the hang of flying so has been left behind. In an effort to help him Owl and Squirrel are called upon to teach the bird to fly, with humorous consequences. (Although, obviously, interaction with talking animals is not part of everyday life, the essential atmosphere of these books is still familiar enough to warrant inclusion in this category.) As the child grows older, the same effect can be found through encountering Francesca Simon's (1994–2012) *Horrid Henry*, Beverly Cleary's (1955–81) *Ramona*, or even Richmal Crompton's (1922–70) *Just William* – perhaps the supreme example of the timeless world, as in 39 books written over a total of 53 years the hero remains 11 years old, and his circle of friends and family unchanged.

Research Focus

Intertextuality

We have identified everyday fiction as a genre, but this is not a term you will necessarily find elsewhere. We have used the term to cover all the books set in the real, modern world which do not obviously fall into any of the other genres considered in this book. Many authors writing within this general definition produce series of novels in which recognisable characters appear in book after book, but the nature of these books can vary from fantasy and magic, as in the *Harry Potter* series, to adventure, as in Blyton's *Secret Seven*. This can be further complicated by the fact that in many stories elements of different genres appear. This can be referred to as *intertextual reference* (Gamble and Yates, 2002) and is a feature of, for example, the Ahlbergs' (1989) *Each Peach Pear Plum*, in which characters from other stories appear, including Tom Thumb and Old Mother Hubbard. Similarly, in *Clever Polly and the Stupid Wolf* (Storr, 1967), our knowledge of other stories and rhymes helps us to understand the text better. This is especially true in stories from the series such as *Songs My Mother Taught Me*.

Because books can be read at different levels, perhaps with the reader enjoying them for their plot, or at a deeper level where allusions are made to other texts and cultural references, some authors include references which may be noticed by more experienced readers, including adults. Thus the biblical references in *The Lion, the Witch and the Wardrobe* and *Wind in the Willows* may pass some readers by, but will be noticed and explored by others.

Perhaps one of the earliest classics of what we describe as everyday fiction was E Nesbit's (1998) *The Treasure Seekers*, which first appeared in 1899, and its two later sequels. The children of the Bastable family try by various means to 'restore the family fortunes', with hardly any success and without any of their adventures involving any circumstances wildly beyond the experience of the Edwardian reader, but with charm and humour which do not date (and which foreshadow the author's better-known *The Railway Children*, 1985 – although there is the added plot device of the falsely imprisoned father and a passing Russian spy, most of the adventure in this book is still very much at the everyday level).

In the title of this chapter, the term 'everyday' (sometimes referred to as 'soap opera fiction') has been used as a catch-all to cover all the writing for children which is set in the normal modern or recent world, without magical or supernatural events, and whose narrative does not fall obviously into any of the other specific genres covered. It is easy to underestimate the appeal of this type of fiction to children, perhaps because as adult readers we come to expect event and adventure in our reading and watching. Even in the world of soap opera, which traditionally offered the same kind of soothing everyday rhythm, there has been a recent move to boost audience figures by the introduction of murders, disasters and other dramatic but improbable storylines.

Of course, not everything in a novel for Key Stage 2 children needs to be completely probable, or the book could be incredibly dull; but the characteristic of a good book is that the writer can make us believe that these things just might happen. Clement Freud's (1974) *Grimble and Grimble at Christmas* has a wildly fantastic cast of characters encountered by one very sensible small boy, but the wit and logic of the story telling keep the reader completely convinced. Roald Dahl's (1974) *Danny, the Champion of the World* is the story of a cunning plan by Danny and his father to outwit a local landowner by spoiling his pheasant shoot. The details of the plan, the descriptions of Danny and his father's life together, the lively rhythm of the conversations and the building of the atmosphere of suspense make a wonderful story out of what could have been a fairly slight plot.

There is a huge range to be considered: domestic and school stories, family holidays, exciting trips abroad, stories centred on sport or particular interest such as animals and, inevitably, encounters with kidnappers, international crooks, gangs of thieves and dastardly plots of one kind or another. The popular adult genre of espionage thrillers has been re-interpreted for younger readers by such authors as Robert Muchamore (the *Cherub* series, 2004–10), Anthony Horowitz's (2000–11) *Alex Rider* series, and Charlie Higson (2005–08) in the *Young Bond* series. These, however, are still aimed at readers older than primary age, though worthy of mention for their possible appeal to older pupils looking to extend their reading. Although it is invidious to make a division into girls' and boys' books, it does seem that such series may represent a deliberate attempt to keep boys' interest in the written word alive at an age when many girls are becoming more involved with family-based series such as Cathy Cassidy's (2010–) *Chocolate Box Girls*, or Hilary McKay's (2001–07) Casson family series.

However, we should remember that in any fiction it is necessary to find some common ground with the characters if the reader is to be engaged; books with animal or alien characters succeed by the perception of human emotions and motivations in the protagonists, whatever their physical form or their situation. If the child is in the world of Shirley Hughes' Alfie with him, then going to a birthday party is just as absorbing a challenge as outwitting a master criminal maybe for Spiderman – and perhaps more so, if the reader is five years old and has faced the same situation himself. The case study below focuses on a similar everyday situation for a young child. Note how Jenny links a story to children's own experiences and develops a writing activity through discussion and role play.

Case Study

Jenny, a Teach First trainee working with a Year 1 class, read *Dogger* by Shirley Hughes (1978) to her children. During the story she involved children in the story by inviting them to the front to 'be' Bella, Dave and Dave's mother. Occasionally, she paused in her reading and asked a character how they felt about what was happening in the story. Other children could ask them questions too.

After the story, Jenny discussed what happened with the children and asked them if they had ever lost anything. Almost all had, including two who had temporarily lost their parents when out shopping. Jenny suggested that they could write a story together as a class about someone who lost something. She invited suggestions for names of characters and wrote some on the board. She then asked children to think about a setting and discuss a way of starting a story.

Using the children's ideas, Jenny modelled writing using shared writing techniques to create the beginning of a story. She found that getting children to dramatise elements of the story helped them to develop ideas which they were able to contribute to the writing task.

Curriculum Links

In the National Curriculum Year 2 Notes and Guidance (DfE, 2013) it is stated that:

> *Drama and role-play can contribute to the quality of pupils' writing by providing opportunities for pupils to develop and order their ideas through playing roles and improvising scenes in various settings.*

(p.31)

Activity

Find a copy of *Dogger* and read it. Why do you think it has remained enduringly popular with children and parents? How could you develop activities using the book as a starting point?

A frequent device used by authors of series is to include a map of the setting, so that readers can locate the homes of the characters and see for themselves how the different events of the stories fit together. This tactic, used by children's authors as diverse as Joyce Lankaster Brisley (*Milly-Molly-Mandy* stories), A.A. Milne and Arthur Ransome, is clearly a popular one – one has only to consider the adult sales for maps of Middle Earth, Terry Pratchett's Ankh-Morpork (from the Discworld series, 1983–2015) and even Ambridge, setting of the radio serial *The Archers*, to see that giving a 'real' geography to fiction increases its appeal.

In the case study below, a series of activities revolve around an imaginary village. Note how work across the curriculum is incorporated, and children are engaged in a range of speaking and listening, and reading and writing activities, including drama and debate. There are opportunities to develop a range of skills through group activity. After reading the case study, consider which examples of fiction you might read alongside such a programme of lessons.

Case Study

Chris, a final-year BA QTS student, planned a range of activities built around the creation of a village within the classroom. The work involved map-making with children creating a plan of a village and deciding on the facilities it would include such as shops, pubs, churches, petrol stations and a village hall. After making a map, they made the buildings in design and technology using a standard scale. Each child in the class was allocated a house in the village and could then suggest a role they might take and create a family with whom they would live. The children were told they could be adults or children in the village and they had to write a short pen portrait of themselves in character which could be displayed for others to read. There then followed a hot-seating session in groups with children asking each other questions which they answered in role.

Chris then wrote the names of all the characters on individual pieces of card and invited children to draw groups of six cards. The six characters then had to meet and talk in role. Once the characters had spent time talking to each other, Chris brought the class together and discussed ideas for developing stories within the village. He invited children to suggest scenarios for each group, pointing out that these shouldn't involve violence or death, but might be the kind of things people encounter within a community.

A list of scenarios was drawn up and modified and revised and included the following.

- One person's dog barks at night and keeps everyone awake.
- One person wants to build a large extension to his/her house which will shut out the light for neighbours.
- Two families fall out because their children have an argument at school.

The groups then discussed which scenario they would like to engage with (there was no restriction on the number of groups which could choose each scenario) and they enacted it. Children worked together on the scenarios, pausing whenever someone called time out to discuss what had happened and what they thought might happen next. Some groups worked very well and had little difficulty in moving a drama forward, while others stopped frequently and argued both

$\longrightarrow$

in and out of role. Having anticipated this, Chris brought groups together for discussions which he arbitrated and he even took part in one group's activity, playing the role of a new neighbour with a noisy motorbike.

Eventually, children worked in their groups to plan performances of their scenarios. Some wrote scripts but most preferred to make notes and then improvise. After two weeks of working together children worked in pairs to write short stories about their characters and the scenarios in which they had been involved.

There are many ways in which you could further develop the work described above. In Chris's series of lessons the focus was on contemporary issues, but there is also potential here for work in history, with the village perhaps being set in Roman, medieval or Victorian times, and links being made to appropriate fiction, as described below.

Curriculum Links

Everyday fiction can be used very effectively for work in history. Sharing stories which tell of families' fortunes in different periods can bring history to life. This was a device used by the BBC in *How We Used to Live* in the 1980s when each period featured both factual input and a short drama in which contrasting families (usually one rich and one poor) played out scenes which made the experience of history more real. There is scope for drama work in the classroom as well as writing in role and investigating lifestyles, diet, housing and education. Caroline Lawrence's (2001–09) *Roman Mysteries* series, set at the end of the first century AD around many parts of the Roman empire, would be an invaluable source for topic work on Roman life, as they explain many details of everyday life and popular features such as gladiators and chariot racing.

Characters

Whatever the setting and storyline of a book, the same is true in this genre as in any other – that if the story is led by strong characters with whom the reader can identify, the book will have a much better chance of survival. One way in which good writers can lead the reader inside the mind of a character is to show us the internal world of his imagination – Richmal Crompton's William, for instance, lives almost entirely within the world of his own imagination, which only makes rare contact with the quiet Kent village in which he lives. Arthur Ransome first introduces seven-year-old Roger, youngest of the Swallows and Amazons children, as he is zigzagging across a field,

The wind was against him, and he was tacking up against it … He could not run
straight against the wind, because he was a sailing vessel, a tea-clipper, the Cutty Sark.

(*Swallows and Amazons*, 1930, p.13)

There is a world of difference between telling us *he was* …, and *he was pretending to be* …

Ransome, although not as widely read these days, was also one of the first writers to share the action and role of protagonist in his stories among a group of children instead of having one lone hero. There are obvious advantages in this, both for the narrative and for the reader; the writer can use dialogue and discussion to carry his story, and a wider range of readers will find a character with whom to identify.

Caroline Lawrence (2009), author of the *Roman Mysteries*, has identified her own archetypes from 'myth-based' journey films such as *Dorothy and the Wizard of Oz, Star Wars, Star Trek, Lord of the Rings,* Pixar's *UP* and others, and this classification is also very useful when looking at the conventions of series fiction.

- You must always have a hero, be they old or young, male or female, heroic or ordinary … Flavia fills this role in her *Roman Mysteries* but she also cites Dorothy, Frodo and Mr Karl Frederickson from *UP*.

- The 'faithful sidekick' is the best friend, sometimes a faithful animal. Their gifts complement the hero's. They often bring the hero back from near death or even actual death. The sidekick shares many of the characteristics of the main character; supports and helps; and is of course on hand at the end to say, *But there's still one thing I don't understand* …, thus enabling the author to give his readers an explanation of points which they may have missed. Nubia, the beautiful slave-girl, is Flavia's sidekick, though she will become a hero in her own right. Among other faithful sidekicks mentioned by Caroline are Toto (or the Scarecrow), and R2-D2 in the *Star Wars* film canon. William Brown has Ginger, Harry Potter has his Ron, and even My Naughty Little Sister has Harry-next-door.

- The 'funny one' adds comic relief when things get tense. In *Dorothy and the Wizard of Oz*, the Tin Man is funny. George Lucas has his own version of a 'tin man' in C-3PO. Other funny ones include Jonathan from the *Roman Mysteries*, Neville or Ron in *Harry Potter*, Roger in *Swallows and Amazons*, Phyllis in *The Railway Children*.

- The 'wild one' is for surprises. This character has aspects of an animal and often betrays the hero. In the *Roman Mysteries*, tongueless Lupus ('Wolf') is the wild one. In Tolkien's work there is Gollum, in *The Wizard of Oz* there is the Lion (albeit a cowardly one!).

- Finally, an archetypal character who usually doesn't go on the journey or take an active part in the adventure but gives instructions at the beginning (and often a Talisman) is the 'mentor' – a wise counsellor, sometimes a parent. Dumbledore and Gandalf are obvious examples here.

These types are not always separate people – in the *Harry Potter* books, for instance, Ron is both sidekick and oddball. In *The Lord of the Rings* (Tolkein, 1994), to take another example many will be familiar with, Aragorn and Gandalf share the role of mentor, and Merry and Pippin share that of funny one.

Activity

Think of books or series you are familiar with and see whether this pattern can be recognised. What advantages does this type of fiction have over that with a single character at the centre?

Enid Blyton

The notion of a group of central characters engaging in adventures was developed by two trainees, who built upon children's knowledge and love of Enid Blyton's many series of everyday fiction to develop a quite sophisticated series of activities. The case study below introduces us to Alice and Mazara who worked together on a children's literature project. The case study continues after a discussion about Enid Blyton, whose work is both controversial and very popular.

Case Study

The Super Six (introduction)

Alice and Mazara undertook a paired first placement with a Years 4–5 class in a small school as part of their PGCE course. Their university required them, in consultation with the class teacher, to conduct a small scale study of children's reading habits and to develop activities with the class which deepened children's understanding of texts.

They began in a preparatory visit by preparing a short questionnaire for the children which asked them about their favourite stories. Alice and Mazara were surprised to find that more children named Enid Blyton as their favourite than strong modern favourites such as Roald Dahl, J.K. Rowling, Jacqueline Wilson and Michael Morpurgo. They discussed this with the class teacher who told them that although neither he nor any of the other teachers ever read Blyton to their classes, the children had a thriving informal book exchange which mainly involved swapping copies of *Famous Five* and *Secret Seven* tales. The teacher was reluctant to be negative about the children's reading choices, especially as many children who had been reluctant readers seemed to devour Blyton's stories. Although he had read some Blyton stories as a child,

→

he had not reread the stories since and was aware of the frequent criticisms of her work on the grounds that the stories sometimes contained material which might now be thought sexist or racist, and that the quality of writing was inferior to that of many other children's authors.

Alice and Mazara decided that they would read as many *Famous Five* and *Secret Seven* stories as possible and then meet to discuss their thoughts and to plan activities and a study which related to the children's reading preferences, but which had scope to broaden their horizons. You will be able to read about the ways in which this led to classroom activities shortly, but first it is important to consider the popularity and output of Enid Blyton.

Research Focus

Popularity and output of Blyton

Enid Blyton wrote 21 *Famous Five* books between 1942 and 1962, with one appearing every year except 1961 and two in 1962. During this time, Julian, Anne, George, Dick and Timmy the dog take part in a range of adventures during the children's school holidays from their boarding schools. The children hardly age over the 21-year period, with the eldest, Julian, being 12 in the first novel: *Five on a Treasure Island* (1942). Although in a later book Julian is *sixteen and very sensible*, charming farmers' wives with his good manners, the level of conversation and interests of the children remain very constant. This freezing of the characters' ages was cited by J.K. Rowling as something she did not want for Harry Potter and his friends:

> *in book four the hormones are going to kick in – I don't want him [Harry] stuck in a state of permanent pre-pubescence like poor Julian in the Famous Five!*

(Carey, 1999)

The 15 *Secret Seven* books were published between 1949 and 1963. Blyton wrote over 600 books, many of which were part of series including *Malory Towers*, *The Magic Faraway Tree* series and *St Clare's*.

Why do some people object?

A glance through some of the key academic works on children's literature shows that Blyton is either scarcely mentioned or, where she is, is portrayed in a poor light. Knowles and Malmkjaer (1996), for example, afford her three mentions, with one being: *Arthur Ransome's (1884–1967) Swallows and Amazons was published in 1930 and represents the new fiction at its best while Enid Blyton (1897–1968) with her Famous Five shows it at its most ordinary and unoriginal* (p.22). Later in the book a survey of 10–12-year-olds' reading preferences shows

Blyton coming second to Roald Dahl. Given the response to her work of many adults, there is little surprise that Blyton was quoted as saying that she took no notice of any critics over the age of 12.

Objections to Blyton's work focus on the perceived sexism in the stories, with boys generally taking the lead while girls, with the frequent exception of George (Georgina – who wears shorts, refuses to be treated as a girl and constantly claims that she is *as good as a boy*), perform more menial tasks. There are also elements of racial stereotyping and use of language which are certainly not acceptable in the twenty-first century and were often regarded as offensive at the time Blyton wrote. For example, *black as a nigger with soot* appears in *Five Go off to Camp*, and she also wrote *The Three Golliwogs* whose characters are named Gollie, Woggie and Nigger.

Research Focus

Carter (2000) points out that judgements about the quality and suitability of children's literature are predominantly made by adults rather than children and reminds us that even the awards which are given to children's books are determined by adults. Shavit (1986 cited in Carter, 2000) sums up the issue:

> The children's writer is perhaps the only one who is asked to address one particular audience and at the same time appeal to another. Society expects the children's writer to be appreciated by both adults and … children.

(p.108)

Shavit goes on to discuss the different tastes of adults and children and their potential incompatibility and concludes:

> But one thing is clear: in order for a children's book to be accepted by adults, it is not enough for it to be accepted by children.

It is interesting to consider attitudes to Enid Blyton in light of these comments. It may be that many children no longer encounter the stories because their parents and teachers avoid them, but could there also be an element of *the appeal of forbidden fruit* which leads some children, such as those in Alice and Mazara's class, to read them anyway.

What has happened to the Blyton stories?

The response to this criticism from publishers has been to remove much of the language which causes offence and to issue revised editions of the books. It should, however, be remembered that some terms which we find offensive today were commonplace when Blyton wrote and carried less pejorative overtones.

Case Study

The Super Six (continued)

Having read some of Blyton's books, Alice and Mazara discussed their views on them and distilled these into the following points.

- The stories feature a lot of action which engages children.

- The children tend to outwit adults or at least be the driving forces in solving crimes, etc.

- Food features strongly and often appealingly.

- Although boys tend to take a lead in many adventures, there are strong female characters such as George (Georgina) in the *Famous Five* series.

- The stories are not badly written, as in being grammatically incorrect, but do include devices such as addressing the reader or the characters, as in *Fun for the Secret Seven* (1963): *Good old Secret Seven! Think hard, and see what you can do!* which appear dated and a little patronising.

- The language is very simplistic and repetitive – for example, 'said' is used almost to the exclusion of any alternative in speech, and exclamation points spatter nearly every page.

The Super Six

Alice and Mazara planned a series of lessons in which the children could create their own characters in discussion with others on their tables of six. Each child was to be a member of a gang called the Super Six, which would have adventures. Children were asked to work together to produce pen portraits and pictures of the characters, with Alice and Mazara bringing in football and theatre programmes to show how these can be presented.

In another lesson, Alice and Mazara produced a series of pieces of dialogue and asked groups to decide which, if any, of their characters might be most likely to say what. Other lessons followed in which groups developed scenarios for their characters' adventures and made notes on what might happen. They went on to improvise dramatic situations and to make notes for scripts and stories. Finally, children worked together to write stories, considering setting, character and plot. It was clear that the Blyton stories had influenced many children's writing, and buns, cakes and fizzy drinks as well as scary adventures made frequent appearances.

Conclusions of the study

Reflecting on their work with the children, Alice and Mazara concluded that:

- on the whole it is better to let children read what they enjoy, especially if it hooks them into books, than to criticise their choices;

→

- teachers need to be aware of a range of literature if they are to guide children to other choices (see Cremin, et al., 2008);

- Blyton's stories have been 'sanitised' and many of the elements which people once objected to have been changed or removed;

- while neither trainee felt it likely that they would read a Blyton story to a class because they thought there were so many better books available, they recognised that the books engaged young readers, and possessed qualities which could be discussed with children and offered opportunities for a range of activities.

Activity

Consider the approach Alice and Mazara took to developing children's appreciation of characterisation in everyday fiction. How could you develop activities which were stimulated by other stories, for example *Swallows and Amazons, Just William?*

Conclusion

Portrayal of groups in everyday fiction means that characters can be developed over a period of time, even if they never actually grow up. In many cases the characters remain easily recognisable by their manner and habits and readers can predict their reactions to different situations. They can also make educated guesses at whom they might attribute pieces of dialogue to, based upon their developing knowledge of their personalities. Anyone who has read *Just William*, for example, would be able to tell which character might say:

> *I'll scream and scream until I'm sick.*

Similarly, followers of the *Famous Five* would be able to identify the speakers for the following:

> *You heard what I said, George. You are not to go! I'll take the papers and hide them on the island.*

> *In fact, I've a good mind not to go. I think I'll live in the summer-house with Timmy, at the bottom of the garden!*

> (*Five Are Together Again*, 1962)

However, while there is a comforting security in getting to know characters well, there is a danger too, if characters never surprise or develop beyond clearly defined roles, that children's own depictions of characters in their writing and drama will be limited.

Everyday fiction represents a range of stories of varying quality, and it has wide appeal for children who enjoy getting to know characters and following their fates, just as soap operas like *Coronation Street* and *EastEnders* attract and engage adults. It is a genre which deserves to be given serious attention in the primary classroom.

Learning Outcomes Review

You should now be aware that there is a significant body of children's literature in which stories revolve around the same group of characters, and that in many of these the characters are 'frozen in time', remaining at the same age throughout series. You should also have ideas for using this literature as part of classroom activities.

Self-assessment questions

1 What is meant by the term 'intertextual'?
2 It has been argued that children's authors need to appeal to more than one audience. Why?

Further Reading

A chapter of such a broad scope can obviously only scratch the surface of what is available. Such books as Marcus Crouch's *Treasure Seekers and Borrowers* (Library Association, 1967) or Margery Fisher's *Intent on Reading* (Brockhampton, 1961) offer very wide-ranging reviews of books from the first 60 years of the twentieth century, many of which are still available and well worth introducing to a new generation.

Nicholas Tucker's *The Child and the Book* (Cambridge, 1981) also discusses fiction for this age group in a very readable and entertaining way.

Above all, if there are titles mentioned in this chapter which are new to you, track them down and try them out.

References

Adamson, J. and G. (1960–2000) *Topsy and Tim* series. London: Ladybird.

Ahlberg, A. and Ahlberg, J. (1979) *Each Peach Pear Plum*. London: Puffin.

Berg, L. (1952) *Little Pete*. London: Puffin.

Blyton, E. (1942) *Five on a Treasure Island*. London: Hodder and Stoughton.

Blyton, E. (1962) *Five are Together Again*. London: Hodder and Stoughton.

Blyton, E. (1963) *Fun for the Secret Seven*. London: Hodder and Stoughton.

Brisley, J.L. (1928–55) *Milly-Molly-Mandy* stories. London: Harrap.

Butterworth, N. (1997) *The Owl's Lesson*. London: Harper Collins.

Carey, J. (1999) Who hasn't met Harry? *Guardian*, 16 Feb.

Carter, D. (2000) *Teaching Fiction in the Primary School*. Abingdon: David Fulton.

Cassidy, C. (2010–) *Chocolate Box Girls* series: London: Penguin Books

Child, L. (2000–10) *Charlie and Lola* series. London: Orchard Books.

Cleary, B. (1955–81) *Ramona* series. London: Puffin.

Cremin, T., Mottram, M., Bearne, E. and Goodwin, P. (2008) Exploring teachers' knowledge of children's literature. *Cambridge Journal of Education*, 38(4): 449–64.

Crompton, R. (1922–70) *Just William* series. London: Newnes.

Crouch, M. (1962) *Treasure Seekers and Borrowers*. London: The Library Association.

Dahl, R. (1974) *Danny, the Champion of the World*. London: Puffin.

DfE (2013) *The National Curriculum in England: Key Stages 1 and 2 Framework Document*. London: DfE. Available at: www.gov.uk/government/uploads/system/uploads/attachment_data/file/335133/PRIMARY_national_curriculum_220714.pdf (accessed 12.04.16).

Edwards, D. (1950–56) *My Naughty Little Sister* series. London: Mammoth, Egmont.

Freud, C. (1974) *Grimble and Grimble at Christmas*. London: Puffin Books.

Gamble, N. and Yates, S. (2002) *Exploring Children's Literature*. London: Paul Chapman.

Higson, C. (2005–8) *Young Bond* series. London: Puffin.

Horowitz, A. (2000–11) *Alex Rider* series. London: Walker Books.

Hughes, S. (1978) *Dogger*. London: Red Fox.

Knowles, M. and Malmkjaer, K. (1996) *Language and Control in Children's Literature*. London: Routledge.

Lawrence, C. (2001–09) *Roman Mysteries* series. London: Orion Books.

Lawrence, C. (2009) Talk at Queen Margaret's School, York, November 2009, quoted with permission from the author.

McKay, H. (2001–07) Casson family series. London: Hodder.

Muchamore, R. (2004–10) *CHERUB* series. London: Hodder and Stoughton.

Nesbit, E. (1985) *The Railway Children.* London: Puffin (first published 1906).

Nesbit, E. (1998) *The Treasure Seekers*. London: Puffin (first published 1899).

Pratchett, T. (1983–2015) *Discworld* series. London: Doubleday.

Ransome, A. (1930) *Swallows and Amazons*. London: Jonathan Cape.

Simon, F. (1994–2012) *Horrid Henry* series. London: Orion Books.

Storr, C. (1967) *Clever Polly and the Stupid Wolf*. London: Penguin.

Tolkien, J.R.R. (1994) *Lord of the Rings*. London: Collins (first published 1954–55).

12 Poetry

Learning Outcomes

By reading this chapter you will:

- have a better awareness of the range of poetry which might be shared with children in primary schools;
- appreciate the importance of poetry in its own right;
- appreciate the range and scope of activities which might emanate from reading poetry;
- have ideas to help you to consider how children might be introduced to writing poetry.

Introduction

A poem is worth reading for its own sake, not simply in order to teach something about poetry. Being a reader of literature gives a teacher the confidence to teach powerfully.

(Martin, 2003, p.16)

In this chapter you will find out about a range of poetic forms which can be shared with children. Case studies of a trainee teacher and a newly qualified teacher (NQT) will illustrate how reading poems can lead to successful writing. At the end of the book, in Appendix 2, you will find a short glossary of poetic terminology, which you may wish to turn to when unfamiliar terms appear.

For probably the majority of children in modern Britain, poetry – rhymed and structured text – is the form in which they first meet the written word, and even before that songs and poems are likely to be the first material they encounter from the world of literature. Babies and toddlers learn to recognise the rhythm of simple nursery rhymes and will respond with clapping, rocking or joining in long before they are vocalising themselves. When they begin to have books read to them, rhymed narratives such as Julia Donaldson's (1999) *The Gruffalo* and countless other books for small children encourage the child to join in and supply the rhyme completing each couplet, making the sharing of the story telling an intrinsic part of the experience. The exuberance of rhymes such as Quentin Blake's *All Join In* stays in the memory and should help encourage a lifelong love of form, structure and the pattern of sound in reading aloud.

And if Ferdinand decides to make
A chocolate fudge banana cake,
What do we do? For goodness sake,
We ALL JOIN IN!

Research Focus

Knowledge of rhyme and reading ability

Bryant, et al. (1990) looked at 64 children aged four to age six from different socio-economic backgrounds and tested them on three occasions. Children's ability to detect rhyme was tested at ages four years and seven months and five years and eleven months, when they were asked to look at three words with pictures: two rhymed and the third did not (for example, peg, cot, leg; fish, dish, book). They were asked to pick out the words which did not rhyme.

At six years seven months, children were given three different reading tests to assess the understanding of words and simple sentences, knowledge of frequent words and spelling. There was a strong correlation between high scores in the rhyme test and scores in reading and spelling. Interestingly, this relationship was found regardless of the influence of the mother's educational level, and child's IQ and vocabulary level.

However, something clearly goes amiss with this. By the time children reach the point of choosing their own reading and picking up books for pleasure, the charm no longer seems to work and few children will select a poetry book; poetry has become something met only in school, and unlikely to be interesting or exciting. Indeed, a primary teacher, seeking to inspire his class, once started the lesson with, 'Who knows what poetry is?' One hand was raised in the sea of blank faces. 'It's chickens and ducks and that,' offered an eight-year-old. Clearly there is some way to go.

The power of rhyme

Of course, not all poems rhyme, but we tend to find it easier to remember the words when they do, just as we can remember song lyrics because the first of a pair of rhyming couplets gives us a clue about the second. This is evident in our use of rhyming *mnemonics* (memory rhymes) to help us remember everyday facts. These include one which many people recite when working out dates:

Thirty days hath September,
April, June and November.

All the rest have thirty-one,
Excepting February alone,
Which has twenty-eight days clear
And twenty-nine each leap year.

We also learn a rhyme to help us remember the fates of Henry VIII's wives:

Divorced, beheaded, died
Divorced, beheaded, survived.

And the spelling rule which most people come up with, when asked to give an example, tends to be:

i before e except after c

Even though this is a rule with many exceptions and is far less reliable than many which do not have a rhyme to help us remember them, it is the rule which most people remember.

Activity

Look at the opening lines of some other rhyming mnemonics. Can you complete them and say what they help us to learn? (Answers at the end of the chapter.)

Red sky at night …
In fourteen hundred and ninety-two …
Never eat …

Now try to make up your own rhyming mnemonics which might help you or your pupils to remember things.

However, poetry can offer much more than an aid to memory. Carter (1998) argued that *the scope of poetry is wider than that of any other kind of writing* (p.9) and maintained that as well as telling stories, poetry also plays games with language, reflects the poet's hopes, fears, hates, loves, responses to the world and to dreams. Poetry, and in particular nursery rhymes, can also benefit children as they develop literacy skills. Citing Bryant and Bradley (1985) and Goswami and Bryant (1990), Whitehead (2007) argues that phonological awareness can be developed in young children through their encounters with rhymes. She asserts:

Many poor readers are remarkably insensitive to rhymes and to the beginning sounds of words, but very young children with an interest in the sounds and poetry of language may well be on the road to reading, writing and spelling successfully.

(p.38)

Why teach poetry?

Apart from its benefits as an aid to learning, there are many reasons why poetry should be an important part of the school curriculum. These include the following.

- Listening and reading skills can be developed as children are engaged by the repetitive patterns of poetry.

- A focus on rhyme can provide opportunities to explore how different graphemes can be used to represent the same phonemes. For example, the opening lines of *Matilda* by Hilaire Belloc show that every rhyming word has a different grapheme sequence from its partner:

    *Matilda told such Dreadful **Lies**,*
    *It made one Gasp and Stretch one's **Eyes**;*
    *Her Aunt, who, from her Earliest **Youth**,*
    *Had kept a Strict Regard for **Truth**,*
    *Attempted to Believe **Matilda**:*
    *The effort very nearly **killed her**,*
    *And would have done so, had not **She***
    *Discovered this **Infirmity** ...*

    [NB capital letters are placed as in Belloc's original poem.
    We added the bold type for rhymes.]

- Children's own writing can be developed as they draw upon the patterns used by poets.
- Poems enable us to tell stories in fewer words than prose.
- Short, structured poems such as haiku, cinquains and triolets develop the skill of distilling ideas into the fewest possible words.
- Many narrative poems tell stories which are part of our culture.
- The moods and feelings expressed by poets can lead to discussion and can influence children's own writing.
- Poetry, in its various forms, shows how we can play with language and encourages experimentation and creativity.

However, some reports and pieces of research have suggested that many teachers either do not recognise the value of poetry or their own knowledge of poems is limited.

Research Focus

Teachers and poetry

There is even a name for dislike of poetry: *metrophobia*. Cremin, et al.'s (2008) research suggests that it is a condition which may apply to some teachers.

A questionnaire was used with 1200 teachers in 11 English local authorities who were asked about their personal reading habits and their knowledge of children's literature. The questionnaire was used to find out about their use of children's literature in the classroom. Cremin, et al. found that:

> *Very few indeed (1.5%) noted poetry as their favourite childhood reading, although this may, in part at least, have been a function of the question which referred to a favourite 'book' as a child, triggering perhaps a memory of a narrative. Nonetheless, this response is in line with the limited mention of poetry in the question on recently recorded reading, and is reinforced by the extremely limited knowledge of children's poets known to these teachers.*

> (2008, p.7)

(See also Chapter 1 where more details of this research are reported.)

Ofsted (2007) surveyed poetry teaching in both primary and secondary schools and found:

> *Many teachers, especially in the primary schools visited, did not know enough about poetry and this was reflected in the limited range of poems studied. Classic poems and poems from other cultures were rarely studied and too many of the poems chosen lacked sufficient challenge. Weaknesses in subject knowledge also reduced the quality of teachers' feedback to pupils on the poetry they had written.*

> (p.5)

Part of the problem may be the fact that historically so much poetry written for children has been somewhat saccharine and trite in its nature. Verses were written not so much to entertain as to give moral instruction – even when couched in humour, like the verses of *Struwwelpeter:*

> *Snip! Snap! Snip! the scissors go;*
> *And Conrad cries out 'Oh! Oh! Oh!'*
> *Snip! Snap! Snip! They go so fast,*
> *That both his thumbs are off at last.*
> *Mamma comes home: there Conrad stands,*

And looks quite sad, and shows his hands;
'Ah!' said Mamma, 'I knew he'd come
To naughty little Suck-a-Thumb.'

These verses, translated from the German, were first published in England in 1848, with the subtitle 'Merry stories and funny pictures'. It is hard not to think that they must have resulted in many merry nightmares and funny traumas.

Even those nineteenth-century verses which are still read, like Robert Louis Stevenson's *Child's Garden of Verse*, often combine simple and charming descriptions of childhood experience, such as make-believe games or going to bed by daylight in the summer, with the casual and complacent attitudes to class and race which were ubiquitous and unquestioned at the time when they were written: for instance *Little Turk or Japanee – Oh! Don't you wish that you were me?* or *The child that is not clean and neat, With lots of toys and things to eat, He is a naughty child, I'm sure – Or else his dear papa is poor.* Perhaps these verses are somewhat ill advised for the modern classroom. A.A. Milne's *When We Were Very Young* (1924) and *Now We Are Six* (1927) have stood the test of time rather better; though occasional references to nannies and nurseries may strike an alienating note, the mixture of fantasy, the daily routines of childhood and ballad-style stories are a good introduction to the appeal of poetry.

Activity

Which rhymes do you remember learning as a young child? Which can you still recite?

Can you, for example, remember all of the lines for the following:

*   'Baa, Baa, black sheep';
*   'Little Jack Horner';
*   'Mary, Mary, quite contrary'?

Janet Adam Smith, in her introduction to the *Faber Book of Children's Verse* (1953), commented that *the poetry we most enjoyed reading in those years (ages eight to fourteen) has stuck in our minds in a way poetry learnt more recently has not. So it seems reasonable to give children poems to read that they will like to find in their heads twenty or thirty years later ... to stock up the attics of the mind with enjoyment for the future* (p.20). This seems to be an excellent justification for giving the children in our classrooms the widest possible range of poetry to read, enjoy and understand.

The ability of poets to condense feeling and ideas into a few words enables them to convey concepts which can promote discussion and reflection in the classroom, as well as inspiring children's own work. Read the anonymous poem below and then consider how you might follow this up with your class.

I Asked the Little Boy Who Cannot See

I asked the little boy who cannot see,
'And what is colour like?'
'Why green,' said he,
'Is like the rustle when the wind blows through
The forest; running water, that is blue;
And red is like a trumpet sound; and pink
Is like the smell of roses; and I think
That purple must be like a thunderstorm;
And yellow is like something soft and warm;
And white is a pleasant stillness when you lie
And dream.'

(Anonymous)

There is scope here for considering the concept of colour and what it means to us, as well as ways in which someone who cannot see colours can have ideas about them. The poem might be read as part of a sequence of lessons in which poems and stories which explore colour are studied. Mary O'Neill's poem, *Mimi's Fingers*, also examines a blind child's perception of the world around her and her lack of understanding of colour, while Betsy Byars' story, *The Midnight Fox*, includes a wonderful passage in which the central character imagines what it would be like to discover a new colour. (For further ideas see Waugh and Jolliffe, 2012, and look online for *I Asked the Little Boy Who Cannot See* – you will find lots of examples of children writing their own versions, and some ideas for lesson plans and sequences of lessons.) First, look at the case study below which shows how an NQT enhanced a project on Victorians while stimulating children's writing and encouraging discussion.

Case Study

Research-based learning

Molly, an NQT, was studying the Victorians with her Years 4–5 class and was eager to develop their understanding of the topic through a series of literacy lessons based on poetry. The class began by looking at a variety of poems written from the perspective of a poor, working Victorian child. The poems included *Housemaid's Letter* by Clare Bevan, *Chimney Boy's Story* by Wes Magee and *Workhouse Boy* by Louise Ward.

The children used talk partners to discuss the similarities and differences between the poems, both structurally and thematically, and a common theme of 'hopes, dreams and fears' emerged.

→

Molly then planned for her class to write individual poems about their own hopes, dreams and fears in order to compare their own lives to those of the Victorian children studied throughout the term. She decided that the children would be more enthusiastic about writing their own poems if they were able to choose the poetic form through which they would express the theme. So that the children were not restricted by poetic forms previously studied in school, the class collected a list of poetic forms they already knew on the interactive whiteboard, and several new types were introduced by the teacher. The list included haikus, clerihews, cinquains and kennings.

The children were then split into pairs and asked to choose a type of poem they had not had previous experience with. Using computers, the children researched the type of poem they had chosen and created a poster which defined the rules (rhyming patterns, syllable counts, number of lines, etc.). The pairs were also asked to include an example of their type of poem and worked hard to find examples which were funny, moving, on-topic and eye-catching.

In the next lesson each pair was asked to present their poetic form to the rest of the class, using the example to demonstrate each of the rules. The act of teaching the rest of the class about their type of poem ensured that the children's understanding was secure and the children rose to the challenge, taking pride in their presentations. The posters were then stuck up around the classroom and the children were given 15 minutes to look at all of the posters and choose the type of poem they would like to use to express their own hopes, dreams and fears. This not only enabled the children to take ownership of their learning, but also significantly increased the children's breadth of knowledge about poetic form. The following lesson the children planned and wrote their poems. They were given time to self- and peer-assess before editing and improving their work and creating a final 'neat' draft on coloured card. The class produced a huge variety of poems and, at the end of the series of lessons, were extremely eager to share them not only with each other, but with friends in other classes.

The activity enabled the children to develop their understanding of their topic on Victorians, their ICT skills, and speaking and listening skills, while simultaneously allowing all children to work with a type of poetry about which they felt enthusiastic and knowledgeable.

Curriculum Links

The example provided by Molly's case study illustrates the possibilities for enhancing history work through poetry. See Moses and Corbett (2002) for examples of poems suitable for a range of subjects.

Poetry, then, has the capacity to be a catalyst for exploring aspects of the world around us. There are poems available to enable us to reinforce or explore ideas across the curriculum, many of which will add to children's understanding of subjects and help them to remember facts or concepts. (For a good selection of poetry for use across the curriculum, see Moses and Corbett, 2002, *The Works 2: Poems on every subject and for every occasion*).

You will see elsewhere in this book (for example in Chapters 3 and 8) that literature offers us many opportunities to promote thinking and to enhance learning. The activity below provides a chance for you to consider how you might use some stimulating and thought-provoking poems in this way.

Activity

All of the poems listed below can be easily found online. Look at some of them and consider how you could use them as a starting point for or an integral element in discussion or study across the curriculum.

Summer Storm by John Foster
It Hurts by John Foster
Growing Up in the 1930s by Trevor Harvey
For the Fallen by Laurence Binyon
The Great Lizards by Dave Calder

When reading progresses from the early rhymed texts to stories told in prose, there are many classic and popular books in which songs or poems are embedded in the text, which can add a great deal of pleasure when a book is read aloud – the 'hums', for instance, in *Winnie the Pooh,* or the poems in *Through the Looking Glass,* many of which have become comic classics in their own right. As readers becomes more independent, however, and find poems in the text of such books as *The Hobbit and Lord of the Rings*, the stories of Rudyard Kipling, or Roald Dahl's *Charlie and the Chocolate Factory* and *James and the Giant Peach*, they are increasingly likely to skip them from their reading on the grounds that they are not expected to be part of the story.

Much of the poetry best known to and remembered by children is comic verse – Hilaire Belloc's (1907) *Cautionary Tales*, for instance, which have been often imitated and updated, are wonderfully funny and well-written, with clever use of rhymes and a good sprinkling of vocabulary which may challenge children but which is always easy to understand in the context of the poems. The poems centre upon children whose particular misdeeds lead to unfortunate consequences, including death for several. However, the presentation and humour are such that children are not horrified, and tend to laugh at Jim being eaten by a lion because he would not hold his nanny's hand, or Rebecca Offendort being crushed by a marble bust as a result of her repeated slamming of doors.

Kit Wright, Spike Milligan, Michael Rosen and Roger McGough have all written volumes for children in which exuberance and form which invite reading aloud are combined with some more reflective and thought-provoking verses. Allan Ahlberg's *Please, Mrs Butler* (1983) and its successor, *Heard it in the Playground* (1989), have become modern classics for their warm but never patronising depiction of life from a primary school point of view. There are many anthologies of comic verse for children to choose from, several of which are listed at the end of this chapter.

Narrative poems

Many narrative poems are ideally suited to the imagination of primary-age children and can be introduced simply for the stories they tell; the rhythm, the form, the repetitions and other 'poetic' effects can come in for discussion at a later stage. Good examples here would be Browning's *The Pied Piper of Hamelin*, Robert Southey's *The Inchcape Rock* and *Bishop Hatto*, splendidly Gothic stories in both of which the evil wrongdoer ends up destroyed by his own wicked deed, or Alfred Noyes' *The Highwayman*, which has a bit of everything – love, drama, death, the supernatural and some highly memorable similes. Gibson's *Flannan Isle*, which is discussed in Chapter 2, is also well worth exploring.

Learning about language through poetry

Poems are also a wonderful way of meeting and experimenting with vocabulary, including made-up words – the obvious and best-known example is Lewis Carroll's (1871) *Jabberwocky*, which starts:

> 'Twas brillig, and the slithy toves
> Did gyre and gimble in the wabe:
> All mimsy were the borogoves,
> And the mome raths outgrabe.

In the case study below, you will see how a trainee teacher linked an exploration of a nonsense verse with modern foreign language study.

Case Study

Poetry and modern foreign languages

Jabberwocky has been translated into French, German and even Latin. (All of these versions are easily accessible on the internet.) Natalie, a PGCE student who was also teaching some French to a Year 6 class, gave her class the French translation and the children worked in pairs finding, guessing and working out which French nonsense words had been created as the equivalent of 'brillig', 'slithy' and so on. This led on to discussion about parts of speech. How could you tell which words were adjectives, nouns or verbs from the structure even when the word itself was completely unfamiliar? This encouraged their confidence in knowledge of patterns in language formation, and led on to creative work in inventing their own 'nonsense' words and poems.

Curriculum Links

The strong emphasis upon knowledge about word classes in the National Curriculum means that teachers will need to devise interesting ways to help children to identify and name them. Word class mobility, which describes the way in which the same word may be a different word class in different situations (for example, book: *I read a book* (noun); *I'll book a ticket* (verb)), can lead to confusion. Therefore, it is important to find ways to teach word classes in context. Exploring word usage in poetry may be an interesting and meaningful way to do this.

Many children's poems achieve comic rhythmic effects by the use of nonsense syllables – for instance, Spike Milligan's *On the Ning Nang Nong* or Roger McGough's *Harum Scarum* – while others use new words to introduce an element of fantasy (try R.J. Scriven's *I'm a Marrog from Mars*). Misspellings to make contrived rhymes are always popular – for instance, Ogden Nash's *Parsley* (*Parsley / Is gharsley*) or the same author's *Shake and shake / The ketchup bottle / None'll come / and then a lottle*. And while on the subject of Nash, it is worth mentioning his *Very Like a Whale* which begins:

> *One thing that literature would be greatly the better for*
> *Would be a more restricted employment by the authors of simile and metaphor*

and ends with the splendid:

> *And they always say things like that the snow is a white blanket after a winter storm.*
> *Oh it is, is it, all right then, you sleep under a six-inch blanket of snow and I'll sleep*
> *under a half-inch blanket of unpoetical blanket material and we'll see which one keeps*
> *warm,*
> *And after that maybe you'll begin to comprehend dimly*
> *What I mean by too much metaphor and simile.*

This is surely a valuable inclusion in any lesson on the structure of poetry.

Poetry can also experiment with onomatopoeia – for instance, the horses' hooves in *The Highwayman go tlot-tlot, tlot-tlot* in a way that would be unlikely in prose. John Masefield's *Cargoes* (first published 1902) in which two images of beautiful and elegant cargo ships from history are contrasted, in the last stanza, with a prosaic early twentieth-century tramp steamer, gives a wonderful example of rich and luxuriant vocabulary chosen for its extravagant sound.

> *Quinquireme of Nineveh from distant Ophir,*
> *Rowing home to haven in sunny Palestine,*
> *With a cargo of ivory,*
> *And apes and peacocks,*
> *Sandalwood, cedarwood, and sweet white wine.*
> *Stately Spanish galleon coming from the Isthmus,*
> *Dipping through the Tropics by the palm-green shores,*
> *With a cargo of diamonds,*
> *Emeralds, amethysts,*
> *Topazes, and cinnamon, and gold moidores.*
> *Dirty British coaster with a salt-caked smoke stack,*
> *Butting through the Channel in the mad March days,*
> *With a cargo of Tyne coal,*
> *Road-rails, pig-lead,*
> *Firewood, iron-ware, and cheap tin trays.*

This is an example of a poem which benefits enormously, as most do, from being read aloud, and has also been set to music very effectively.

It remains important, however, to resist the temptation always to use poetry simply to amuse, and to show how poetry can express or distil a memory or an emotion often more effectively than prose. Use of anthologies such as Seamus Heaney and Ted Hughes' classic anthology *The Rattle Bag* – still arguably the best and most comprehensive available – can introduce the children gradually to more serious and provocative poems. Many of the classic poets wrote at least sometimes in metre and style easily comprehensible by younger children – Thomas Hardy, Robert Browning and Edward Thomas can provide useful examples, and such well-known classics as Shelley's *Ozymandias,* although certainly not written for children, are by no means inaccessible. And to quote again from Janet Adam Smith, *One of the greatest pleasures of poetry is the discovery that a poem which you have always known means far more than you could realise when you first read it and liked it* (1953, p.20).

Another advantage of introducing 'adult' poetry to children rather than a diet of poems written expressly for younger readers is that the earlier readers meets more complex poems, the less likely they are to persist in the belief that it is necessary and logical to stop at the end of each line. Poetry written for children is nearly always constructed in simple forms with a full-stop or comma at each line-break, and it is easy for children to get into the habit of stopping at the end of each line whether the sense demands it or not. The idea of *enjambement* – the use of phrases which go straight over a line-break in the poem – can be difficult for children to get used to.

It might be helpful to introduce children to the old classroom punctuation exercise:

> *Caesar entered on his head*
> *A helmet on each foot*
> *A sandal in his hand he had*
> *His trusty sword to boot.*

This rhyme makes no sense if read with a pause at the end of each line, but needs correct understanding of *enjambement* and punctuation to be read. *Caesar entered; on his head, a helmet; on each foot a sandal. In his hand, he had his trusty sword to boot.* From looking at this, we can go on to introduce children to poems which contain lines where the thought continues uninterrupted by punctuation from one line to the next, so that they will eventually be able to cope with, for instance, such lines as these from Keats' *Endymion*:

> *A thing of beauty is a joy forever:*
> *Its loveliness increases; it will never*
> *Pass into nothingness but still will keep*
> *A bower quiet for us, and a sleep*
> *Full of sweet dreams, and health and quiet breathing.*

Short, structured poetry

Poetry takes many forms and some of these are highly structured and, often, short. Poetic forms such as haiku, limericks, triolets and cinquains enable us to express complex ideas very concisely. Their brevity often appeals to children, as in Molly's case study, and it can provide an excellent introduction to poetic form. The case study which follows is divided into three parts and shows how a trainee teacher developed children's knowledge and understanding of poetry through activities involving short, structured poems.

Case Study

Part 1: Haiku

Daniel, a third-year undergraduate trainee, was asked to plan a series of lessons on poetry for his Year 4 class. After discussions with his tutor, Daniel decided to focus initially on short, structured poems and discovered that there were several different forms which would enable

→

him to look with his class at rhyme, structure, scansion and the power of poetry to convey a lot of meaning in a few words.

He found several examples of haiku in anthologies and online and brought suitable examples to school to share with children. He began by discussing syllables and getting children to clap the syllables* in their names and in the names of TV programmes and football teams. Once the class had understood syllables, he looked at some haiku with them and asked them to try to work out the rule for haikus in terms of syllables.

Daniel went on to do some shared writing of haiku with the class, using interesting photographs as stimuli, and focusing on pictures of the seaside since the class would be making a visit to a nearby resort later in his placement. He displayed the pictures on the interactive whiteboard and asked children for their thoughts on what they could see in single words and short phrases. A beach with a setting sun and colourful sky in the background elicited, among other suggestions, the following: *light reflecting on the water; last rays of sunshine; end of a perfect day; a chill in the air after a baking hot day; ball of orange fire sinks below the horizon.* Daniel took some of the ideas and with the children's help and using revision and drafting wrote:

Ball of orange fire
Reflected in darker sea
Cool end to hot day.

Children were keen to make use of the ideas they had about the picture and Daniel asked them to use mini-whiteboards to try out ideas in pairs. They then worked together on paper to produce haikus which were read aloud to the class and displayed. The work was followed up by each pair being given a different picture to write a haiku about and these too were shared in a display and a PowerPoint presentation, which was played on a loop in the school hall.

(*Another way to count syllables is to place your hand under your chin as you say words. Each time there is a syllable change your chin touches your hand.)

Case Study

Part 2: Developing structured poetry

After the success of the lessons on haiku, Daniel wanted to introduce his class to limericks and cinquains. Cinquains have five lines, each line with a fixed number of syllables:

line 1: 2 syllables
line 2: 4 syllables
line 3: 6 syllables
line 4: 8 syllables
line 5: 2 syllables

To demonstrate this, Daniel did some shared writing modelling a cinquain for the picture he had used as an initial stimulus for haiku:

Lonely dark beach
Last rays of sunlight glow
Crashing waves in the pale moonlight
Darkness

He then asked children for suggestions for changing his cinquain using their own words, reminding them about the need to keep the number of syllables in each line constant. This was followed by writing about another picture, drawing upon children's ideas as they worked together in pairs to make notes on mini-whiteboards.

Although Daniel had anticipated that children might find producing five-line cinquains more challenging than three-line haikus, in fact they found it easier, being already familiar with counting syllables and trying ideas out. The children's work, which drew upon a selection of colour pictures Daniel had downloaded or cut from magazines, included, for a picture of Bonfire Night:

Fizzing
Booming, bursting
Cascading, glittering
Bright colours fill the dark night sky
Fireworks!

Case Study

Part 3: Rhyme

For the third stage of Daniel's poetry lessons he focused on limericks. His class teacher suggested that children may find these more challenging since, although they now had a good appreciation of syllables and should be able to write lines of the correct length, they would now have to introduce rhymes and these often proved difficult.

Daniel therefore decided to create a rhyme wall with a bank of words suggested by the children which they could draw upon when writing. To create this, he gave pairs of children people's names on cards based upon the 20 English vowel phonemes and asked them to create as many rhyming words as possible, regardless of whether the spellings had the same graphemes. For example, he gave one pair the word Kate, which they then rhymed with late, wait, great, mate, grate, slate, gate, weight, eight, ate and date. Another pair had Fred, which they rhymed with head, bed, said, dread, led and lead. Children wrote their rhyming words neatly onto cards which were placed beneath each name on the rhyming wall.

$\longrightarrow$

Daniel then discussed the different ways in which many rhyming words could be spelled, and encouraged children to add to the wall whenever they thought of a new word by placing blank cards next to it.

The wall proved a great success and children produced several amusing and well-constructed limericks. Daniel shared these with the class and read them some examples from poetry anthologies.

Activity

The three poetry activities Daniel and his class undertook demonstrate the importance of sharing poetry with children before asking them to write and of preparing them by looking at different poetic structures. Consider how you would plan for lessons in which children learned about and wrote triolets (poems with eight lines in which there are two rhymes and five of the eight lines are repeated or refrain lines. The first line is repeated as the fourth and seventh lines. The second line is repeated as the eighth line). For instance:

I've been reading Lorna Doone
A stupid thing to try in June
It's far too hot.
I've been reading Lorna Doone,
It kept me up from night till noon,
I am a clot.
I've been reading Lorna Doone,
A stupid thing to try in June.

Curriculum Links

The National Curriculum Years 3–4 programme of study requires that pupils should be taught to:

- *prepare poems and play scripts to read aloud and to perform, showing understanding through intonation, tone, volume and action*
- *recognise some different forms of poetry {for example, free verse, narrative poetry}*

(DfE, 2013, p.36)

Daniel's lessons provided a range of opportunities for children to broaden their knowledge and understanding of poetry, as well as to produce their own poems for sharing.

Conclusion

You have seen that poetry can present challenges for both children and teachers, but you have also seen that it offers tremendous potential for enhancing study across the curriculum, as well as for developing an appreciation of language and its many exciting possibilities. If you were previously unenthusiastic about poetry, we hope that you will now revisit it and explore some of the recommendations we have made. If you were already an enthusiast, we hope you will pass your enthusiasm and knowledge on to your pupils and colleagues.

Learning Outcomes Review

Having read this chapter and engaged with the activities, you should have a better awareness of the range of poetry which might be shared with children in primary schools. You should also be able to appreciate the importance of poetry in its own right and the range and scope of activities which might emanate from reading poetry. The case studies should enable you to consider how children might be introduced to writing poetry.

Self-assessment questions

1   Can you describe the features of each of the following types of poem: haiku, limerick, cinquain?
2   What is enjambement?

(Definitions can be found in the glossary in Appendix 2.)

Further Reading

Ahlberg, A. and Ahlberg, J. (1979) *Each Peach Pear Plum*. London: Puffin.

De la Mare, W. (2001) *Peacock Pie: The Collected Works of Walter de la Mare*. London: Faber.

Donaldson, J. and Scheffler, A. (1999) *The Gruffalo*. London: Macmillan Children's Books.

Frost, R. (2001) *Stopping by Woods on a Snowy Evening*, in *The complete works of Robert Frost*. London: Penguin.

Lear, E. (1947) *The Complete Nonsense of Edward Lear*. London: Faber and Faber.

Milne, A.A. (1924) *Now We Are Six*. London: Methuen.

Milne, A.A. (1927) *When We Were Very Young*. London: Methuen.

Moses, B. and Corbett, P. (2002) *The Works 2: Poems on Every Subject and for Every Occasion*. London: MacMillan.

This book is an excellent resource for enhancing teaching across the curriculum. Poems are divided into subject areas so that it is easy to find something appropriate for a topic.

Nash, O. (1994) *The Adventures of Isabel*. New York: Little Brown.

Nash, O. (1995) *The Tale of Custard the Dragon*. New York: Little Brown.

Ofsted (2007) *Poetry in Schools: A Survey of Practice, 2006/07*. London: Ofsted.

Opie, I. and Opie, P. (1992) *I Saw Esau: The Schoolchild's Pocket Book*. Cambridge, MA: Candlewick.

Stevenson, R.L. (1992) *A Child's Garden of Verses*. London: Everyman's Library Children's Classics.

References

Adam Smith, J. (compiler) (1953) *Faber Book of Children's Verse*. London: Faber and Faber.

Ahlberg, A. (1983) *Please Mrs Butler*. London: Puffin.

Ahlberg, A. (1989) *Heard it on the Playground.* London: Puffin.

Belloc, H. (2008) *Cautionary Tales*. Radford, VA: Wilder Books (first published 1907).

Bryant, P.E., MacLean, M., Bradley, L. and Crossland, J. (1990) Rhyme and alliteration, phoneme detection, and learning to read. *Developmental Psychology*, 26(3): 429–38.

Byars, B. (1976) *The Midnight Fox*. London: Puffin.

Carroll, L. (1871) Jabberwocky, in *Through the Looking Glass*. London: MacMillan.

Carter, D. (1998) *Teaching Poetry in the Primary School*. London: David Fulton.

Cremin, T., Bearne, E., Mottram, M. and Goodwin, P. (2008) Primary teachers as readers. *English in Education*, 42(1): 8–23.

DfE (2013) *The National Curriculum in England: Key Stages 1 and 2 Framework Document*. London: DfE. Available at: www.gov.uk/government/uploads/system/uploads/attachment_data/file/335133/PRIMARY_national_curriculum_220714.pdf (accessed 12.04.16).

Martin, T. (2003) Minimum and maximum entitlements: Literature at Key Stage 2. *Reading Literacy and Language*, 37(1): 14–17.

Milne, A.A. (1924) *When We Were Very Young*. London: Methuen.

Milne, A.A. (1927) *Now We are Six*. London: Methuen.

Moses, B. and Corbett, P. (2002) *The Works 2: Poems on Every Subject and for Every Occasion*. London: MacMillan.

Ofsted (2007) *Poetry in Schools: A Survey of Practice, 2006/07*. London: Ofsted.

Waugh, D. and Jolliffe, W. (2012) *English 5–11*, 2nd edition. London: Routledge.

Whitehead, M. (2007) *Developing Language and Literacy with Young Children*. London: Paul Chapman.

Answers to activity

Rhyming mnemonics activity

Red sky at night
Shepherd's delight (the weather will be sunny if the evening sky is red)

This is often learned alongside:

Red sky in the morning
Shepherd's warning

In 1492
Columbus sailed the ocean blue (set sail for America)

Never eat
Shredded Wheat (Points of the compass in clockwise order: north, east, south, west)

Conclusion

We hope that this book has whetted your appetite for exploring a range of children's literature, and that you will make extensive use of this literature in your teaching across the curriculum. You should now be aware of the breadth of literature available and its potential for enhancing your teaching and children's learning. Above all, you should have recognised the importance of sharing and discussing literature with your pupils and the value of engaging them with a wide spectrum of stories and poems.

Stories and poems are central to our cultural heritage and should, therefore, be at the heart of our work in primary schools. They provide entertainment, as well as opportunities to develop a love and understanding of language. Through engaging with children's literature, children can improve and develop their own writing, as well as their reading skills. If they have teachers who are enthusiastic about stories and poems and who have a wide knowledge of texts, children will develop a love of reading which can be life-enhancing.

Our reading habits are changing constantly. After peaking in 2007, when the final instalment of the Harry Potter series was published, sales of printed books (now referred to as p-books by some publishers) have fallen as those of e-books have risen. No doubt further changes will occur as your teaching career unfolds. It is, therefore, important to be receptive to change and to ensure that, whatever media children's literature is presented in, you help make it attractive and available to your pupils. (See also Baddeley, 2015.) We hope that reading this book will contribute to your ability to do that.

David Waugh
Sally Neaum
Rosemary Waugh
June 2016

Reference

Baddeley, A. (2015) The ebook is dead. Long live the ebook. *Guardian*. Available at: www.theguardian.com/books/2015/feb/01/the-ebook-is-dead-long-live-print-digital-sales (accessed 12.04.16).

APPENDIX 1

Seventy-five books

The books described in this section were chosen by parents, teachers, headteachers and the authors of the present book because they represent a wide range of children's literature and many of the major authors.

We have tried to include classic and modern texts, as well as those which represent our diverse society.

The list, which is presented in no particular order, is bound to induce debate: *Why this author and not that one? Why that book by that author and not one of her others?*

We hope you will join the debate and will send us your own suggestions, but that in the meantime the list might inspire you to read something you hadn't previously tried or even to revisit some old favourites.

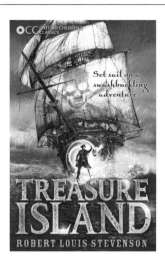

Treasure Island

Robert Louis Stevenson

A classic adventure story of pirates, hidden treasure and a young boy's great adventure. Some of the language is archaic and even Y6 children may need help to access some of it, but it can prove a good introduction to writing from an earlier age. Some discussion of life on large sailing ships might also be necessary. Nevertheless, the excitement of the story should appeal to Y6 classes.

The old film may be useful but some modern revisionist interpretations go a long way wide of Stevenson's original story!

Alice's Adventures in Wonderland

Lewis Carroll

One of the very earliest children's books of the first great Golden Age of children's literature, the classic story of Alice's magical adventures has been interpreted in many different ways. Beware of using any of the film or television versions in class to accompany your reading – many directors have all put their own distinctive take! The poems and songs can set off good imaginative writing, as can ideas such as the magic potions and size changes.

Five Children and It

E Nesbit

Four children, and their baby brother, find a magical creature in a sand-pit, who has the power to grant their wishes. However, these rarely turn out as expected. The book's Edwardian setting adds interest, and though some historical details will need further discussion, the characters and their conversation and actions remain fresh and humorous. An excellent starting point for imaginative work on "What would you wish for?"

The story has two sequels, *The Phoenix and the Carpet* and *The Story of the Amulet*. Nesbit's many other works include both magic-based stories and more straightforward ones such as *The Railway Children*, all told with the same humour and engaging style.

The Magic Faraway Tree

Enid Blyton

This book is the second in Blyton's Faraway series, but seems to be the best-known and loved. The Faraway Tree has an ever-changing rotation of different lands at the top, and the children who climb it explore them in a series of adventures. Although Blyton is often criticised for the blandness of her writing, her simplistic and sometimes patronising style, there is no denying that these books have been favourites for many years and continue to give children a taste for reading, which can only be a good thing! The original stories have been bowdlerised slightly for a new generation – for instance, Dame Slap is now Dame Snap and terrorises her classes by shouting at them rather than with corporal punishment.

Perhaps a book for children to find for themselves rather than to be used whole as a class text, but nevertheless the case can be argued for it having a place.

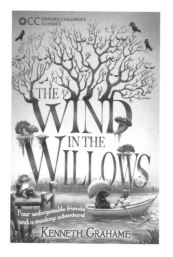

The Wind in the Willows

Kenneth Grahame

Mole leaves his house underground and discovers a whole new life on the river bank with his new friend the Water-Rat, meeting Mr Toad and Mr Badger and helping to rescue Toad from the consequences of his exciting adventures when he steals a motor car and is sent to prison. Although some of the attitudes may need careful explanation with a young audience, and two chapters ("The Piper at the Gates of Dawn" and "Wayfarers All", both of which are outside the main thread of the story) are often omitted for the young, the beauty of the descriptions and the humour of the characters continue to delight new audiences.

In particular, the detailed descriptions of interiors of rooms could be the stimulus for writing activities.

The Wind on the Moon

Eric Linklater

Two sisters have a "year of naughtiness" while their father is away: their adventures include the magical (turning themselves into kangaroos and solving a mystery in a zoo) and the exciting (rescuing their father from imprisonment in the wicked Count's castle). A wide cast of characters and a constant pace of events make this book sheer comical entertainment, and a possible starting point for imaginative work. Who hasn't wanted to stow away in a removal van? What animal would you choose to turn into?

Danny the Champion of the World

Roald Dahl

Danny is initiated by his father into the excitement of poaching pheasants from the local unpleasant landowner. Dahl's eye for detail, and for narration at the right level, makes this a real page-turner. It has been made into a film starring Jeremy Irons with his own son, Sam, playing Danny. The film sticks closely to the text and would be very suitable for classroom use. The story could lead into PSHCE discussions of right and wrong and breaking the law.

Roald Dahl's other works are mostly too well-known to need listing – always original and sure to engage children.

The Weirdstone of Brisingamen

Alan Garner

Susan possesses a bracelet with an unusual stone in it: she does not know that this is an ancient and magical weirdstone, which is being sought by dark forces from many centuries ago. With her brother Colin, and with the assistance of a mysterious wizard, she must save the stone from the enemies who are trying to seize it, including a shape-shifting witch. A fast-paced and action-filled story, imaginative and exciting.

There is a sequel, *The Moon of Gomrath*. Some of Garner's other writing is more suitable for older readers, as his style became more elliptical, but those who enjoy this might also enjoy *Elidor*.

The Secret Garden

Frances Hodgson Burnett

Mary is a lonely and disagreeable orphan when she arrives to live at her uncle's vast and remote house, but gradually discovers the pleasures both of watching the neglected garden come to life and of developing friendships. Her relationships with Dickon, the maid's brother who is a straightforward Yorkshire boy, and Colin, her spoilt and self-centred cousin, are described with sensitivity and realism.

This book has been filmed and televised many times, and has a charm not always found in the author's *Little Lord Fauntleroy* which was a bigger success in her lifetime. Children who enjoy it are likely also to enjoy *A Little Princess*, which again has an independent-minded orphan heroine. (In this book, filmed and televised several times, Sara suffers a downturn of fate and being made a maid in the school where she had once been prize pupil.)

Swallows and Amazons

Arthur Ransome

Two families of children in the Lake District spend the summer sailing, camping and having self-reliant adventures which, although perfectly prosaic on one level, are always enhanced by the imagination of the children. A girl alone on a lake island becomes Man Friday to herself, a man who lives on a household is a retired pirate... Although Ransome's world of the 1930s is one of considerably more freedom from adult interference and such concerns as Health and Safety, the personalities of the characters and their relationships have not dated and Ransome's own maps and illustrations bring the stories vividly alive.

The first of Ransome's 12 children's stories, *Swallows and Amazons* has been filmed several times in a sympathetic and faithful way.

The Tiger Who Came to Tea

Judith Kerr

Sophie and her mother are surprised when a tiger turns up at their house for tea – and more surprised by his unending appetite! He eats and drinks everything in the house, so that when Sophie's father gets home the family have to go out to a café for tea. A very simple story whose appeal has not dated, with Kerr's detailed and charming illustrations in which the tiger is smiling and saturnine rather than wild or threatening.

Harry Potter and the Philosopher's Stone

J K Rowling

Eleven-year old Harry suddenly learns that he is a wizard, and finds a whole new world in which he can escape from his boring life. The first story to introduce the whole detailed world of Hogwarts and its magical education, which is now captivating a second generation of readers. Humour, fast-paced adventure, magic and a range of thoroughly convincing and varied characters make this story a practically universal pleaser. J.K. Rowling kept complete editorial control of the film script, which means that the film is totally faithful to the book and can enhance any classroom reading.

Stig of the Dump

Clive King

Barney makes friends with Stig, who seems a mysterious survivor from Stone Age times. Their adventures lead to a magical night when time zones cross and Barney, with his sister, sees the building of a great monument of standing stones. Much of the book's enduring appeal lies in the efforts at communication between the boys from different worlds, and Stig's reactions to aspects of modern life – a good starting point for many imaginative activities.

Stig has been filmed and also made into a television series, largely available on YouTube.

The Lion, the Witch and the Wardrobe

C S Lewis

Almost too well-known to need introducing, the first story in C.S. Lewis's *Chronicles of Narnia* continues to enchant new generations of children from the first moment when Lucy finds a strange snowy country in the back of a wardrobe, to the final conflict between the great lion Aslan and the wicked White Witch. Sometimes criticised for its underlying Christian message, the book and its successors are still wonderful imaginative stories which can be enjoyed at face value.

The recent films of this and the next two books, *Prince Caspian* and *The Voyage of the Dawn Treader,* are fairly faithful to the text and would be useful in the classroom. Although *The Magician's Nephew* is a prequel in the time-sequence of the books, it is better read later.

The Hobbit

J R R Tolkien

Despite the recent expansion of this story into three epic films, the original remains a fairly straightforward magical adventure with a range of lively characters, and a range of humour, wit, excitement and suspense. The introduction of a range of creatures, both nice and nasty, can inspire the imagination and enthral audiences. The story lends itself to possibilities of drama and illustration, and the songs and poems in the story could be a basis for creative writing activities.

Winnie the Pooh

A A Milne

The adventures of the original well-meaning but often rather dim bear, and his friends in the Hundred Acre Wood, remain fresh and the humour of the characterisation and situations continue to delight, despite their exploitation by the Disney studios. These stories were written to be told or read aloud, rather than tackled by young readers, so sometimes the language is slightly more demanding than the stories – a wonderful opportunity for a range of voices!

The sequel, *The House at Pooh Corner*, carries on the story and introduces new characters such as Tigger, Kanga and Roo.

Nurse Matilda

Christianna Brand

The countless and unbelievably naughty children of the Brown household are tamed into order by the fearful and magical Nurse Matilda. The riotous behaviour and the terribleness and logic of the punishments make these stories a perennial delight, ideal for reading aloud and sharing. For example, when the children refuse to get up in the morning they find themselves confined to bed with measles for the day; when they refuse to say please and thank you they must repeat their actions over and over until they will say "Please stop!". Edward Ardizzone's illustrations capture the humour of the stories beautifully.

Although the recent "Nanny McPhee" films were based on the idea of the stories, they represent a very watered-down and saccharine version.

The Gruffalo

Julia Donaldson

Only 700 words long, this rhymed story is a delight for children who will enjoy joining in with the ends of the lines. A small mouse walks through the woods, and warns off all the fierce animals who want to attack her by threatening them with the Gruffalo... then she comes face to face with the real Gruffalo. The endearing pictures are never too scary, and there are useful lessons about not being afraid of things which seem alarming.

The book has rapidly achieved classic status since its first appearance, and the sequel *The Gruffalo's Child* is becoming equally well-loved.

Just So Stories

Rudyard Kipling

Stories to be read aloud, for the best appreciation of Kipling's love of the sounds of words and the pleasure of repetition. "How the Elephant got his Trunk", "The Cat that Walked by Itself", and "How the Armadillo Became" are humorous delights of fantasy. In some of the stories Kipling's nineteenth-century colonialism might need some explanation or editing; strange gods appear, for instance, and attitudes which are no longer within the range of political correctness. Nevertheless, the life and humour of the stories continues to appeal to new generations of readers.

Little House in the Big Woods

Laura Ingalls Wilder

This is the first of the series in which Wilder recounts the true story of her childhood and early life on the Great Frontier in the nineteenth century, as her pioneering father wants to move the family ever further West. The close family atmosphere and the relationship between Laura and her older sister Mary keep the interest lively, and the detailed descriptions of such events as butter-churning and "sugaring-off" the maple trees would enhance history work on the USA or farming.

There are six more books waiting for readers who want to follow Laura's growing-up: *Little House on the Prairie*, probably the best-known, has vivid descriptions of Victorian-style schooling, and *By the Shores of Silver Lake* describes the building of the railroad heading west across the undiscovered continent, all through young eyes at first hand.

Clever Polly and the Stupid Wolf

Catherine Storr

There are four volumes of these stories, in which a clever little girl constantly outwits a fierce and hungry but extremely stupid wolf, most of whose plots to catch her are based on familiar stories and rhymes. In the classroom, a reminder of the original story first might help with understanding where the wolf goes wrong – as he does, every time.

The wit and humour of the writing goes well beyond the enjoyment of the very small, and these stories can be enjoyed for years. Polly is a sensible and matter-of-fact girl, whose reasoning and explanations always outwit the wolf.

Professor Branestawm

Norman Hunter

This series of books featuring the adventures and inventions of an eccentric professor was first started in the thirties, and the settings have a period charm, although Hunter wrote the later volumes until as late as 1983. They are filled with comic characters and ideas, and could be the trigger for imaginative or serious work on inventions and discoveries. The naming of the characters (Colonel Dedshott, Mrs Flittersnoop) could also be a spark for creative writing.

Heath Robinson's illustrations add much to the early books, and there have been films of the Professor made by the BBC and starring Harry Hill, as recently as Christmas 2015.

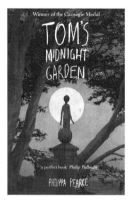

Tom's Midnight Garden

Philippa Pearce

Tom goes to stay with his uncle and aunt when his brother has measles, in a flat which forms part of an old Victorian house. When he goes downstairs at night he finds the house and garden as they were 50 years ago, and gets involved with the life of Hatty, who lives there, also with an aunt. His understanding gradually grows, and the final scene has often been called one of the most moving in all of children's literature.

Although the book was written in 1958 and some context may need explaining – measles and quarantine, for example – the characters and dialogue remain fresh and original.

The book can also provoke discussion about how houses, landscapes and people change over time, and even about the nature of reality. One of those books everyone should encounter, it has come to be regarded as a classic of the second Golden Age of children's books.

Bill's New Frock

Anne Fine

Bill Simpson wakes up one morning to find that everyone sees him as a girl and he has a new frilly pink frock to wear to school. As the day progresses, he finds unfairness and frustration on all sides at the differences from his life as a boy. These range from practicalities (no pockets in his clothes) to attitudes and perceptions – his anger is dismissed as "being a bit upset". Interestingly, we are never told whether he has actually *become* a girl for the day – Bill's own self-image is still firmly set in being a boy. Still relevant 40 years after publication, the story challenges and raises consciousness about differences in attitudes towards girls and boys.

Funny, memorable and provocative, the book has been filmed and also has a range of classroom resources available online, as well as a book published by Scholastic on further ideas for its use in schools.

The Jolly Postman

Janet and Allan Ahlberg

This wonderful interactive book uses many well-known traditional stories as its springboard, as the postman goes from house to house delivering messages to familiar characters such as Cinderella and the Three Bears. The book includes eight separate and removable letters, each in its own envelope. An excellent starting point for early writing – replying to the letters, or imagining the scene when each letter is received.

A wide range of well-designed classroom resources for using this book is available online, many of them free.

Flat Stanley

Jeff Brown

Stanley Lambchop is flattened into two dimensions when a heavy board falls on him. He soon discovers the advantages of his new state – entering rooms by sliding under doors, for instance, or posing as a picture on the wall to foil art thieves. The fast and funny adventures of Stanley and his younger brother first appeared in 1964 but have a perennial appeal.

Twenty years after the original book, the author started to write the first of six sequels following further adventures of Stanley. The idea of the books has given rise to the *Flat Stanley Project*, an international initiative in which letters, journals and ideas are sent to other schools around the world in envelopes with a Flat Stanley cut-out – more information on this can be found on the project's website.

Meg and Mog

Helen Nicoll and Jan Pienkowski

This timeless series of books for the younger reader – 22 books in all – feature the comic adventures of the world's least scary (and least efficient) witch and her cat, often accompanied by their friend Owl. The clear lively drawings and simple text invite discussion and engagement.

The stories are also widely available on YouTube and on DVD.

Kensuke's Kingdom

Michael Morpurgo

Every child has probably had the "What if you were all alone on a desert island?" idea: this book takes this ubiquitous thought further. Michael is sailing round the world with his parents when he is washed overboard one night and lands on a remote island; while he is working out how to live there alone, he discovers that there is another inhabitant, Kensuke, a Japanese doctor and WWII soldier, who has been there since 1945. The two gradually and realistically build a working relationship which is totally convincing for the reader.

All of Morpurgo's many books can be recommended without reservation for use in schools – he has a gift for narrative and dialogue which are clear and natural.

Dogger

Shirley Hughes

Dave takes his favourite toy, Dogger, everywhere with him, and when Dogger goes missing a huge search is launched. This is a very engaging story for younger children, with pictures full of interest and detail, and a happy ending. A good starting point for discussion of favourite toys, and looking for lost things, which could lead into writing activities.

Shirley Hughes' books are always full of visual detail which can be enjoyed in depth, and often deal with simple but familiar situations (feeling shy at a party, going to the shops or the seaside).

Handa's Surprise

Eileen Browne

This colourful book for younger children has won a number of awards for diversity. Handa sets out through an African landscape with a basket of fruit for her friend, but as she walks a variety of animals steal the different fruits. When she arrives there is a fresh surprise for her. The pictures help children to predict and follow the story.

There is an animated version of *Handa's Surprise* available on the internet, and a wide range of associated teaching resources.

The Suitcase Kid

Jacqueline Wilson

One of Jacqueline Wilson's first and best "issue" novels for children, in which she confronts the experience of children for whom separated parents, step-siblings, and commuting between two households, become the pattern of their lives. Andy is ten and dislikes both her mother's new partner and her father's partner's two children. Her only friend is the toy Sylvanian rabbit she has had since she was tiny... Andy gradually becomes more isolated at school and dreams of a return to her secure childhood. By the end of the book she has learnt to accept the new order to a greater extent, and to found better relationships with her new families.

A good book for helping children in similar situations to talk about their own lives and problems; the first-person narrative makes the story personal and accessible.

The Queen's Nose

Dick King Smith

Harmony is ten and wants nothing more than an animal of her own – then her uncle Ginger sends her a coin which grants her ten wishes. The familiar theme of "what would you wish for?" is given an original and involving narrative offering plenty of opportunity for discussion, role-play and creative writing.

The book was adapted into several television series, and also a radio adaptation, all fairly faithful to the novel.

Would You Rather?

John Burningham

A cheerfully revolting series of choices, from the mildly silly (Would you rather an elephant drank your bathwater or a hippo slept in your bed?) to the downright disgusting (Would you rather be made to eat spider stew, taste slug dumplings, chew mashed worms, or drink a snail shake?), presented with lively pictures and a rhythm built for reading aloud. This book is guaranteed to provoke discussion and entertainment! Younger children will enjoy making their choices and suggesting more of their own.

The Boy in the Dress

David Walliams

Twelve-year old Dennis has an ordinary life of school, home with dad and big brother, and football, but always feels different – until he becomes friends with Lisa, an older girl, and discovers the thrill of wearing glamorous dresses and shoes. The story is told with humour and incident, and Dennis's friends and family show remarkable ease, after initial shock, in accepting his choices. This is a light story with no overt references to sexuality or life-style; an underlying reaction to Dennis missing the softer side of life since his mother left is there to be picked up, but is never spelt out.

Children's books by celebrity authors are often criticised for elbowing their way onto the shelf; nevertheless, this one is original and written in a voice and idiom which appeal to the junior age-range.

The Worst Witch

Jill Murphy

This series of books – seven in all – combines traditional boarding-school stories with the added element of magic. The magic is mostly light-hearted without the darker elements of the Harry Potter canon, and much of the books' humour arises from the central character, Mildred Hubble, getting things wrong and her spells having unexpected effects.

A good range of characters and original stories make these books favourites in an increasingly popular genre.

The Very Hungry Caterpillar

Eric Carle

This much-loved book for very young children introduces the idea of an egg changing to a caterpillar and finally to a butterfly, and is good for simple counting practice. Much of the appeal lies in the novelty of having holes in the pages through which a caterpillar, or a finger, can poke as the caterpillar eats its way through an ever-changing diet. Reinforce the edges of the holes before you let small children handle the book!

Charlotte's Web

E B White

The opening line, "Where's Pa going with that axe?", sets the mood – Wilbur the piglet, runt of the litter, is threatened with untimely death. He is befriended by Charlotte, a spider who lives in the barn, and is eventually saved by becoming a celebrity on the agricultural show circuit, thanks to the mysterious slogans which Charlotte weaves for him.

This book defies categorisation in many ways – a favourite since it appeared more than 60 years ago, it has a heroine who dies near the end of the book, a mixture of human and animal characters, and an ending neither wholly happy nor sad. It has been filmed both in animated and live versions.

A Traveller in Time

Alison Uttley

While staying in an old Derbyshire farmhouse, Penelope travels to and fro into the world of the same house in Elizabethan times, and gets involved in the family's plots to save Mary Queen of Scots. The book gives well-researched domestic detail of Elizabethan life, and a good introduction too to the politics of the day. Some of the locations described are still standing and open to visitors, so for those within range a trip might be possible.

Finn Family Moomintroll

Tove Jansson

The Moomins are a carefree and adventurous family who live in a magical valley somewhere in Scandinavia, though they sometimes travel to distant and exotic places. The author's own illustrations show us the creatures, white and cuddly, without any unnecessary detail in the writing as to exactly what and why they are. The nine books detailing their adventures are filled with humour, excitement, magic and above all a cheerful family optimism.

The Wolves of Willoughby Chase

Joan Aiken

Timid, orphaned Sylvia comes to stay with rich and daring Bonnie in her great house in Yorkshire. But soon Bonnie's parents are missing and the horrible new governess is making many changes to the household... A splendidly Gothic series of adventures ensue, in a lively and exciting story. This is the first in Joan Aiken's long series set in a parallel history, in which the Jacobeans are the ruling house and the wicked Hanoverians constantly plot to overthrow them.

This book can be enjoyed as sheer entertainment, but could also tie in with history work on the nineteenth century and conditions of child labour.

My Naughty Little Sister

Dorothy Edwards

These stories of a stubborn, mischievous and constantly inquisitive little girl are excellent for reading aloud to younger readers. There are five volumes, all in finite five-minute episodes which are constantly fresh and entertaining. Although they were first written in the 1950s, the situations (such as going to a party or sharing toys) are still those relevant to small children's lives.

Shirley Hughes' illustrations add to the charm of these stories: there are resources online illustrating their use in a KS1 classroom.

The Revenge of Samuel Stokes

Penelope Lively

A new housing estate is built on the site of an old manor house and country park. This enrages the eighteenth-century landscape gardener who first designed it, and the new occupants are haunted by the ghost of the original grounds, in a completely unexpected way. Tim, Jane and Tim's granddad set out to solve the mystery.

A funny and original story which could be a starting point for discussion of how and why landscapes change and towns develop.

Diary of a Wimpy Kid

Jeff Kinney

Greg Heffley struggles with the expectations of his family, friends and school about what a red-blooded all-American boy should be like. He tries to cope with life in his middle school but his ideas and strategies do not always work out well. The books are presented as a hand-written and illustrated diary, with short chunks of text and frequent cartoon-style drawings, which can enhance their appeal to reluctant readers.

This series of books makes good reading and discussion material, especially for boys at the upper junior age-range.

Iggie's House

Judy Blume

Winifred is astonished when the new owners of her friend Iggie's house turn out to be African-Americans – the first in the neighbourhood. As she gets to know them and sees some hostility from certain neighbours, she comes to reconsider her own feelings about people different from herself. Although this story first appeared in the UK in 1980 and some of the reactions from neighbours may seem out-of-date, the story is still funny and provocative, with strong characterisations and dialogue.

Judy Blume's books always confront issues such as religion, family problems, changing schools or growing up, with humour, wisdom and realism. An excellent author to use as an introduction to sensitive topics which might arise in PSHCE.

Amazing Grace

Mary Hoffman and Caroline Binch

Astonishingly, this book is more than 25 years old, but still rings fresh and true. Grace wants to play Peter Pan in the school play but is told by friends that she can't because Peter Pan wasn't a girl and he wasn't black. The strength of the story and the power of the beautiful illustrations send as clear a message today as they always have. A wonderful introduction to equality issues in the classroom.

Not Now Bernard

David McKee

A picture book for the younger age-range, with a wealth of possibilities and online resources (including an animated version) for classroom use.

Bernard's parents are too busy to pay attention when he finds a monster in the garden: they ignore his successive appeals to them, and don't even seem to notice when the monster eats Bernard, simply accepting the monster in his place and putting him to bed in their son's place. The story can be enjoyed at face value, or possibly interpreted as the "monster" representing Bernard having, and giving way to, a tantrum.

Carrie's War

Nina Bawden

Carrie and her brother Nick are evacuated to deepest Wales during World War 2 and learn gradually to come to terms with the new world they find themselves in: the strict shopkeeper who runs the household and his sister with inflexible severity, the mysterious sister who lives down in the valley, and the kind but downtrodden "Auntie Lou" who wants to make the children happy.

Nina Bawden's many books for children all show strong characterisation as well as a narrative which constantly engages and surprises the reader, as well as giving a strong sense of place. This is a worthwhile book in its own right, but would also fit well with history work on World War 2 or evacuation.

Dear Zoo

Rod Campbell

A tried and tested favourite for early readers; a child repeatedly writes to the Zoo to send him a pet, but there is something wrong with all the Zoo's offerings until they finally get it right. This book is a gift for "all join in" activity – guessing what animal is inside each book, working out what is wrong with each one, and recognising the simple and repetitive elements of the text.

A Bear Called Paddington

Michael Bond

The recent feature film, and various television animations, have helped keep the small bear from darkest Peru popular for more than 60 years. Much of the humour is derived from Paddington's reactions to the everyday life of the Brown family with whom he lives, finding the absurd and unexpected in such situations as travelling on the underground, shopping in a big store, or going to a party. His literal interpretation of idioms, and a good range of characters, make this book and its sequels continuously entertaining.

Pippi Longstocking

Astrid Lindgren

Pippi is nine, the strongest girl in the world: her father is a sea captain and she lives alone with a horse and a monkey. From the first page it is obvious that these stories are going to be different and exciting! The humour and inventiveness of the adventures into which Pippi leads her friends from next door, Tommy and Annika, remain fresh 70 years on from their first appearance.

Pippi's reaction to such situations as school, and her own brand of logic applied to life, are always original and engaging.

The Demon Headmaster

Gillian Cross

Dinah starts at a new school with her foster-brothers but soon finds that something very strange is going on: the prefects and her fellow-pupils have their minds and memories controlled. How and why this is done is the mysteries the three set out to solve. They find themselves pitting her wits against a very strange Headmaster who thinks everything would be better under his complete control. This is an exciting and lively story, which has been made into a television series. The first book was followed by a sequel, *The Prime Minister's Brain,* and then a number of other books featuring the Demon Headmaster in the title.

Horrid Henry

Francesca Simon and Tony Ross

Naughty children are guaranteed to appeal, and the constant variety of Horrid Henry's evil schemes, plots and practical jokes, often directed against his brother Perfect Peter, are lively both in their narration and in Tony Ross's illustrations. The stories are told in accessible language and although Henry's machinations are unusually sophisticated for his age, they are engaging and usually result in a satisfactory comeuppance for him.

All the children in the books, of which there are currently 24 as well as 33 "Early Readers", have alliterative nicknames (Moody Margaret, Gorgeous Gurinder etc.) which could be a starter for writing activity. Many episodes and materials are available online.

Goodnight Mr Tom

Michelle Magorian

During World War 2, Will is evacuated from his deprived life in London to find a whole new world of friendships and experiences in the country, where he is billeted with an ageing widower. The story of his stay is both moving and full of interest, full of event and well-drawn characters. The book was faithfully filmed with John Thaw in the title role.

Details of wartime life are often explained, and the book would fit well with a historical project work set in this era; however, death and cruelty to children are both themes which occur in the book, and sensitivity may be needed.

The Snowman

Raymond Briggs

A boy builds a snowman, who comes alive at night and takes him on a magical adventure – but by the morning he has melted away. A wordless picture book, with an animated version which has become a classic of Christmas television.

The detail in the pictures, and the wordlessness, make this a perfect stimulus for imaginative story-telling work with younger children.

Raymond Briggs' detailed pictures in his *Father Christmas* books are also a delight which can be enjoyed over and over again.

An Illustrated Treasury of Hans Christian

Hans Christian Andersen

Andersen's Fairy Tales

Andersen's stories have contributed so much to the heritage of British childhood reading that their inclusion needs no explanation. Every child should have the chance to read the original, unDisneyfied telling of such stories as Andersen's *The Little Mermaid* and *The Snow Queen*, as well as the lesser-known tales. Poignancy and even sadness are elements in these stories, reflecting Andersen's own unfulfilled life, but the stories in their original versions are the richer for it.

Where the Wild Things Are

Maurice Sendak

The night Max wore his wolf suit… This story has become the subject of much psychological analysis, and has been adapted into a stage show, a feature film and even an opera. However, for the age-group who love it best it remains a simple story of how Max's bed becomes a boat which sails to the island of the wild things, where Max has a "wild rumpus" with them before returning home to find his supper is still hot.

The monsters are never too frightening, and they make Max their king in a most endearing way. The story has been interpreted as that of a little boy having a tantrum, giving rein to it and then returning to normal; however, this analysis is not necessary for the enjoyment of this favourite.

We're Going on a Bear Hunt

Michael Rosen and Helen Oxenbury

Clear pictures of a family expedition make this an ideal book to share with a young class joining in with the simple and repetitive text, going through the traditional chant. This is a book for reading aloud and sharing, with plenty of opportunity for sound effects and all joining in.

I Will Never Not Ever Eat a Tomato

Lauren Child

Charlie and Lola, the sensible big brother and the wilful little sister, have become familiar through television and comic off-shoots, so the original books have some appeal and acquired glamour from these. Lola is full of the prejudices of toddlerhood and is gradually persuaded into new experiences. A popular book with small children, this can be a starting point for discussions of their own likes and dislikes.

There are several similar titles in the series, such as *I Am Not Sleepy and I Will Not Go to Bed* (2001) and *I Am Too Absolutely Small for School* (2003)

Grimms' Fairy Tales

Jacob and Wilhelm Grimm

The Grimm brothers devoted much of their time to collecting old folk stories, and not all of them were comfortable or even originally intended for children. However, the Grimms' telling of *Hansel and Gretel* or *Snow White* have charm and detail which are often lost in simple retellings, and the Gothic atmosphere of many of the stories has a perennial appeal to imaginative children.

The Midnight Fox

Betsy Byars

Ten-year-old city boy Tom is sent to spend the summer on his uncle and aunt's farm while his parents are away. At first he is lonely and dislikes everything, but after he sees the black fox and her cubs in the wood his view changes and he comes to develop a relationship with the natural world. But his uncle is a farmer and has no time for foxes, so how can Tom try to save his new friend? Tom's real problems in life are mingled with his fantasies and ideas, which make the story continuously involving. Classwork on this book could offer plenty of opportunities for drama, debate and writing in role.

Betsy Byars has written many children's books and is a winner of the Newbery Medal for *The Summer of the Swans*.

The Tale of Peter Rabbit

Beatrix Potter

The perennial appeal of this and all of Beatrix Potter's stories lies as much in the charm of the illustrations and the format as in the simple stories. The books are small and child-sized, and neat squares of writing are framed on white pages which make the stories look accessible to young readers. Peter Rabbit is naughty and disobeys his mother, always a winning feature, and has a narrow escape from the wrath of Mr. McGregor.

Modern children may be surprised by the realism of the fact that a gardener may actually shoot a rabbit for his wife to put in a pie! Peter is appealing and wears a little blue coat, but Potter's sentimentality goes only so far.

Oliver's Vegetables

Vivian French

At the beginning of the story Oliver only eats chips. He tells his grandpa that he doesn't like vegetables. But grandpa has a wonderful garden where he grows his own, and after a week of munching through beetroot, rhubarb and spinach, Oliver declares that vegetables are delicious! An appropriate book for exploring healthy eating.

A Wizard of Earthsea

Ursula le Guin

Earthsea is a world of islands and ocean. Ged, an orphan, is a goatherd on one of the more remote islands, until he finds that he is to be sent to the school of the Mages and learn to be a wizard or Mage. The beginning of the story, then, has much in common with others from Harry Potter to Star Wars. Le Guin's skill in atmospheric writing and characterisation, and in developing the ideas of her magic world in which "to light a candle is to cast a shadow", makes this an exciting and gripping read for the older primary age-range.

This is the first book of a trilogy, followed by *The Tombs of Atuan* and *The Farthest Shore.*

Northern Lights

Philip Pullman

Lyra, who lives in a version of Oxford which is both similar to and unlike the real modern city, becomes involved in a magical quest to discover the nature of "dust" and to stop the State-sanctioned "Gobblers" from separating children from their daemons or souls. In this world, the daemon is a small familiar animal which accompanies its owner everywhere and all the time. In children, the daemon changes form frequently; when adulthood is reached, the form becomes fixed in the creature which best reflects the person's inner nature.

A book for more mature readers at the top end of the primary school, both because of the complications of the story and the sophisticated level of the subject matter itself. This is the first story in Pullman's *Northern Lights* trilogy, which continues through a range of universes in the epic search to establish "the republic of Heaven". It has been suggested that this trilogy and its underlying ideas offer a direct rebuttal of Lewis's overtly Christian messages in the *Chronicles of Narnia*.

The Family Book

Todd Parr

Simple, bright drawings and a clear multi-coloured text present for early readers the idea that although families come in different shapes and sizes, all are important and strong, and your family is special no matter what it's like. A good starting point for discussion about all kinds of diversity.

The Tunnel

Anthony Browne

Once upon a time there lived a brother and sister who were complete opposites and constantly fought and argued. One day they discovered the tunnel. The boy goes through it at once, dismissing his sister's fears. When he doesn't return his sister has to pluck up the courage to go through the tunnel too. She finds her brother in a mysterious forest where he has been turned to stone...

This story could lead into discussion of sibling relationships and feelings towards one's brothers and sisters.

The Borrowers

Mary Norton

The idea of miniature worlds is always one which fascinates, and the world of the tiny Borrowers who live under the floorboards by "borrowing" from the giant worlds of Human Beans has a wide appeal. A hatpin and a scissor blade are their tools and weapons, a postage stamp makes a picture for the wall. The details of their life are complemented by the story of Arrietty's growing friendship with a real full-size boy, and the family's constant fear of discovery and extinction. The Borrowers was filmed starring Ian Holm and Penelope Wilton: the film keeps the basic concept, but changes the story beyond recognition. A more faithful adaptation is the Japanese anime *Arrietty*, which retains more of the original charm.

Four sequels (in which the Borrowers are consecutively *Afield, Afloat, Aloft* and *Avenged*) follow the further adventures of the family; the same author also wrote *Bedknobs and Broomsticks*, which was made into a very successful Disney film. Children could enjoy creating a Borrowers–style house or room, looking at everyday objects from a quite different perspective.

Can't You Sleep, Little Bear?

Martin Waddell

Little Bear can't sleep because his bed is in the dark part of the cave. Big Bear can't read his bear book because Little Bear repeatedly disturbs him. But Big Bear is very patient and takes Little Bear a series of lanterns that get bigger and bigger. Finally, Big Bear takes Little Bear outside to see the biggest lantern of them all – the moon. The story has a reassuringly repetitive style, and explores the ideas of light and dark, shadow and being afraid of the dark.

The Great Wave

Véronique Massenot, and Bruno Pilorget

Hokusai's classic woodcut of a majestic wave becomes the starting point for a storybook children will want to read again and again.
On a stormy winter's day, a baby boy, Naoki, is swept into a fisherman's boat by a great wave. Years pass, but still Naoki does not grow. Must he return to the ocean in order to become a young man? The answer arrives in the form of a mythic fish.

Rumble in the Jungle

Giles Andreae

In this lively, poetic book we meet many jungle creatures, such as a gangly giraffe, ravenous rhino and galloping gazelle. Each animal is described in a verse that contains lots of rhyming and alliteration. The verses are accompanied by colourful, humorous illustrations by David Wojtowycz. Children enjoy writing further verses about other animals, in a similar style. The book could be used as a starting point in developing a fact file about jungle animals. The verses are also ideal for performing aloud, and can be effectively used as a stimulus for music and drama.

The Rainbow Fish

Marcus Pfister

The Rainbow Fish has colourful, sparkling scales, making it the most beautiful fish in the ocean. Other fish are amazed by its beauty, until The Rainbow Fish refuses to give a scale to another fish, and then he is ignored by everyone and becomes lonely. He seeks the advice of the wise octopus, who suggests he give his scales one by one to the other fish. The story is accompanied by illustrations complete with shiny, foiled scales. It raises many issues, including pride and cherishing things that are precious, selfishness and sharing and being lonely and isolated from a group. It provides opportunities for discussion about being an individual and a member of society.

Heaven

Nicholas Allan

An amusing and yet poignant story about Lily and her dog Dill's discussion about what heaven might be like. Dill is told by an angel that it is "time" and leaves a temporarily bereft Lily, but she soon find another puppy and remembers all the things that Dill had described as heavenly. The story provides a gentle and engaging starting point for discussing bereavement.

How to Live Forever

Colin Thompson

At night, when the library is closed, the book shelves come to life. Doors and windows appear in the back of books, lights appear along the shelves, and the library is transformed into a bustling miniature city. But on a shelf of cookery books beginning with 'Q' lives a boy called Peter, who has discovered a secret in the library – there is only one book in the world missing from its shelves, a book called *How to Live Forever or Immortality for Beginners*. This is the story of Peter's labyrinthine journey through the library to discover the lost book and its secrets.

King and King

Linda de Haan and Stern Nijland

When the Queen insists that her son, the Prince, gets married she arranges for a series of princesses to visit so that he can choose one to be his wife. But none of the visitors appeal to him until Princess Madeleine arrives with her brother Prince Lee. The two princes fall in love at first sight and are soon married. This is an engaging tale presented very much in the traditional style, but with a thought-provoking element which is very relevant now that same sex civil partnerships and marriages are common.

Skellig

David Almond

When he moves house, Michael finds a strange creature living concealed in the garage of the new house, and gradually establishes a relationship with him. At first, seeming to be an old man, Skellig is later found to have wings and – maybe – life-saving powers. Michael befriends the girl next door, Mina; a home-schooled child who is into birds, nature and William Blake.

This is a strange book, defying classification: even the author remains uncommitted as to who or what Skellig actually is or represents. There are references to the Persephone story, to archaeology, to medicine – and yet the book is not "about" any of these. A thought-provoking read for imaginative children. There is a prequel, written some years later: *My Name is Mina*.

APPENDIX 2

Glossary of terminology for poetry

Acrostic A poem which uses the initial letters of a key word to begin each line:

Sunshine
Primroses
Rebirth
Ice has melted
New growth everywhere
Green has replaced brown.

Alliteration A phrase or nearby words begin with the same phoneme: *Sweet, succulent, silky smooth and satisfying.*

Assonance A form of rhyme where the vowel sounds are the same, but linked by different consonants; for instance *bottle* and *cockle*, or *magic*, *if* and *adjective*. This kind of 'nearly-rhyme' is very often used in rap lyrics.

Ballad A poem or song which tells a story.

Blank verse Poem with rhythm and metre, five feet to a line ('iambic pentameter'), but no rhyme.

Calligram A poem where the formation of the letters represents an aspect of the poem's theme. e.g. a scary poem might be written in a shaky hand.

Cinquain A poem invented by the American, Adelaide Crapsey, containing 22 syllables on five lines in the sequence: 2, 4, 6, 8, 2 (see above).

Clerihew A four-line comic verse with two rhyming couplets. The first line is the name of the person about whom the poem is written:

> *Jeremiah Smith*
> *Is boring to be with;*
> *The company he doth keep*
> *Will send a person to sleep.*

Concrete poem A poem in which the layout of the words represents an aspect of the subject.

Couplet Two consecutive lines of poetry which are paired in length and rhyme.

Elegy A poem which is a lament, usually for someone or something that has died.

Enjambement Sometimes called 'run-on lines', enjambement is the continuation of a phrase from one line to the next of a poem, with no punctuation break. For instance, *And would have done so, had not she Discovered this infirmity* – from *Matilda* by Hilaire Belloc.

Epic A poem about the adventures of an heroic figure.

Free verse A poem without patterns of rhythm or rhyme.

Haiku A Japanese form of poetry with 3 lines, 17 syllables in the sequence: 5, 7, 5.

> *Rivers burst their banks*
> *Fields, towns and houses flooded*
> *Rain, rain go away!*

Half-rhyme Words which almost rhyme. *polish/relish.*

Jingle A short verse or rhyme used to attract attention: often used in advertising.

Kenning A poem written as a list of the characteristics of the subject without naming it:

> *Ball-chaser*
> *leg-nipper*
> *bone-eater*
> *paper-fetcher*
> *fast-eater*
> *loud-barker.*
> [dog]

Limerick A five-line comic verse following the sequence of syllables: 8, 8, 6, 6, 8 and the rhyming scheme: a, a, b, b, a (see example):

> *There was a young person from Crewe*
> *Who didn't know quite what to do.*
> *He went for some shopping*
> *But ended up dropping*
> *His purchases straight down the loo!*

Metaphor 'Imaginative substitution'. The writer describes something as if it were something else:

> *The sea is a hungry dog*
> *Giant and grey.*
> *He rolls on the beach all day.*
> *With his clashing teeth and shaggy jaws.*

> (From *The Sea* by James Reeves)

Narrative poem A poem that tells a story.

Onomatopoeia Words which sounds like their meaning, for instance Snap, splash, plop.

Personification A metaphor which attributes human characteristics and actions to non-human subjects. *Winter grabbed us with his icy fingers.*

Riddle A question or statement, often in rhyme, which is a puzzle to be solved by the reader.

Shape poem A poem which is laid out to take the shape of the subject of the poem.

Simile The writer compares one thing to another in order to create an image.

Sonnet A poem of 14 lines which may follow any rhyming scheme.

Stanza A verse or set of lines of poetry, the pattern of which is repeated throughout the poem.

Tanka Japanese poem based upon a Haiku but with two additional lines to give a more complete picture of the event or mood. (A poet would write a Haiku and then give it to another poet, who would then add two lines to create a poem of 31 syllables with the sequence: 5, 7, 5, 7, 7. This would then be returned to the original poet.)

APPENDIX 3

Model answers to the self-assessment questions

The answers provided are suggestions. You will probably think of many more.

Chapter 1: Developing a love of reading

1. What are the key features of dialogic book talk?

    Key features of dialogic book talk include:

    - using language for thinking;
    - helping children to make connections to things they already know;
    - asking questions of books;
    - exploring books at different levels;
    - children giving reasons for what they say.

Discussions can be planned to focus on settings, characters, relationships and events. Questions can be prepared which should not be simple checks on children's knowledge about events but should challenge them to think and discuss.

2. Why is it important for teachers to have a wide knowledge of texts?

It is important that teachers develop a wide knowledge of children's literature so that they can:

- enhance study across the curriculum by introducing children to appropriate fiction and poetry;

- help children to broaden their range of reading by being able to recommend suitable texts and guide them towards those which might interest them;

- be better able to conduct successful guided reading and dialogic book talk sessions, drawing upon a strong knowledge and understanding of children's literature.

Chapter 2: Sharing literature with children

1. How would you justify spending time reading stories and poems to children if a parent or colleague questioned your approach?

It is important to emphasise that reading aloud to children is much more than simply a way of entertaining them, although that in itself is a good reason for doing so. You might refer to *The National Curriculum in England: Key Stages 1 and 2 Framework Document* (2013, London: DfE) which states that:

> *By listening frequently to stories, poems and other books that they cannot yet read for themselves, pupils start to learn how language sounds and increase their vocabulary and awareness of grammatical structures. In due course, they will be able to draw on such grammar in their own writing.*

(Programme of study for Year 1)

You might further justify devoting time to reading aloud by explaining the importance of children experiencing stories read by an experienced reader, who is able to bring them to life and model reading skills which children are still acquiring. This also enables them to hear stories which they would not be able to read independently and introduces them to a wider range of texts. In addition, as children hear language structures and vocabulary they are more likely to be able to introduce it into their own writing. You might also emphasise the value of discussion and drama which can follow reading aloud, and the opportunity this gives for children of different abilities to participate.

Chapter 3: Using children's literature across the curriculum

Consider your last teaching placement.

1. Identify a successful lesson that you taught. How could you have enhanced it by including the use of children's literature?

2. Identify a lesson that could have been better. How could you have used children's literature to improve the lesson?

Answers to these questions will vary depending on the lessons that you have identified in your last placement. The chapter content will support your analysis of the lessons and offer you some ideas for how you can incorporate literature into lessons across all curriculum areas.

Chapter 4: Books for younger children

1. Choose a book for babies or young children. Identify the benefits of that book for children's enjoyment and engagement with books and stories and suggest how it might support language and literacy development.

    Your answer to this question will depend upon the book that you have chosen. However, you should have identified aspects of the book that support some of the following benefits of books and stories for young children. They:

    *   are a rich source of engagement and enjoyment;
    *   enable the expression of a wide range of emotions;
    *   are an opening for sensitising children to the needs and feelings of others;
    *   open up experiences beyond the child's own experience;
    *   are a safe way into understanding experiences beyond a child's own experience;
    *   enable a child to see social patterns and relationships beyond their own experience;
    *   make a connection to children's own cultural heritage;
    *   provide a connection to a range of different cultural heritages; both in the content of the story and different cultural patterns of stories and story telling;
    *   are an authentic way of extending and enhancing children's language capability;
    *   encourage focused listening;
    *   provide a way of promoting 'storying' in their play and responses to books and story telling which supports learning about story structure, language and plot;
    *   are an authentic introduction to literacy.

2. Refer to Wade and Moore's (2003) evaluation of Bookstart. What are the implications of their findings for Early Years policy?

> *The most important finding of the Bookstart project is that when there are books in a home, most families will read and talk about the books with their children. This enhances the chance that the children will reap the benefits from early exposure to books outlined in question one. The important implication for Early Years policy and practice is to support parents in having books at home and reading and discussing books with their child. The project is an excellent example of the importance of parents in children's learning, and bears out the research evidence that it is more important what parents do with their children than who they are.*

> (Sylva, et al., 2003)

3. Recall a story time that you have led for young children. Undertake an analysis of your planning, preparation and delivery of the session. What worked well? What could have been better?

In your reflection on story times that you recall you need to consider:

- your choice of book;
- how you prepared;
- how you read the story;
- how you followed up the reading.

Chapter 5: Picture books

Choose a picture book.

1. What is the relationship between the pictures and the narrative?

2. What social and cultural understandings do you bring to understanding the book?

3. How may the pictures support children's meaning-making from the text?

4. Describe the illustrative style. What is the effect of the illustrator's choice of materials and techniques? What are the affective aspects of the book?

5. Identify ways in which this book could be used as part of your teaching.

Answers to these questions will vary depending on the book that you have chosen. The chapter content will support your analysis.

Chapter 6: Stories and poems from and about different cultures

1. What do you consider to be the value of finding stories and poems about different cultures which are written by people who have experienced those cultures first-hand?

   Your answer might include some of the following points.

   - Writers with first-hand experience of a culture may write about it more accurately, avoiding some of the fanciful elements included by those who have never experienced the culture (animals which do not live in the environments described, for example).

   - The focus of a member of the indigenous population may be on the content of the story rather than using the setting purely as a vehicle to describe a culture or society. Thus, we learn about the culture incidentally.

   - Many feel that stories about different cultures should not simply be created to 'tick boxes' by portraying different people in certain ways. Stories which are written by members of a cultural group as stories rather than as vehicles for political agendas may be more appealing to readers and still help them to learn about another society.

Chapter 7: Traditional stories and fairy tales

1. What are the key features of fairy tales? Think about character, setting, plot and language.

   The features of fairy tales may include some of:

   - kingdoms and castles;

   - princes and princesses;

   - animals which talk and have human characteristics;

   - wishes that come true;

   - a moral or an embedded message that gives a truth about life;

   - speed of time passing;

   - absence of extraneous detail and description;

- recurrence of 'lucky numbers' of characters;
- one-dimensional characters – people tend to be good or bad.

For further definitions see Phillip Pullman's comments in the chapter.

Chapter 8: Fiction which addresses issues

Choose one of the books identified in the chapter and read it carefully.

1. What are the issues raised?

2. How are they raised?

3. What, if anything, would you need to consider about the presentation of the issue or the language used in the text?

4. What age range would you consider the book appropriate for? Why?

5. How could you incorporate use of the book in your teaching?

6. What aspect of the issue would you have to be sensitive to? Why? How would you achieve this?

Answers to this question will vary depending on the book that you have chosen. The chapter content will support your analysis.

Chapter 9: Fantasy and magic

1. What do you understand by the terms high and low fantasy?

   In low fantasy the rational world is the setting for non-rational happenings (see Gamble and Yates, 2002 – details on page 144), while in high fantasy events take place in an alternative world. Therefore, *The Hobbit*, which takes place in Middle-Earth, and the Narnia books, which predominantly take place in Narnia, are high fantasy, while *Flossie Teacake* and *Matilda*, which take place in a familiar world but include extraordinary occurrences, may be referred to as low fantasy.

2. Are there any aspects of magic and fantasy fiction which you would avoid?

   You may need to be sensitive to individual children's backgrounds when selecting stories. For example, some religious groups are opposed to children experiencing stories about witches and the celebration of Hallowe'en. You might also consider whether some stories might be disturbing or frightening for some children. There is such a huge range of stories available that it is not difficult to find alternatives which may avoid upsetting children and their parents and carers.

Chapter 10: Classic fiction

1. Having read the chapter and considered the issues raised about classic children's literature, consider the following.

   • Books regarded as classics for children are dated in their language, social context and social attitudes. Therefore, they have little relevance for children today and so should have no special place within the English curriculum.

   Discuss your views with a colleague.

   Answers to this question will vary depending upon your point of view. The chapter content will enable you to construct your argument. A number of sections in the chapter are particularly relevant to this debate.

   • Why read classic books?
   • The literary canon
   • The golden age of children's books
   • Conclusion

The case studies and research focus sections in the chapter will also support your consideration of the place of classic texts in the curriculum.

Chapter 11: Everyday fiction

1. What is meant by the term 'intertextual'?

   Intertextuality is the shaping of texts' meanings by other texts. It can include authors transforming a prior text, as in C.S. Lewis's use of the resurrection of Christ when he describes Aslan's resurrection in *The Lion, the Witch and the Wardrobe*, or to a reader's referencing of one text to another. For example, in *Each Peach Pear Plum* there are several allusions to well-known stories, which the reader will notice. In other stories we can draw parallels with traditional tales such as those which involve rags to riches stories. Readers make intertextual connections and comparisons by looking at what they are currently reading in the light of what they have read before.

2. It has been argued that children's authors need to appeal to more than one audience. Why?

   It has been argued that for a children's novel to succeed it needs to be attractive not only to children but also to parents, librarians and teachers who are the people who make decisions about which books to purchase.

Chapter 12: Poetry

1. Can you describe the features of each of the following types of poem: haiku, limerick, cinquain?

2. What is enjambement?

   You will find definitions for all of the above in the glossary in Appendix 2.

Reference

Sylva, K., Melhuish, E., Sammons, P., Siraj-Blatchford, I., Taggart, B. and Elliot, K. (2003) The effective provision of pre-school education (EPPE) project: findings from the pre-school period. Available at: http://eppe.ioe.ac.uk/eppe/eppepdfs/eppe_brief2503.pdf (accessed 12.04.16).

Index

Glossary entries are denoted by page numbers ending in 'g'